Brazil's Culture of Corruption--

Travels through a Cleptocracy

By

J.Q. Jacobus, copyright 2016[1]

Acknowledgments

This project involved many interviews with Brazilians. Since the current government might not welcome criticism, I will thank my informants by first name only:: Tatiana, Adam, Alice, Bena, Beth, Carla, Carlos, Carlos F., Cassandra, Cecília, Darrell, Elaine, Ester, Fabio R., Gabriel, Gisella, Guilherme, Ines, Izabel, Jacques, John, Leonardo, Lessio, Marcelo C., Marcelo, Maria, Mario C., Mario, Michel P., Michel, Nelson R., Nelson, Onaldo, Paulinho, Paulo R., Paulo W., Reginaldo, Riva, Samuel, Sergio, Sergio M., Sofia, Solomon, and Teresa. Many thanks to all and to others whose names I never learned.

Thank you also to Wikimedia for making the cover art available.

Foreword

This work was originally published under a different title and a different pseudonym. Why use a pseudonym? The Brazilian government is currently receiving constant criticism from its citizenry. The politicians could silence their domestic critics by cleaning up Brazil's "cleptocracy," but they are resisting reform to their last breath. However, they could easily silence a visiting critic by cancelling his visa; so Brazilians have suggested I employ a pen name to avoid complications.

Most of the corrupt practices described in these pages took place before 2010; and though in retrospect they seem minor compared to more recent criminal acts, the underlying causes remain the same.

Brazil's corruption rarely makes international news, but foreign investors paid attention when news came out that officials of the national oil company, Petrobras, had been diverting billions of dollars from the company to the Worker's Party (PT) of then-President Dilma Rousseff. It became big international news only because Petrobras shares had been sold on the New York Stock Exchange. Meanwhile, Petrobras executives were pocketing more than $2billion in bribes from construction and engineering companies. Subsequently, Petrobras' market value has fallen from nearly $300 billion to less than $20 billion, resulting in at least lawsuits by the city of Providence, Rhode Island, Universities Superannuation Scheme of Liverpool, England, and by another led by North Carolina's treasurer and including the Employees' Retirement System of Hawaii."

The lawsuits did not turn out well for one set of victims, the bribe *payers*. On 12/21/16, BBC headlined, "Brazils Odebrecht fined at least fined at least $2.6billion for bribery" paid to Petrobras. The article explained, "The company and Brazilian petrochemical firm, Braskem, have agreed to pay at least $3.5 billion to the authorities in the US, Brazil, and Switzerland..."

As the scandal was being announced in a televised news conference, I heard President Dilma Rousseff say under her breath, "Maybe this will change how we do business in Brazil."

If these lawsuits are going to change Brazil, they haven´t yet. The "Lavo Jato" investigation ("Car Wash" a name chose in homage to *Breaking Bad*'s car wash money-laundering scheme) has indicted numerous bribe-payers and bribe-takers, including (to-date) four-times-accused former President Lula. Never indicted by Lavo Jato, President Rousseff was impeached for signing a national budget containing illegal accounting irregularities, something which she said, "Previous presidents have done." Subsequently, President Lula has been indicted five times for bribery, but never arrested. The President (Speaker) of the Camara (House of Representatives) was removed from office and has served some jail time, but no one else in the government who took bribes has been convicted or returned any embezzled money; and it would take major structural changes if, as ex-President Rousseff said, "...this will change the way Brazil does business."

Recently the fastest growing economy in the world, Brazil is currently in the midst of a depression. According to a recent report, they have the poorest functioning economy of the G-20 countries. Governments cannot make payroll. Engineering firms aren't getting new contracts. President-elect Trump complains that his hotels aren't getting built on schedule.

The interviews and writings reported in these pages document the sources and intransigence of Brazils corruption. It has been suggested that international awareness and disapproval may provide the impetus to change how Brazil does "business" (William Easterly, *The Economics of International Development*). One would hope that the lawsuits would next target the perpetrators of the bribery schemes, i.e., Brazil's government officials. Odebrecht executives have signed a deal to cooperate with that investigation into Petrobras… naming more than two hundred politicians allegedly involved in the kickback scheme. In a related report, the headline reads, "Brazil's [former president] Lula hit with fresh charges." (To date Lula has been charged with eight counts of taking bribes.)

No Brazilian thinks Lula will be punished. In most countries, the government is designed to obey and enforce the law. As the interviews and testimony presented in the pages which follow suggest, the story is backwards in Brazil: In Brazil the government is built to steal. "Corruption" starts with the government and the constitution on which it was built in the ´80´s. (As an interviewee will point out in the following pages, "If a government is built to be dishonest, there is nothing which can be corrupted.")

This book documents the structure of this cleptocracy and the culture which produced and maintains it.

Table of Contents

Preface

Brazilians don't take kindly to criticism from foreigners, especially when it comes from North Americans. Who can blame them? Looking through the windows of his own glass house, a neighbor can easily see the faults of others. This book did not set out to find flaws in my home away from home. It grew innocently enough from my frustration learning Portuguese and from my professional training, which involved questioning people. I wanted an excuse to speak Portuguese with Brazilians and decided to interview them. I started by asking simply, "What do you like and not like about your country?"

Several interviews were conducted in English, but most took place in Portuguese and were recorded and then reviewed twice, once by the interviewer (me) and once by a native speaker. In translating these interviews, as well as quoted texts, I have translated everything into English except the names of people and places, words which have no one-word English translation, and words which are used in English, like *favela*. The term for Brazilian currency is the *real*. The text substitutes the English *dollar* and uses a one-dollar : four-reals exchange rate. To facilitate comprehension by English speakers, the names of Brazilian institutions of government are replaced by the names of the equivalent U.S. institutions when they exist.

These interviews should not be read as a random survey or accurate tabulation of Brazilian public opinion. I intended, rather, to ask people with varying life experiences and areas of expertise to tell about their country. Their answers raised new questions, which forced me to read what social scientists had already said about Brazil's people, history, culture, and political systems. This account tells the story just as it happened—a foreigner traveling, seeing sights, following the news, talking to people, asking questions, and recording their answers.

The document available for this revision made it impossible to replicate all of the more-than-four-hundred footnotes in the original addition. For this reason, footnotes will be included where possible. In addition, a complete list of references is included for those who wish to check the information being quoted.

Responsibility for the book's informal tone falls upon me and a young man I heard speak at his brother's funeral. The brother died in a car accident shortly after beginning college. The speaker, still in high school, said, "My brother thought everything in life could be laughed at, not that it wasn't serious or important, just that life is better lived happily." I hope to tell a sad story happily.

The happy telling of this story begins with some of writer Sebastião Nunes' eight reasons for using footnotes, but first the reader must be warned. When reading the words of Mr. Nunes and a writer named Millor Fernandes, one cannot think literally. These two write with a quill soaked in irony.

With this warning, I quote some of Mr. Nunes' reasons for using footnotes:[2]

(1)   "To appear as erudite as possible . . .

---

[2] Nunes, *Historia do Brasil*, Sao Paulo: Atlanta, 2000, P. 11-12.

(2)   To support weak work which without such notes would sound false, inappropriate, foolish, or, who knows, maybe all at the same time.

(3)   To function as a parallel text, frequently superior to the main text, which is sometimes just a pretext for the footnotes.

(4)   To pursue a modern tendency to appear cultured at all times, in books and in the bathroom, in bed and bars, in palace and in pigpen . . .

(5)   To bore critics and drive away friends with . . . irrelevancy . . . "

Each of the eleven cities I describe provides new information about Brazil. In the future, other cities and different citizens will surely tell me more as I continue trying to know this complicated place.

Who is . . . Pedro Alvares Cabral? . . . Thirty years of age, more of less, commanding a hopeful armada of 15 ships and a stagnant multitude of 1,500 passion fruits, . . . swimming in an ocean of doubt.

Sebastião Nunes

Chapter 1: Cabrália—discovery and early patterns

When my pharmacist heard I was going to Brazil, she said, "Can I go with you? I get off at 5:00." I told her my plane left at 1:00.

I've never met an American who didn't want to visit Brazil. They see it as a fun, exciting, and exotic place where beautiful, barely-clad people play on the beach during the day and dance all night. One of the first people I interviewed, a doorman named Mario, saw it just this way: "It is a beautiful country. I like soccer, Carnival, the music (especially Jobim), the culture, the theaters, . . . and the beaches."

A Brazilian clergyman would tell me, "When Europeans first settled Brazil, food was easy to come by--fruits and vegetables of all kinds, so many kinds of bananas that they had different names for them. If you wanted a mango, you picked one. If you wanted to eat some fish, you plucked one out of the rivers. Later they could pan for gold in rivers or scoop up some dirt and find precious stones. They were everywhere." The clergyman decried the allure of Brazil as a "curse of plenty."

Times have changed. Much of this story tries to explain why a land cursed with plenty has become a land of scarcity for men like Mario. In the opinion of one informant, "The story of Brazil begins with a lie."

In 1493, right after Columbus landed in the West Indies, the Pope tried to prevent squabbling between Catholic countries by drawing an imaginary line running north and south a little west of the Cape Verde Islands, which would have given Africa to Portugal and the Americas to Spain. Though admitting to no previous voyages to the Americas, Portugal seemed to suspect there was more to the new world than had met Columbus' eyes, and Portuguese King João II convinced Ferdinand and Isabella of Spain to renegotiate the deal. In 1494 the resulting treaty at Tordesilhas shifted the line farther west. The new line passed through the still theoretically unknown continent of South America, putting not-yet-officially-discovered Brazil within Portugal's sphere of influence.

According to the official story, Brazil was accidentally "first discovered" and claimed by Portugal in 1500. Pedro Alvares Cabral was leading an expedition of thirteen ships carrying fifteen hundred men (according to Nunes) around Africa to India. However, after passing the Cape Verde Islands, "one of the ships disappeared in the night . . . in calm weather, and . . . [the] other twelve ships spent two days looking for it and . . . lost their bearings."[3]

---

[3] Nunes, *Op. Cit.,* P. 89.

Lost their bearings? For someone who claimed to be lost and searching for Africa, Cabral made pretty good time--a little more than forty days. No sailor believed his story of being lost. Africa wasn't hard to find from Portugal, after all. In fact, it was hard to miss. How convenient that the armada of expert sailors would have lost their bearings and found the coast of South America jutting across this dividing line innocently drawn up just a few years before. According this version of history, the story of Brazil began with not just a lie, but the first example of the famous *jeitinho brasileiro*, which I translate as a "little brazilian trick" or "scam." And Spain was its victim.

(An alternative, less cynical explanation says that Cabral swung west to pick up winds and currents that would take them around the southern end of Africa. Why they would need the new line drawn by the treaty at Tordesilhas to travel farther west is not at all clear.)

When Cabral's armada pulled into the bay that now bears his name, twenty or so indigenous Tupi awaited them. They welcomed the visitors with a picnic, some dancing to the Portuguese tambours and the Tupi horns, and eventually a mass. After partying with the locals and claiming the territory for Portugal, Cabral left behind two convicts to see how they'd fare, and one ship sailed back to Lisbon to inform King Dom João of the discovery. The other ships spent a week surveying the coast and then resumed the trip to India.

Three years later a wooden sailing ship took a little over a month to sail from Portugal to the easternmost point of South America. The commander of this ship went by the name Coelho, meaning rabbit, Gonçalo Coelho. Coelho and navigator, Vespucci, followed Cabral's directions to a particular bay, which he modestly named Cabrália after himself. The opening was narrow but the bay in what is now Santa Cruz Cabrália in the state of Bahia was wide, deep enough for their ships, and a calm, safe harbor. Coelho's ships approached the harbor at its north end and entered at the mouth of a river eventually named Rio Mutary. After dropping anchor in the mild, tropical waters, the passengers rowed to the north shore of the river.

No soldiers, police, or tax collectors accompanied them. Of course, the passenger list included priests, but they came in search of different treasure, souls for the Church. Justice and safety took a backseat to religious hunting and gathering. While the immigrants began to build their new home, the commander and the Italian continued on their way, mapping the coast before returning to Portugal.

When Coelho sailed south from Cabrália, he followed white sand beaches and mangrove forests, which extended for thousands of miles (4578) to the north and south from the landing site. Traveling south, explorers would sail into a subtropical climate. If they had ventured north, they would have found hotter and wetter equatorial weather.

Immediately inland, later explorers would come upon patches of parana pine forest along a narrow area of lowlands running from Parana River valley in the south to the Amazon and São Francisco river valleys in the north. At the mouth of the Amazon, they would enter the gateway to the inner life of the continent. This massive flood slowly carried one-fifth of the world's fresh water down a decline of only about 100 yards. Treasure hunters would eventually follow the river upstream to the world's largest tropical rainforest, its variety of life forms sustained by the water which fell when wet easterly winds were forced to rise above the rocky slopes of the mountains to the west and north.

The colony's first capital stood on the beach of Bahia at Salvador. Moving west, explorers would find the slope rising slowly as mangroves gave way to tropical, deciduous forests. There they would discover the *pau brasil*, a type of redwood which produced a red dye.

By the middle of the century, this tree piqued the homeland's interest in the continent. Europeans apparently wanted red clothing.

At first the Tupi would harvest the trees and take them to the ships, trading them for metal tools and firearms. It seemed as though the supply of wood was inexhaustible. Trade in the redwoods would prompt exploration of woodlands of the interior and give Brazil its name, but much of the colony still remained unknown to the Europeans.

Moving still further west, explorers would have to climb a little to higher, drier land, eventually discovering the Central Plateau, this land's hottest and driest area and home to scrub woodlands evolved to survive in the dry escarpments and mesas. Though considered the highlands, it would have an average elevation of only a little more than half a mile, and about two-fifths would be less than a couple of hundred yards above the ocean. The highest mountains of the Portuguese colony would lie far to the north at its boundary with the lands claimed by Spain.

A clergyman used the term, "curse of plenty," to describe the life of the early settlers: "Since the beginning the Europeans had an easy life. Brazil had so many natural resources . . . Public property was considered to belong to no one, so people did whatever they wanted with it. Its resources were free." Plus, though the first settlers did not know it, the indigenous population had recently been decimated by the quick spread of smallpox following the landing of Columbus in the Bahamas. No one remained to defend Brazil from the acquisitive Portuguese.

The social life may have been grim at first due to the fact that the first arrivals did not bring wives. The immigrants soon displayed an appreciation of indigenous women, and eventually mixed-race children appeared, a tradition which would greatly affect the demographics of a nation.

Before they found the gold, the Europeans realized they could grow sugar. This brought more immigrants with an interest in agriculture, but the new farmers did not intend to make homes and feed their families. The immigrants to Brazil were not fleeing a hierarchical society in order to establish a democracy; rather, they sought to create wealth for themselves and the nobility of Portugal. Agribusinessmen, they grew sugar for export; and profit depended on cheap labor.

First they tried forcing the indigenous people to work for free, but the indigenous people didn't take well to slavery, causing high rates of absenteeism as the workers fled west into the highlands. Plague, smallpox, and other diseases killed thousands and sent more away from the Europeans. Soon men and women from Africa were captured, sold, and enslaved to sweeten the tea of the Europeans. Slave ships brought some three million slaves, six times the number transported to the English colony to the north. Slavery was so rampant, even slaves had slaves. The Portuguese, to a degree not seen in the northern continent, interbred with them as well.

Unlike the British Protestant proponents of inalienable human rights to the north, the Portuguese did not have to pretend a person was subhuman in order to enslave him. Perhaps accustomed to a hierarchical society, the Portuguese immigrants needed no rationalization to excuse slavery. Perhaps their Catholic consciences had evolved over centuries of feudal society, punctuated by the Inquisition and other purges of the rebellious, allowing them to accept economic causes of slavery. Maybe being poor was reason enough to be a slave; and being rich and armed was reason enough to enslave another person. The slaves were not rationalized to be subhuman, just unlucky enough to have been born poor. Accustomed to a hierarchical society, the Portuguese immigrants needed no rationalization to excuse slavery. Their Catholic consciences had evolved over centuries of feudal society, punctuated by the Inquisition and other purges of the rebellious. Unlike their British, protestant proponents of "inalienable" human rights farther to the north, they did not have to pretend they were subhuman. The slaves were simply unlucky enough to have been born poor. As a result, the ships brought some three million slaves, six times the number transported to the English colony to the north. The Portuguese, to a degree not seen in the rationalizing northern continent, interbred with them as well. Lacking a crisis of conscience, however, the Portuguese immigrants retained the institution of slavery until 1887. Slavery was so rampant, even slaves had slaves. Brazil was the last place on earth where slavery was legal, ending in 1887.

It took almost two hundred years after the landing in Bahia before prospectors reported finding gold nuggets in the highland streams of the south-central region. Once it became clear that there was money to be made from this land, the French began to show more interest, and the Portuguese crown needed citizens on-site to manage the process of extracting its treasures.

The mineral-rich south-central region became the focus of this activity, and the city of Vila Rica (Rich Town) housed the administrators who policed and taxed the miners. The wealth of the city showed in the ostentation of its churches, paid for in gold. The miners called the best ore *ouro preto* (black gold) because it came coated with black iron oxide. Clearly signaling the reason for the town's existence, they renamed it after the ore. My first questions about Brazil arose in the city of Ouro Preto.

A doorman in an apartment building answered my first question this way: "What do I like? It is um pais bonito... the beaches, going to bars with my friends to drink some beer and laugh, see soccer on TV, and watch the young women." In these few ways Brazil remained a land of plenty, but only in these ways. Much of this book is dedicated to understanding why Brazil is a land of scarcity for men like Mario. We will return to his interview, but first a brief history. Patterns laid down early are hard to undo. In the opinion of one informant, "the story of Brazil begins with a lie":

A man stands at the railing of a wooden, sailing ship in the year 1503. Over a month since leaving his home in Portugal, he hopes to see a shoreline soon. A poor but experienced sailor, he barely notices the ship's rolling and pitching, which have many of his companions leaning over the railing--all male, his passengers, all willing to risk everything because they have little to lose. He hopes to find land on which he can grow food and live simply, but others have higher ambitions, if you can call them that. He sleeps lightly because some of his companions are released convicts who are convinced they will find riches to sell to the homeland. They will wade onto a beach without the King's army to uphold the law. Of course, the passenger list includes the priests, but they come in search of a different treasure, souls for the Church. Justice and safety must take a backseat to this form of hunting and gathering.

Three years have passed since the first visit to this un-named place. It took more than forty days for Cabral's armada to arrive three years earlier and claim it for the Portuguese empire. For someone who claimed to be lost and searching for Africa, Cabral made pretty good time. No sailor believed his story of being lost. Africa isn't hard to find from Portugal, after all. In fact, it's hard to miss. Apparently without permission from the Crown, Cabral had continued the search for a shorter voyage to the East. Such men sought wealth through trade.

Like him, few of the men onboard have come to stay. They wish to return to their homeland as wealthy men. The commander goes by the name Coelho, meaning rabbit, Gonçalo Coelho. Fortunately, an Italian navigator named Americo Vespúcci accompanies him. If Vespucci had not drawn and signed the maps, the New World might have been named after a bunny. These two are following Cabral's directions to a particular bay, which he modestly named Cabralia, after himself. He said the opening was narrow but the bay, itself was wide, deep enough for our ships, and a calm, safe harbor.

They approach the harbor at its north end and enter at the mouth of a river, which someone would name Rio Mutary. Coelho drops them off on the north shore of the river. They begin to build our new home, and then he and the Italian continue on their way, mapping the coast and then returning to Portugal, which many of them would never see again. We are left in a land which is, physically at least, a paradise. Not far from the beach, they set up camp and talk about building a settlement. The visitors know the natives watch and hope the indigenous people remain friendly or at least frightened.

The landing took place in what is now Santa Cruz Cabrália, which lies in the state of Bahia, in a Portuguese colony one day called Brazil. Along the beach, the weather is tropical—mild and usually sunny. The narrow white sand beach and mangrove forests extend thousands of miles (4578) to the north and south. The white sands continue further south to subtropical climates. Immediately inland, explorers find patches of parana pine forest along a narrow area of lowlands running from Parana River valley in the south to the Amazon and Sao Francisco river valleys in the north. At the mouth of the Amazon, they enter the gateway to the inner life of the continent. The massive flood slowly carries one-fifth of the world's fresh water down a decline of only about 100 yards. Treasure hunters would eventually follow the river upstream to the world's largest tropical rainforest, its variety of life forms sustained by the water which falls when wet easterly winds collide with the rocky slopes of the mountains to the west and north. There, the climate is equatorial—hot and humid.

Moving west from the beach of Bahia, explorers would find the slope rising slowly, and mangroves give way to tropical, deciduous forests. There they would discover the *brazil pau*, a type of redwood which would by the middle of the century greatly interest the homeland and lure lumberjacks to harvest the trees for dye. It seemed as though the supply was inexhaustible. Europeans apparently wanted red clothes. The trade picked up, so much so that the colony began to be called by the name of the tree it produced, as if China were called Tea or Rice. Interest in the redwoods would prompt exploration of woodlands of the interior and give Brazil its name, but much of the colony still remained unknown to the Europeans. The colony's first capital stood on the beach of Bahia at Salvador.

Moving further west, explorers would have to climb a little to higher, drier land, eventually discovering the Central plateau, this land's hottest and driest area and home to scrub woodlands evolved in the dry escarpments and mesas. Though considered the highlands, it has an average elevation of only little more than half a mile, and about two-fifths is less than a couple of hundred yards above the ocean. The highest mountains of the Portuguese colony lie far to the north at its boundary with the lands claimed by Spain.

Five hundred years later a Rabbi would diagnose his land to be the victim of a "curse of plenty." Since the beginning, he would say, "the Europeans had an easy life. Food was easy to come by, fruits and vegetables of all kinds, so many kinds of bananas that they had different names for them, fish from the streams and the sea, game if they wished to spend our ammunition on hunting. Later they could find gold in rivers and precious stones if they scratched the surface of the land." Plus, though the first settlers did not know it, the population had recently been decimated by the quick spread of smallpox after the arrival of Columbus to the Bahamas. There was no one to defend Brazil from the acquisitive Portuguese.

The social life may have been grim at first due to the fact that the first arrivals did not bring wives, but necessity gave birth to an appreciation of indigenous women, and eventually to the birth of mixed-race children, a tradition which would greatly affect the demographics of a nation.

Though the first treasure hunters were disappointed by their failure to find gold and precious stones, almost two hundred years after the first settlement, reports came of gold nuggets washing down the streams in the highlands of the south-central region. Once it became clear that there was money to be made from this land and the French began to show more interest, the Portuguese crown needed citizens on-site to manage the process of extracting its treasures. They tried the Hereditary Captaincies system which divided the colony into strips of land which were given to Portuguese noblemen, who would in turn take responsibility for the occupation of the land and the extraction of valuable commodities. When only two of the lots were successfully occupied, the king reclaimed control of the others. In other words, well into the seventeenth century the colony known as Brazil was settled, not for religious freedom, not to create a new form of democracy, but to fill the treasuries of the Portuguese crown and to perpetuate an oligarchy.

The rush of prospectors in the 1690's opened the interior of the colony. On the south slope of the mineral-rich highlands, where the sea came up against the craggy peaks of an escarpment, the city of Rio de Janeiro became a busy harbor and much later a capital city, but not the capital of a nation called Brazil.

The systematic and very rough Tiradentes, though young and handsome, not the very nice Jesus Christ, lost first his breath, then his head.

Sebastião Nunes

Chapter 2: Ouro Preto—Brazil's failed hero

In the late 1950's when my girlfriend, Tatiana, was a little girl, her father bought their first car and drove his wife and three daughters through the mountains of Minas Gerais to the old city of Ouro Preto. The young family drove up the steep cobblestone streets to a large, brick parade ground in the center of town where stood a statue. When the car came to a halt, Tatiana stepped out onto the stones and asked her father, "What is that smell?"

It was not a very important question, but she soon followed it with one that was. Looking up at a statue in the middle of the square, she asked, "Who is that?"

The statue honored one Joaquim Jose da Silva Xavier; but after he died, Brazilians knew him by another name. During the year 1746, Joaquim's mother delivered him in the Portuguese colony of Brazil at a place they called Pombal. He died in 1792 in Rio de Janeiro. Over the course of forty-six years, he worked as a dentist, a miner, a soldier, a businessman, a mule driver, a garlic salesman, and a traitor to the Crown of Portugal.

"He is Brazil's only national hero," my girlfriend told me as we stood on that same spot fifty years after her first visit, "but he did not become a hero until many years after his death."

I found that statement strange. Hot and only half-interested, I asked her, "So, how'd he get to be a hero?"

To answer my question, she led me up some steps to the top of a hill. There perched a two-story, stone colonial building housing the Museum of the Conspiracy. The museum gave some of the answers.

In the 1770's, revolutionary ideas were circulating in France and in the British colonies to the north of Brazil. France already had a distinct self-concept, whereas the thirteen British colonies in North America struggled to think of themselves as a nation. Meanwhile, Portugal's huge colony, occupying almost half of South America, had little sense of identity.

As a journalist trained in economics would later explain, "The Portuguese King tried the Hereditary Captaincies system. They divided the colony into fifteen strips of land, starting at the coast and going inland who-knew-how-far. These were given to twelve Portuguese noblemen who would be responsible for sending everything of value back to Portugal."

One of these captaincies was the mineral-rich Minas Gerais, the state in which we were standing. Only two of the lots were successfully managed; the king reclaimed control of the others.

My informant went on, "The Portuguese had no interest in developing the country, only in extracting its treasures. Gold was discovered around 1690 in the Rio das Velhas on the coast. At first they panned most of the gold from rivers and streams. There were lots of prospectors, and they were difficult to track down and tax."

From Lisbon's point of view, the colonists were there to make money for the Crown. In other words, well into the seventeenth century, Europeans immigrated to the colony not for religious freedom, not to create a new form of democracy, but to work for the noblemen of Portugal.

Money does funny things to people. They have trouble sharing it. This being the case, things changed in Minas Gerais after the discovery of gold. Soon the lords of Portugal realized a lot of money could be made from the colony, and they stepped up their efforts at taxation, just as the British did on the northern side of the Gulf of Mexico.

According to the journalist, the situation began to escalate: "When the prospectors attempted to sell their gold, they were charged a 20% tax called the *quinto*, the fifth. The king's cut came right off the top."

Rebellions seldom justify themselves with words like, "I want to be rich, so I want freedom to keep all my money for myself." They seek other explanations. People are more likely to attend a Tea Party in Boston, for example, when the invitation reads, "No taxation without representation!" In Portugal's colonies, the homeland provided ample slogan material. The rebels of the Minas Conspiracy would come up with *Libertas Quae Sera Tamen*, translated first from Virgil by them and then from Portuguese to English by me to say, "Liberty even if it comes late." In the view of some, the clock is still ticking on Brazil's quest for freedom.

My informant continued: "This money did not go to public works or investment in industries. Portugal had contracts with France and England, allowing these countries to sell their goods in the colonies, so they didn't encourage the production of goods for sale, just extraction of resources."

Thus, the colonists had to give up 20% of their money; and in exchange they got no improvement in their lives, no investment in their futures, and no freedom to create businesses. They remained poorly paid miners who could buy stuff from the company store, except unlike the coal miners of West Virginia in the U.S., the company store was French or English, not even Portuguese, and certainly not locally-owned. And what did Portugal do with the money it made off its colonies?

With the production of gold, the colonies became the economic engine of the entire Portuguese empire. In the eighteenth and early nineteenth century Portugal used the Brazilian gold to repay its debts, largely to England. Thus, Brazilian miners indirectly financed the expansion of the British Empire. The miners of Minas Gerais were working to strengthen the British.[4]

Not unexpectedly, people developed ways to cheat on their taxes. In a museum I saw a table with hidden drawers. Folks used these drawers to hide their money from tax collectors. Tatiana also told me how the colonists hollowed out wooden statues of saints and stuffed them with cash.

Things went from bad to worse in the colony. As the gold lying around the surface ran out and production slowed, the Crown raised taxes. In 1785 Portuguese Queen Maria I, "the Crazy," intensified her control over the colonies by prohibiting the manufacture of anything. She also required the region to produce a quota of 1500 kilograms of gold per year and taxed them accordingly.[5]

---

[4] Hudson, Rex A., *Brazil: A Country Study,* ed., Washington: GPO for the Library of Congress, 1997, http://contrysutdies.us/brazil.

[5] *Ibid.,* P. 63.

Some people didn't like the tax hike very well. Like the Boston Tea Party, the Minas Conspiracy was sparked by anger over taxes. Its conspirators plotted in the town of Ouro Preto. According to the local museums, the malcontents included poets (Cláudio Manuel da Costa and Tomás Antônio Gonzaga), military colonels (Domingos de Abreu Vieira and Francisco Antônio de Oliveira Lopes), priests (José da Silva and Oliveira Rolim e Carlos Corrêa de Toledo), a canon (Luís Vieira da Silva), a sergeant-major (Luís Vaz de Toledo Pisa), at least one miner (Inácio José de Alvarenga Peixoto), and our very own Joaquim José da Silva Xavier, referred to these days as Tiradentes, the puller of teeth.

Like their American contemporaries, the rebels never intended universal liberty, nothing so radical as freeing *all* the slaves, since many apparently owned slaves. According to some sources, the conspirators never even intended to unify the colony into one nation. More modestly, they sought to turn the captaincy of Minas Gerais into a republic. Arguing that Minas had all it needed to prosper and that Portugal was a parasite, they pledged to lift restrictions on mining and mine iron ore as well, set up factories, create a university, form a citizens' militia and a parliament, pardon debts to the royal treasury, free slaves *born in Brazil*, and form a union with São Paulo and Rio de Janeiro similar to the new-born United States.[6]

Nowadays, everyone in Brazil knows that this first effort did not succeed. Still, on Tiradentes Day, April 21, 2009, Belo Horizonte's courageous newspaper, *Estado de Minas* (*State of Minas*), celebrated the national holiday with a headline calling Tiradentes a "Martyr to Liberty." It wrote, "Today Brazilians celebrate the Day of Tiradentes, the major symbol of liberty in the country and the great hero of the Minas Conspiracy."

Two days after this national holiday I sat outside a second-floor meeting room in downtown Belo Horizonte, Brazil's third largest city. A journalist trained in economics had agreed to meet with me. When she invited me in, I asked her about Tiradentes and got the following answer:

"The conspirators met and complained about the state of poverty to which they were being reduced. They wanted freedom, especially freedom from taxes."

The conspiracy was uncovered and squelched in 1789, ironically the very year of the successful French Revolution. Joaquim Silvério dos Reis betrayed his fellow conspirators by squealing on them in order to win forgiveness of debts he owed the Crown of Portugal. The leaders of this insurgent citizen movement, to use Holston's term, were arrested and jailed in Ouro Preto, where one of them (Cláudio Manuel da Costa) died of mysterious causes. (Some believe he was murdered by order of the governor.) The others were shipped off to Rio de Janeiro and charged with the crime of being unfaithful to the King. All but Tiradentes denied involvement in the conspiracy and were exiled to Africa. Tiradentes assumed total responsibility for the movement. On April 21, he was hung, then drawn and quartered, and his head was shipped to Ouro Preto, apparently to remind the discontented miners to behave themselves. One of them must have stolen Tiradentes' head because it disappeared and was never found.

Generally speaking, his crime of unfaithfulness (*Inconfidência*) has become synonymous with *freedom*, as if (1) it were somehow the cause of Brazil's independence from Portugal thirty years later and (2) Brazil's independence from Portugal had anything to do with freedom. Thus, on the 2009 anniversary of Tiradentes' hanging, the paper trumpeted, "Brazil became free three decades later" in 1822. If that were true, there would be no reason for this book.

---

[6] Holston, James, *Insurgent Citizenship: Disjunctions of Democracy and Modernity in Brazil,* Princeton: Princeton University Press, 2007, P. 3-4, 33-34, 416 pp.

I liked the colonial look of the old city of Ouro Preto. Much like other colonial towns I would visit later on, white masonry topped by red tile roofs walled in cobblestone streets. Balconies opened onto the street, and most often a bright blue sky or a starry night sailed above. But in the big, modern cities built during the past 217 years, cities with schools of all types and plenty of homegrown industries, one can see proof of Brazil's development. Clearly Tiradentes would be happy with some of the changes since his death. Brazil is now the world's tenth largest economy.

But what tax reduction did this independence produce? The journalist in Belo Horizonte explained, "At that time 20% was considered a very high tax, and the miners felt that it stole all of their profits. They had an expression, 'They go a fifth of the way into hell.' It led to a movement for independence. We continue to celebrate Tiradentes, the leader of the movement, even though he didn't succeed at the time."

I wondered if he would even be considered successful today and told her, "I interviewed a businessman who said that taxes comprise 40% of his costs."

(Actually, the man had said, "The tax rate is abusive and absurd. In 1990 taxes for business totaled 23%. Now they make up 40% of total expenses. I would not mind paying this amount if so much of it were not wasted in corruption and inefficiency. This rate is found in undeveloped countries without services. We have a very inefficient system, low productivity, and corruption.")

The journalist concurred, "Yes, our tax rate on business has doubled and is headed toward 50%. We are almost halfway to hell."

At that point, I assumed Tiradentes would be appalled at the current tax rate and wondered how average Brazilians felt about it. A political scientist had told me, "Tax collection is a problem in Brazil." That could have meant many things—computer glitches, difficulty tracking income, not knowing how to deal with people who have no CPF number—but he didn't mean that. He meant people cheat.

A few days later I would discover that tax collection remained a problem in modern Brazil where at that very moment Brazilians were filing their income tax returns. I watched as one private citizen, a young graduate student, worked on the taxes of a middle-aged professional. When he got done, he told his client how much she owed. She was disappointed, but she knew her tax rate (27.5% for income tax. Her overall taxes exceed those in the U.S.) and expected to be paying tax and interest for months. Then she told him she wanted to retire in the near future.

He looked at her quizzically and explained, "You will be paying last year's taxes until November of this year. If you keep paying the way you are now, you will never be able to retire. But if you can start setting aside money in anticipation of the coming year's taxes, eventually you will catch up and retire. I don't know how long it will take you."

"Never be able to retire," she repeated. She looked as though she'd seen a ghost--her ghost, slaving at her job long after her death.

Her young mentor grew concerned. "Most people don't pay this much. There is no way to reduce your tax legally. Most people cheat. They don't report all their income, or they buy fake medical receipts to reduce their tax."

"But if they get caught, the fines are huge."

"That's true. Some get caught, but some people have no choice. They just don't have the money to pay and have no way to get it."

She said, "I am a slave of the income tax. I haven't bought anything new in years. Every year I work to survive and pay last year's taxes. I worked constantly to raise my children, build my career, and pay my mortgage. My salary has not gone up in over fifteen years, but prices and taxes have gone up. I still work constantly because even though the mortgage is paid and the children are raised, I cannot make enough to save anything. I work simply to pay taxes. I feel like a gerbil in a cage on one of those exercise wheels. I understand why Brazilians hide their income and cheat on their taxes. Being middle class in Brazil is a form of slavery."

She sounded like Tiradentes to me and like someone else too. A hundred years after Tiradentes was executed by employees of the Portuguese monarch, another man was hunted by the new republic's army. Antônio Vicente Mendes Maciel became well known as an itinerant preacher who said, among other things, that taxes were driving people back into slavery. Long after Brazil's independence, the authorities considered him, like Tiradentes, a criminal.

I continued to listen while she and her son discussed her tax problems. He asked to look at her paperwork; and after one glance, he began to chastise her for declaring all of her income:

"No one does that," he said. "If you are going to declare everything, you have to invent some fake expenses."

She wasn't willing to cheat. "It is a moral issue for me. I do not want to do anything illegal; but I feel dumb, like I'm the only one paying."

He could barely contain his outrage. "Every business keeps two sets of books," he argued.

("In Brazil, it is common practice for businesses to keep double books. The 'second box' . . . is usually used to hide excess profits from taxation, but is also used for 'illegal disbursements,' such as campaign contributions . . . ")

"I know," she said. "[Two colleagues] have already been caught. They had to pay huge fines."

"It's worth it. Did they stop cheating?" the son asked rhetorically.

"No, and they haven't been caught again," she explained. "But the owner of Daslu, the chic store on Avenida Chedid Jafet in São Paolo, got caught twice. And she got arrested. I don't want to go to jail like her. A few years ago the Federal Police investigated her for tax evasion. She was sending money abroad. She paid all of that back and continued operating the store. The Federal Police kept investigating her, though, and found more irregularities. The police said she was smuggling clothes in to evade taxes and charged her again. She was sentenced-- sentenced!-- to a 94-year prison term. Is that justice? Do you know why she was given such a stiff sentence? It is to give the impression of justice. I think she has been chosen as the sacrificial lamb for the wealthy class to receive a symbolic punishment, not that she isn't guilty."

I checked the internet and found one report that the owner, Eliana Tranchesi, did owe a half billion dollars and another that pegged the amount at $218 billion dollars. At last report, she was serving time. Soon, I would get an example of the more common course of events:

Reputed billionaire Daniel Dantas was charged with tax evasion, and a year later he had not seen the inside of a jail cell. As a matter of fact, the federal policeman who investigated and arrested Dantas was fired the day after the arrest. The day after that, President Lula rehired him. (I was surprised that the president had the power to rehire a policeman.) On the third day, a news report said the cop "voluntarily" resigned and that the case remained under investigation.

"No Brazilian thinks that banker will go to jail," the woman continued. "This owner of Daslu just didn't pay the right judge. That is the way justice works in this country. If you don't pay a bribe, you'll sit in jail. It's not fair. If the money went to people who needed it, I wouldn't mind, but it goes to crooked politicians and their friends. Only the middle class suffers under the weight of taxes. The rich have ways to hide their income."

I found ample justification for her complaints. Brazil has one of the worst distributions of income in the world. Among 177 countries in the world, Brazil's wealth is the ninth most concentrated. With so much land and wealth in the hands of so few, the very rich have the money to pay the taxes. Many of those considered to be middle class do not have such money. The woman who was complaining about being a slave to her taxes, for example, said she had worked to pay off her mortgage. Thus, she owns property, which to a slum dweller would mean she was rich.

While this woman was stopped at a traffic light, a young man broke her car window with a rock, stole her purse from the seat next to her, and sauntered into the nearby *favela* (variously known as an *aglomerado*, a self-built neighborhood, a slum, or a shanty town). He would also rob her apartment if he could get in. If he knew the apartment had three bedrooms, he would be angry that someone could have so much space. It would not matter to him that two adult children occupied the other two bedrooms because they could not yet afford to move out.

He would point to her car as a sign of wealth, but the car takes her to three different work sites. To prove she is rich, he would protest that she has enough money to have a housekeeper, which is true. She pays the salary and social security taxes for someone who cooks and cleans. The robbery victim knows how to cook, of course, but when would she have the time, working until after 8:00 p.m. five days a week? It is true that twenty years ago, by working six days a week, she had enough money beyond expenses to pay off her mortgage. But with the inflation of everything but her income, she now has no extra money. She didn't really realize how much things had changed until she heard the words, "You will never be able to retire."

I asked her, "So, what did Tiradentes accomplish? Are you still slaves working to pay a government?"

At that moment her son was sitting at his computer to compute his taxes. When he realized how much tax he owed, he bellowed, "This country is crap!"

"I do feel like a slave," repeated his mother.

When I told others about this woman's determination to pay all of the taxes she owed, they laughed in disbelief. "Yes, if they catch you, you pay a fine. But there are lots of ways to do it. It isn't a moral issue at all. They aren't taxing us to develop the country. Yes, some money goes to good causes like the program to feed the poor, but lots also goes to pay their relatives huge salaries for jobs they never do. They are stealing that money from us."

A whole new can of Brazilian worms had been opened. This was beginning to sound like the colonists secreting their money away in the hollow statues of saints. Once again Brazilians were hiding money from a government which they considered to be selfish and exploitative. In no country do people give their money to the government happily or completely voluntarily, but it helps if the government is perceived to be legitimate and reasonable in its demands. A selfish, greedy, and/or wasteful government will have trouble finding money to tax.

I had begun by asking, "What do Brazilians celebrate on Tiradentes Day?" and I heard stories of corruption and high taxes. Now I wondered whether the Brazilian government was actually so corrupt. If so, why did the Brazilian voters tolerate it?

The answers would begin to emerge during my travels in Brazil, for which I would need another visa. I asked a friend about visas, and he told me a nightmarish tale of his encounter with the Brazilian government.

Someone must have defamed Joseph K. because he was arrested one morning without having done anything wrong.[7]

The Trial, Franz Kafka

Chapter 3: Bureaucrazy—Obedience and passivity

In *The Trial* K famously becomes ensnared in an authoritarian web and is helpless to understand his crime, let alone defend his innocence. His plight has relevance to this chapter, which concerns Brazilian bureaucracy. A traveler's first introduction to Brazil takes place at its consulate. How a country treats foreigners might tell nothing about how it treats its own citizens, or it might tell a great deal.

Several friends preceded me to Brazil. About one's experience I heard the following story:

"Getting to Brazil the first few times presented no problem. I simply bought a tourist visa, which would allow me to stay for at most six months per year, and every year I'd need a new one. When someone mentioned that the price had just gone up because Brazil was trying to keep up with the rate charged by the Americans, I did the math and decided to apply for a permanent visa.

The website told me I could qualify as a retiree. The most difficult part of the application seemed to be proving I had sufficient income. No problem. Along with a criminal background check, birth certificate, copy of my passport, evidence of sponsorship, proof that my bank would wire money to Brazil, and a transcript of each confession I ever made during my five years as a Catholic, I sent documentation of my income. This came from two sources, the Social Security Administration and the company handling my personal investments, which one needs to know was affiliated with Merrill Lynch but had its own name, Hometown Investments *(neither being the names of the actual companies). I was told the process could take as long as six months.*

A few weeks after sending in the complete application and three hundred and some dollars, I received a call from an angry-sounding man at the consulate who explained that the printouts from Merrill Lynch would be confusing to the good folks in Brasília:

"You don't know those guys," he said. "They are very picky, and their English is no good. They won't understand these columns of numbers. Just write a letter summarizing your investments."

It occurred to me that numbers were the same in both languages, but I did what I was told. I summarized my investments, reported only one number, and sent the letter back to the angry man.

---

[7] Kafka, Franz, *The Trial,* SAo Paulo: Abril S.A.Cultural e Industrial, 1979, 279 pp., P.7.

Some weeks later, I got another phone call: "These guys aren't going to take your word for this. You have to get a letter from your investment company, Hometown Investments. *They just have to say that you will have enough monthly income. The amount of your investments doesn't matter."*

"I did it that way because you told me to," I said, but he was relentless, and I would need another letter.

I no longer lived in Maine, but my money did, so I had to email Hometown Investments *in Maine and ask for another letter, which I eventually received and forwarded on to my local consulate. Sometime in early October I got another phone call:*

"How do you think they will know that you are not making this up? You cannot just send a letter like this. It has to be notarized, and then the notarization has to be authenticated. But this Hometown Investment *place is in Maine. I cannot authenticate a notary in Maine. You have to send this to the Boston consulate to have it authenticated."*

I had no idea what it meant to "authenticate a notarization," but I dutifully sent a letter to the Boston consulate along with another check. In a matter of weeks, I got back the following note:

"We do not authenticate notarizations. In order to get your visa to go to Spain, you must send this to Minnesota. They will authenticate it."

I had no idea why a Brazilian consulate thought I was asking them for a visa to go to Spain. As for the confusion between Maine and Minnesota, I got the same thing from a guy who'd lived in New York City all his life and went to an Ivy League school. He said, "Maine, Minnesota, it's all the same—pine trees."

I sent my request to the Maine capital and received a rejection, leading me to believe erroneously that bureaucracy is bureaucracy in every country. They said they could not authenticate the notarization of the letter because the notary's signature was not dated.

Now I was getting impatient. I was pretty sure someone in the Maine Department of State was simply going to look in a directory and assure the Brazilians that this office manager was a registered notary in the state of Maine. Why did they care if the notary's stamp and signature were dated? But I got Hometown Investments *to redo the letter with a dated signature of Terri the notary and resubmitted my request. Much to my surprise, the Secretary of State authenticated the notarization, which I then immediately sent to my local consulate. By now winter was approaching.*

Good enough? Not by a long shot. The angry man insisted the authenticated notarization had to go to Boston.

I cracked. Unraveling completely, I yelled, "Why? They said they don't authenticate these things. They don't know what they are doing. They told me my request for a visa to Spain had to be sent to Minnesota, for God's sake!"

It took two more weeks for Boston to put some official stamp on the letter from Maine, which authenticated the notarization, which notarized the signature, which substantiated my income as a retiree.

"Good," said my local guy, but by then the stock market had crashed, and the world economy was in crisis. He insisted, "You need to show where this money is coming from. You have to show your investments."

"I gave you the printouts from Merrill Lynch, and you said I didn't need them and that they'd be confusing. Now, what exactly do you want?"

He'd forgotten he'd said that and paused for a moment but then quickly threw up another hurdle. "Oh, but they won't understand the connection between Merrill Lynch and this other company, Hometown Investments. How do I know the printouts refer to the same money as the letter?"

"It's the same amount!"

"You don't know these guys in Brasília," he repeated. "I'm trying to help you. If I send it in like this, they will reject it. It has to be notarized."

Good cop, bad cop. I said, "Fine," hung up, and commenced to assemble a paper trail of letterheads and communications showing that Hometown and Merrill Lynch were dealing with the same money.

Then I went to my bank. I had to go there anyway to get a different letter, a better letter, saying that the bank would indeed send my money to Brazil every month. They'd already written me one, but it wasn't good enough. While I was getting that letter signed and notarized, I pulled out my Merrill Lynch printouts and asked them to notarize them too.

"We can't notarize this information from Merrill Lynch," said my banker.

I was ready for that one. "I am going to sign that I received this, and you are notarizing my signature," I said. "I know it's strange, but I've figured out that these guys are more interested in appearances than reality."

He shrugged and signed as witness to my being the man in my driver's license picture, but nothing more.

Was I done? No. I never expected the next phone call:

"You need a letter from the Social Security Administration, saying how much money they give you."

"I gave you that."

"But it doesn't say that you actually have gotten the money, only that you are eligible."

Who is eligible and doesn't take the money? I didn't argue. I just spent an afternoon getting a new letter from the local social security office and sent it in, only to hear back, "How do I know it is official? It needs a notarization."

"They don't have a notary."

"Then you have to get a letter from Washington."

"The information won't be any different."

"Other people have gotten nice letters from Washington."

"Ok, I'll ask them."

I sent the request to an address in Bethesda, Maryland, with another check and in a week or so received a call from a lady at the Social Security office:

"This letter was sent to me, but I don't handle this kind of thing, so I sent it to a friend in another office. She'll take care of it. What do you want me to do with the check?"

"You friend won't need the money?"

"No."

"Tear it up."

"You sure you don't want me to send it back?"

"Are you kidding? If there is anyone in the world I trust right now, it's you."

In another week, I got a letter from an office in the Washington area. It had the same information and looked the same except for a bright, red ribbon attached. I wasn't there, but I could guess how the ribbon got affixed. After they printed out the same statement of benefits, *with the word, receive, instead of the word, eligible, I'd bet the ladies got together on their lunch hour and had this discussion:*

"How can we make this look official?"

"How about a stamp?"

"What stamp? We don't have a stamp."

"What country is it for?"

"Brazil."

"Brazil is beautiful. How about a ribbon then?"

"A ribbon. That's nice. I have some Christmas ribbon in my desk. What would be better—green or red?"

"Better make it red. Red's in our flag."

Priscilla did the ribbon cutting.

"That's nice, but it's long."

Priscilla said, "I think we need some kind of bow. Will you do it, Alice? Your bows are so pretty."

"Sure. Hand it over." Alice made a bow.

"That's pretty. Now, where do we send this?"

After six months since starting this process, my criminal background check had expired, and I needed to secure another. It required another afternoon in a waiting room and another check.

As I waited for evidence of my innocence to arrive, my then-girlfriend flew in from Brazil. We planned to deliver all of the new documents to the consulate after picking up the criminal background check. The drive would take over three hours, and we wanted to arrive at 8:45 a.m. in order to secure a place in the front of the line. We ended up second; and when our turn came, my girlfriend was appalled by what she witnessed.

When I introduced myself to my tormentor, he had no idea who I was even though we'd had many conversations and I had announced I would be coming. He did, however, recognize my girlfriend from the I.D. photo I'd been required to send six months before because she was my sponsor. Despite his apparent liking for her, he was still not satisfied with my application:

"You need to prove that the letter you have from Hometown *refers to the same money as the printouts."*

I explained, "Well, they are the same amounts, and I have all of these documents to show they are affiliated." Then came the clincher: "And I have this notarization. Here, take a look."

"You need a letter from Merrill Lynch," he declared.

We left empty-handed. No permanent visa. When I did ask local Merrill Lynch offices to write a letter, none seemed very interested. Forgery became an appealing option/

But we decided to get married instead. In a few weeks we returned to the consulate with all of the documentation needed to get a permanent visa based on my marriage to a Brazilian citizen. We carried old divorce decrees, new marriage certificates, and a new marriage license, all of which had to be authenticated at the cost of twenty-five dollars per document.

We had everything we needed, everything except proof that my bride had not gotten remarried to someone else in Brazil in the past few days. To prove she could not be in two countries at the same time, my new wife had to ask her lawyer in Brazil to schlep down to the office of records and get proof of non-marriage, whatever that might entail. After another week, we hauled this document back for our third seven-hour round trip, and the consulate finally accepted my application--accepted it, not approved it.

I have saved the last straw for the end. During that visit to the consulate, I passed my birth certificate through the slot in the now-understandably bulletproof glass. Confident that I couldn't shoot her through the slot, the lady pointed out that the name on my passport was different than the name on my birth certificate. My parents had failed to officially add a III to my name. I told the lady behind the glass had been a III all my life--on diplomas, on driver's licenses, on passports, in marriage, and in divorce.

"We can't accept the application this way," she said.

"Look, I have the documents. Doesn't that prove that I am me? My birth certificate proves my father had the same name as me and was a Junior, which makes me a III. It has the same day of birth as all of my other documents. If the question is whether the birth certificate is actually mine, I will redo my application without the III. You can't very well doubt that my passport and driver's licenses with the III are mine since that's my picture." I immediately began to fill out another application without a III.

She looked irritated by this and left the window, disappearing into the back room. After some consultation, she returned.

"We will do you a favor and accept the application as it is."

There may be a profound lesson about Brazil in this interaction between citizen and government. They allowed my friend to keep *his* name, and he was supposed to be grateful. He was not a Brazilian citizen, so maybe he was treated differently from a Brazilian. I suggested this to Tatiana. She smiled prettily and said sweetly, "In Brazil if you get something from the government, it is as though they are doing a favor." My friend's saga continues:

My application would fly back and forth from Brasília *to the U.S. for at least 90 days. In the meantime, I wished to return to Brazil with my wife, which meant (1) I had to buy another tourist visa and (2) I would be out of the country when my visa application returned to the States from Brazil.*

A sympathetic clerk at a different window voluntarily approved a tourist visa good for five years instead of the usual one-year visa. She even accepted cash for the postage to send it to me. I asked my tormentor if he would notify me when my visa returned from Brasília and he declined.

Then I asked the helpful clerk, but she would not say one way or the other. I couldn't just pick it up in six months when my tourist visa ran out. Nothing is that simple. The visa would become invalid if I did not pick it up and then use it within three months of its arrival in the States.

Why wouldn't Brasília just send the visa to him while he was in Brazil? I knew better than to bother asking. "*Why?*" was a wasted question. The correct question to ask when dealing with the Brazilian bureaucracy is, "*How high?*" The story continued:

Back in Brazil, I was shocked and delighted to receive an email, clearly not from my nemesis, saying that my visa had been approved and I had until early August to pick it up. At least I thought I would pick up the visa. I had applied, and they had approved the application, so what else needed to be done?

Upon my arrival at the consulate, I would first nab one of the twenty tickets available for customers. If I arrived in time to be one of the first twenty, which I did, I would then give them

$330 in a postal money order. Cash would not do. I came with a money order. For that I won the right to turn over my passport and return again in fifteen days to pick up the visa-laden passport.

Forty-nine weeks after first applying, I received my permanent visa. The victory came on my fifth personal voyage of 150 miles to the city which housed the consulate. In a fortnight plus one, a friendly and efficient man--not my tormentor for almost a year--handed me my passport with the permanent visa and my original application. As I clutched the passport, the guy told me, "Be sure to register with the Federal Police. If you don't, there will be problems." I found that a little strange because I would be entered into their computers upon arrival in São Paulo, so why check in?

A few weeks later, I appeared at an office of the Federal Police with my permanent visa and prepared to announce my presence. The privilege of introducing myself to them would cost $150, and I would have to present them with various documents which I had and one, the cover page of the original application, which I hadn't packed for the trip. If the man in the consulate had told me I needed to turn in this cover page, I had no recollection. (My brain has trouble remembering things that make no sense, and I couldn't imagine why they'd need the application for something that had been granted.)

"The visa is not enough proof that I have a visa?" I asked the clerk at the Federal Police.

"We must have the signature of the official who granted the visa," she said.

Did they think someone who could forge a visa with all of its official stamps couldn't forge a signature?

Since I did not have the document with me, we were given the phone number for the local office of their State Department. My wife and I decided to pay them a visit immediately. We entered a ten-story federal building but could not go immediately to the office on the eighth floor. Instead, we had to wait our turn in a room which required an electronic key to enter. After a half dozen or so people came down and a half dozen more went up, we realized that there were a limited number of passes, and we could not go up until someone else came down with a pass. Soon we figured out that there was only one pass, one pass for a ten story federal building. Only one visitor at a time could have an audience.

Our turn finally came, and my wife entered the elevator first. "Only one may go up," said the guard's voice, and the elevator closed behind her. The applicant and his visa remained below, which I painstakingly explained to the guard. Meanwhile, my wife made the same explanation to the clerk above. Finally, I was allowed to join her upstairs.

The sullen, tight-lipped young woman listened to our tale and admitted, "This happens all the time." She would ask the consulate to send proof that they had granted the visa.

"Great," I said.

"I will ask, but I can't guarantee they will comply. Not all consulates respond to this request."

"How about consulates in the U.S.," we asked.

"China and the U.S. are the worst," she said.

When I related this story to my girlfriend's daughter, she commented, "Guilty until proven honest."

Tatiana theorized, "This is a projection of the government's dishonesty. They assume you lie and steal because they do. The only purpose of this bureaucracy is to generate money to pay the people who hold up the hoops for you to jump through."

This did not have the ring of someone who considered her government legitimate and fair. The story went on:

"If my daughter could not find the original document at home and mail it safely to me, and the consulate in the U.S. simply could not be induced to cooperate, then I would be fined for every day I spent in Brazil without permission. But if the problem were as unsolvable as they said, and they could not accept visa as proof of my having a visa, then this would go on forever. Forever.

By the way, the fine for failing to comply amounted to four dollars per day, and I planned to stay 340 days in the coming year and to return every year for the rest of my life, endlessly paying a fine but being allowed to enter on my nonexistent visa."

From a young man I heard the story of a woman who deserved better treatment even more than my friend:

"She has been a permanent resident since 1977, but she cannot become a naturalized citizen because one of her requirements is to produce the 1977 article from the government newspaper announcing her becoming a permanent resident. She never saw the article since no one outside the government reads the thing, and the national library no longer has a copy. In addition, since the government was then a dictatorship and that version of the paper is now out of business, there is no one from whom to request the copy. The government wants this proof even though her government-issued residency card shows the date on which she became a permanent resident. She has to petition the Supreme Court to force the bureaucracy to take its own word for her residency. She'll never become a citizen."

As the realities sank in, I realized that along with *The Trial, Catch 22* might make good reference material. Is this treatment just for the non-citizen? My friend's story ends with this:

My wife is a citizen of Brazil. At the Brazilian consulate she was told to be sure to register our marriage within six months of arriving in Brazil. As the deadline approached, we found the appropriate office and paid an incredible amount of money to register a marriage. It only took a few minutes. As we were leaving, the nice lady told us, "Be sure to take the receipt to get your husband's visa registered. They probably won't register his visa without it."

My wife shook her head and said to me, "We have a list of things you need to register your visa, but our proof of marriage isn't one of them. They hold that card up their sleeves to trick the overconfident foreigner."

Ah ha, they save this treatment for foreigners. Brazilian bureaucracy treats Brazilians great then?

It would not take long for Brazil to prove its bureaucracy to be an equal-opportunity torturer. One professional woman's story began in July of 2008. It concerned a routine event that actually went smoothly by Brazilian standards, not the ordinary bureaucratic nightmare. Nevertheless, it raised questions about whom the government serves.

When the professor wanted to retire from her university post, she could not simply announce her retirement date. She had worked for thirty years, more than enough; still, she had to *ask permission* to retire. Apparently she had no contractual *right* to retire and draw her pension.

She said, "Before I can stop working, I have to have my application signed by the President, and it has to be published" in that national publication. "President Lula, or maybe the Secretary of Education," couldn't sign it until the Dean of her university sent it to Brasília, but he would not send it in because he had no one to take over her classes. In other words, she was obligated to continue teaching until a replacement had been found. So, she continued to work and filed her retirement papers, not in July when she was eligible, but in December at the end of the semester.

Even that step wasn't simple. She had a small window of time between the two semesters--before the end of the semester would be too soon; after the start of the next, too late. Teresa, the secretary, would submit the signed retirement application to the Dean for a signature, and only then would it be sent to Brasília. It sat on someone's desk for three months, was finally signed by the President or his surrogate, and the federal newsletter published the notice in March. Only then could she actually stop teaching.

A six-month wait did not create a tragedy. However, her predecessors did not always fare so well. In the past, the government has raised the retirement age while people waited to have their retirements approved, and they would not be able to retire for another five or ten years. But this wasn't exactly slavery. They were being paid. It was more like indentured servitude.

My friend added this story of bureaucracy to my collection:

"After I got to Brazil, my wife tried to add me to her current health insurance. To do this, she had to physically travel to the University."

I asked, "Why was that necessary? She'd worked there for years. Didn't they have all of the necessary information in their computers?"

He answered, *"Yes and no. They had been told all the information; but she found they had a few things wrong, like her CPF (the equivalent of her social security number). She probably could have been cheating on her taxes for years. They also had her birthday wrong. So, she had to drive over to the campus."*

I asked, "Why is it such a problem to drop into the office to do some paperwork?"

He said the problem was traffic. Belo Horizonte stacks 2.4 million inhabitants into the physical space equivalent in size to Poços de Caldas, a city with less than 150,000 inhabitants. This is worth mentioning because in this age of computers, the process of checking insurance coverage had to be handled in person.

His wife lived on one side of Belo Horizonte, and the desk of the woman who controlled his health insurance sat on the opposite side. Between home and office roughly four million people milled, and drove, parked, and honked 1.1 million vehicles. Weaving between the cars, trucks, and busses darted the kamikaze motorcyclists, mostly making deliveries, their wage depending on their speed.

He explained, *"One did not measure the trip across town in minutes; and after one arrived, he did not measure the task in hours. After making her application, my wife had to wait a few weeks and call the insurance office to see whether I was covered. The idea of their calling or writing her never occurred to them or to her. She was flabbergasted when the lady from the Social Security Administration called me about my visa problems.*

"During this call, an employee of the university assured her that the application had been successful and I was enrolled in her insurance plan. But when my wife called to ask another clerk whether a particular service would be covered, the woman on the other end of the phone had no record of me, and no one could solve the problem over the phone. We would have to drive across town again. She and I spent a nice, but hot, hour in traffic to again fill out forms that could have been on a computer.

"When we arrived, she introduced me to Amanda, the secretary responsible for my health. Then I retired to a sunny courtyard and read among feral cats, which kept the campus

free of rodents and scorpions. While I wiled away an hour, the saintly Amanda deduced that I hadn't been enrolled because I didn't have one of those CPF numbers. Outraged, she flushed out the varmint who had lied to my wife and asked her, 'Why did you lie to these people?' The question was rhetorical.

"When Amanda hung up, she said, 'I know why she lied. She just didn't want to have to solve the problem, so she wasted your time and mine.'

"While I waited, Amanda found out that no one in the country would admit knowing what to do about the box asking for the CPF. Amanda could barely contain her contempt: 'This university has foreign visiting professors all the time. They have no CPF's, and they get insurance; yet no one seems to know what to do about this space asking for the CPF of a spouse who doesn't have a CPF. Someone has the power to solve this.'"

(In a college course in political science my professor assigned a paper in which we could argue for or against the premise that the U.S. bureaucracy was inefficient. Because the argument for the premise was so obvious, I took the other position, and I got a good grade for arguing that inefficient bureaucracy protected a government from rash mistakes. Years later in Brazil, a federal employee would tell me, "Federal employees are protected from being fired for incompetence or even failure to work, thereby guaranteeing inefficiency." Good thing my prof didn't know that.)

My friend continued, *"Unaware of any of this, I finished with the things I'd brought to keep myself busy and wondered, 'How long is that form?' I wandered back to the office and found out Amanda had called people in Brasília and was bounced around from bureaucrat to bureaucrat until finally someone said he could help. We had to return the next day to actually get it done."*

"'She had to call the capital over an insurance form?' I asked.

"'No one is responsible for anything locally. Everything is decided in Brasília,' she explained, and none too happily.

"On the second day we dutifully headed back across town to see if Amanda and Deep Throat in Brasília could come through. I might be insured. I might not.

"When Amanda greeted us, I returned to the courtyard and wanted to take my spot with the cats, but one cat--a dirty, flea-bitten, practically toothless, brown, black, and white one--was on my favorite bench, being hand-fed by a woman in an orange dress. Completely helpless in this foreign land, I had no idea if this paper torture would ever end. 'If this doesn't get solved soon,' I vowed, 'I'm going to hang myself right here in this courtyard with the old toothless cat watching.'

"My wife arrived much earlier than I expected. I hadn't even had time to throw the rope over the lamppost. She stopped to pet the toothless cat and greet the lady in the orange dress.

"'She feeds that cat every day,' she explained. 'I don't think it can catch food any more.'"

Amanda and my friend's wife had slain the bureaucratic dragon, and he had health insurance. Next, he simply had to get sick.

Very soon after hearing this story, I had a chance to watch the healthcare system up close. Tatiana, her daughter, and I visited what they called "a new, good hospital." The very allergic daughter had the day before contracted a sore throat and breathing trouble. She'd been put on a

Phenergan drip but nevertheless felt worse the following day. I accompanied the patient inside while her mother parked the car. With a swollen and sore throat, she whispered what she needed, got directions, and steered us to the otorhinolaryngologist. I followed her into the observation room for women. We sat down. No one seemed to be observing her.

In a few minutes the worried, Jewish mother arrived on a whirlwind and stormed into the hiding place of the supposed observers and explained politely, I assume, though I couldn't hear, that her daughter couldn't breathe and therefore needed a little closer observation. The very young doctor who appeared touched the daughter's throat, did not look inside, and ordered a second day of Phenergan drip.

The mother begged to disagree and said that she had to be seen by the ear-nose-and throat guy, who eventually turned out to be a girl. Though he did not yell, the first doctor was clearly displeased and said that a Phenergan drip was standard procedure for a swollen throat. His hurt feelings seemed irrelevant to the mother, who explained that he could not see what was wrong because he never looked, that her daughter had sores in her throat, suggesting an infection, and the specialist was necessary rather than more of the same, which wasn't working.

He directed us to another area, this time a hallway outside a room from which appeared the afore-mentioned female doctor, not more than a few minutes older than her irritated, male colleague. My two ladies disappeared inside the room, and then the boy doctor entered the room seeking vindication. I could hear that vindication would not be given. The specialist had looked in the young woman's throat and cancelled the Phenergan drip. Because the throat had an infection, the patient would receive antibiotics as well as cortisone.

As he skulked off to his hiding place in the observation room, the boy doctor lied, "That is why I sent her to see the specialist."

Outrage radiated from the mother's face. Next door in the treatment room, her daughter received medications. My girlfriend asked why her daughter was being examined without rubber gloves and masks, noting, "She probably got this infection yesterday when she was here for an allergic reaction and got the Phenergan drip."

The doctor appeared not to be concerned and said it was Standard Operating Procedure (SOP), so Tatiana reported having been spoiled by some time spent in a U.S. hospital where masks and gloves were always worn. The doctor laughed it off, saying U.S. doctors lived in fear of malpractice suits. Then she grudgingly admitted that gloves might be a good idea.

What on earth had this to do with visas and health insurance? True, this did not concern a government bureaucracy. However, it did lead me to ask questions about how Brazilians run organizations. The first doctor's hurried error did not concern me in and of itself. Mistakes happen. Organizations have to catch and correct them, which requires that they create a culture which encourages the process. However, the young male doctor acted as if he were trying to cover up a mistake, which is a great way to assure similar mistakes will happen in the future. And why would a well-trained doctor laugh and ridicule infection control measures, especially during a swine flu pandemic?

This story caused me to wonder if they had ever heard of anything resembling Total Quality Management (TQM). This is a management approach made famous by the Japanese when they were pulling themselves out the embers of World War II and into the G7. America's Big Three automakers took a pass on the idea and on their futures.

Looking through a quality assurance filter, one might ask whether the hospital's problems are identified, including mistakes such as treating a throat ailment without an examination. Are action plans agreed upon, such as, "Let's examine and diagnose before treating"? Are measures of success determined, which include feedback from all constituencies, including patients and staff? Are results collected and evaluated, and then are adjustments made in the action plan until the goal is really met? I suspected not in this hospital.

In the eyes of TQM, the doctor shouldn't be covering his ass. He should be suggesting that SOP no longer consist of a Phenergan drip for an unexamined, swollen throat. And the specialist might suggest rubber gloves and masks. They aren't very expensive. In preparation for a flight, I bought a surgical mask for three centavos.

Institutional bureaucracies had thus far proven to be inefficient and difficult for the "customer." Perhaps retailers would be more attuned to customer service. I told an interviewee, "I read a book which says that Brazilians have to know their rights in order to work the system."

He answered, "It's not that we don't know our rights. It's that the bureaucracy makes it impossible. For example, it is the right of a consumer to get a replacement for a product if it proves defective within the first seven days. You are supposed to be able to get your money back or get a new one. But if you take it back to the store, they say 'no.' They will fix it but won't give you money or a replacement. You can go to an ombudsman, and then the store will have three days to respond. In three days, they say, 'No.' You can appeal it, but it will take months. They will make an offer, and most people take the offer rather than drag it out. I had a cell phone with a bad chip, and they wanted to fix it; but I insisted they replace it, so they ordered one from São Paulo, and it took 45 days to arrive. It had a bad chip too, so they told me I could wait another 45 days for the new one."

Not an expert on management theory, I read some articles by a Brazilian organizational psychologist. She had consulted with a company after it instituted some version of TQM and got horrible results. The employees had become dissatisfied, vulnerable to psychosomatic illness, and accident-prone.   This caused me to wonder how the principles of Quality Management were being implemented.

At one point she suggested that "the Japanese model" of Total Quality Management could create psychological problems in a capitalistic work environment. About her client company, she commented, "This type of business is treated as a totalitarian universe."

I then realized that my experience with quality management took place in non-profit companies, not in the capitalistic universe at all. In the nonprofit world the term, *quality*, didn't pertain to the quality of just a product, but of all goal achievement.

I turned to a man with an MBA and told him, "I am surprised to hear that the employees felt so pressured and unhappy. In my personal experience with Quality Management, it was very employee-friendly. The idea wasn't for the people at the top to catch people at the bottom making mistakes. Everyone's performance was evaluated according to measurements of goal-completion, even the CEO's. In one company the employees were considered the equivalent of customers, and their job satisfaction was a primary goal of the company. I've heard that Deming pitched TQM to the North American automakers during the sixties (maybe before), but they were too authoritarian to permit the employees to evaluate management's performance."

He responded, "The manner in which these programs appeared in Brazil was probably quite different than the North American (U.S. and Canada) experience. Even in the public sector they are implemented in an authoritarian form and always from the top down. They never take into account the quality of the workplace."

Then I asked him, "Is capitalism the problem, or is it that the work environment in the large Brazilian company is too oligarchic to permit democratization of quality management? Or maybe you have other explanations."

He responded, "By a happy coincidence, I was responsible for the implementation of a system of quality assurance in a large company which was part of a conglomerate . . . We received a contract worth hundreds of millions of dollars, and the insurance company insisted we implement a quality assurance system. They hired me to manage the contract. At that time, no one talked about quality assurance in Brazil. I had to assemble a team of fifty engineers and technicians and indoctrinate them about their responsibilities for the implementation of the quality assurance system.

"An 'oligarchy' of directors controlled the company and mostly favored old friends who were unqualified and had little technical knowledge. In the beginning this created great difficulties. When the unqualified people found their work controlled by technicians and standards, they felt their power diminishing.

"The stress occurred primarily at the managerial level. Among the workers (welders, mechanics, builders) there weren't major difficulties. The equation appears to be simple: the modern systems of quality assurance require the technical knowledge and intense participation of the workers in its execution. The older, oligarchic management doesn't have much technical knowledge or the inclination to have dialogue with the workers. Therefore, for them to implement systems of quality assurance raises the stress level in the workplace. In the less oligarchic businesses, in which a meritocracy predominates the implementation of a quality assurance system causes little stress." Mario de Oliveira, Filho[8] and others argue that Brazil, itself, is inefficiently, unjustly, and corruptly managed.

Several months later on 7/29/09, *Estado de Minas* headlined, "Traffic changes and disorients pedestrians in Belo Horizonte." The traffic designers had created a new bus lane; and bus riders, not the most prosperous of the city's residents, were dropped off on an island in the middle of traffic with no way to get across safely.

I did not attend the meeting at which this design was approved, and I wondered if any bus-riding, lower-level employee did either. Was the transit authority a place where Oliveira's quality management allowed input from a variety of employees, where criticism could flow from

---

[8] Oliveira, Filho, Mario de, *Brasil--o entulho oculto dos privilegios oligarquicos,* Aso Paulo: Editora Alfa-Omega Ltda, 2006, 384 pp., P. 131.For future reference, the approach suggested by Oliveira includes the following types of ideas:

    1) Goals are stated clearly and publicly. Oliveira lists this first in his "rules of government for results," borrowed from Drucker and his descendents. From the wish list of things to do, two or three priorities are selected. Goals for governing cannot include re-election, only good governance.

    2) The procedure for reaching the goal is identified in terms of more specific objectives. Oliveira advises that the details of reaching goals are determined not by the CEO, but by managers to whom responsibilities are delegated.

    3) The way of objectively evaluating the success of the procedure is established. Where government is concerned, one measure of success should always be public opinion.

    4) If the objectives have not been reached, the cycle begins again until goals are reached or changed. When guided by Quality Management principles, an organization's Holy Grail becomes goal completion. Meetings must have minutes, and the minutes must document efforts at evaluating quality improvement efforts. Thus, they provide a paper trail, which creates a high degree of transparency.

    5) The same process applies to employee evaluations: Oliveira says managers have to be selected by merit, not personal friendship. Otherwise, evaluation of outcomes will not be objective. The employees and the manager identify goals together. Then they come up with a plan of action--goal, procedure, and a way to measure success. If an employee does not meet his goals, the evaluation will not be good and employment may end. This kind of quality management eliminates impunity. Personnel decisions must be based on merit, making nepotism and patronage difficult to hide or defend. No one is immune from the consequences of poor performance.

the bottom up, or was it an environment where "the older, oligarchic management doesn't have much technical knowledge or the inclination to have dialogue with the workers?"

Brazilians trained in management know all about quality assurance; yet Brazil doesn't employ it much. When it comes to hiring and firing, quality of performance ranks low in priority. According to Speck, there are two main sources of corruption in Brazil. First of all, each incoming government can fill at least 25,000 public service posts. It sounds high, but that figure may be too low. The *Estado de Minas* reports new government jobs all the time. Thus, three years after the above number was reported, Abramo cited a figure of 30,000.

As the journalist told me in Belo Horizonte, the economic development of Brazil is delayed by the size of the bureaucracy. She said, "Now the huge public administration adds to the cost of buying and reduces the profits from selling. Brazil must reduce its bureaucracy to stimulate the economy. Inefficiency requires high taxes, which impedes the growth of business. Everyone knows that the tax burden eats the profits of doing business . . . So business is directly related to the question of corruption because bribery is a business cost."

According to Transparency International, "The motive for maintaining a cumbersome, inefficient, costly bureaucracy is no secret. The executive branch gives these posts to lawmakers in exchange for support in Congress. To be an attractive form of payment, the rules permit politicians to fill the posts with friends, relatives, and supporters. Therefore, no selection process whatsoever is spelled out. Through this mechanism, all Brazilian governments, not only the current administration, expand on the legislative support that they have won in elections."

This sounded like a bad way to manage an organization. How could it be changed? Advocates of transparency in government have given two answers. First, Abramo said, "It doesn't need to take too long . . . [The government] has to have the power to nominate ministers, directors, etc. What has to happen is a drastic reduction in the quantity through the establishment of a ceiling that would be proportional to the number of career workers."[9] Sounds quick and easy, but elsewhere he said, "The solution to this is neither mysterious nor complicated; however, it would be laborious. It would require drastically limiting the power that the Constitution gives to the high office holders in all three branches of government. Who can amend the Constitution? The Congress." Would the Congress be interested in this reform?

In 2009 Michel Temer was the top guy in the *Câmara* (equivalent to the House of Representatives). Now he is president. Back in 2009 did he see a problem with the system? When *VEJA* asked him about the number of jobs controlled by his party (PMDB), he said the following:

"When he was re-elected, the President [Lula] wanted to form an alliance [with my party]. As the president of the party, I reached a seven-point agreement with him. This is the basis of the coalition . . . This coalition conducts the filling of these jobs . . . "[10]

Allow me to offer an interpretation of this very economical statement: Brazil has 27 political parties. One party never achieves a majority in either house of the Congress, so coalitions must be formed to get legislation passed. The President went to Temer to form a coalition with his party, the PMDB. As the chief executive, Lula had thousands to jobs to offer Temer as incentive to cooperate. Temer's party could then fill these jobs with whatever supporter, relative, or even qualified applicant it wished. Temer spoke as if it were a perfectly acceptable way to conduct business. He described the transaction as if he were simply fulfilling

---

[9] Transparencia.org.

[10] *VEJA*, April, 2009

his role as head of his party. He did not criticize the system at all. So, one must wonder whether Mr. Temer would be an agent of change.

I asked Tatiana if I were being too negative in my assessment. She said, "This is not a democracy. It is a dictatorship of the crooks. This is why they are there, to give and get favors." So, if I sounded disrespectful, I will follow Mr. Temer's example: Don't blame me; I got my tone from Tatiana; I'm just doing my job.

Luiz Eduardo Soares sounded even less respectful than I. He compared the State of Brazil to organized crime and commented, "There is no organized crime without corruption . . . The history of Brazil . . . [includes] patrimonialism . . . a tradition of authoritarian elitism. Justice is synonymous with a consolidation of democracy and overcoming the vestiges of our atavistic patrimonialism . . . "[11]

This patronage system gives the President bargaining power. What does it do for the legislature or judiciary?

A Brazilianist told me, "I once wrote a chapter for a book on *institutional duplicity . . .* Duplicitous institutional environments, it seemed to me, must have some degree of corruption to work. Even the career bureaucrat might not want to clean up his act, though. If ten signatures are needed on a document, that requires ten bribes. To these folks, increasing efficiency means 'Pay cut.'"[12]

There are many ways patronage consolidates power. For example, a bright, young jurist from Belo Horizonte sat in front of a coffee table laden with wine and *hors d'oeuvres* and explained, "For someone from the Workers' Party to get a job in a ministry, he must agree to give 33% of what he earns to the party. By the time someone gets elected to an office, he will be completely compromised by his agreements with the party. The political structure is built to remain as it is with no chance for change."

But what if people find out an employee is incompetent or unnecessary? The jurist explained that it was virtually impossible to remove any government employee from his position. If a Supreme Court Justice or the clerk in the prosecutor's office chooses not to work, he or she will continue to receive a paycheck until mandatory retirement age. Thus, not only is the quality of work performance irrelevant to the Brazilian government's hiring and firing, the very idea of a meritocracy is a threat to those in power.[13] What does the Brazilian citizen think of this?

One of the clichés Brazilians repeat about their country is, "We have good laws. They just aren't enforced." Apparently the Portuguese liked to promulgate lots of laws against which Tiradentes rebelled. Not only do they write lots of laws, but to this day Portugal is number one in the world in adhering to protocol regardless of the situation.[14]

Number one in the world! This means they are more rigid than anyone else now, but maybe not more than the Scotch riflemen in the War of 1812 between the U.S. and England:

"A regiment of almost two thousand Scottish infantrymen stand at attention in the muck, while from behind the bunkers, Jackson's riflemen shoot them down one at a time . . . because their commander ordered them to halt so he could assess their situation, at which point he was shot. None of the subordinates took charge, so the Scottish riflemen just stood there awaiting their next order, which never came . . .

---

[11] Soares, Luiz, "Crime Organizado," Corrupcao--Ensais e Criticas, editoraufmg, 2008, p. 401-411.

[12] Reames, Benjamin, *Creating Accountability in Federal Democracies: The Diffusion of Police Oversight Policies in Brazil and the U.S.,* New York: Columbia University, 2006.

[13] Araujo, Marcelo Cunha de, *So e preso quem quer!,* Rio de Janeiro: Brassport Livros e Multimidia Ltda., 2009

[14] Gladwell, Malcolm, *Outliers--the story of success*, NY: Little Brown & Co., 2008, 309 pp.

Dominique looses a thirty-two pound cannonball directly at a column of Scots. It hits the first man in the column and doesn't stop until it kills two hundred of them. Not till two-thirds of the Scots have been shot down do the riflemen turn and flee."[15]

The U.S. citizen is the most likely to openly defy authority. Neither Portugal nor Scotland is #1 in submission to authority. What country possesses that distinction? It's Brazil, of course.[16]

This came up over breakfast as my theoretically submissive girlfriend and I discussed the Portuguese language:

"In Portuguese you cannot simply say something is 'evocative,'" she instructed. "You have to say what it evokes."

"Portuguese is so rigid," I rebelled. "In English we use *evocative* without further explanation to leave things purposely vague, but I cannot do that here." Then I reported the above findings saying that Brazilians were the world's most submissive people while Americans were the most assertive in the face of authority.

"That can't be," she resisted. "Americans obey the law, and Brazilians don't."

"But they are *our* laws. They aren't imposed upon us. And when they *are* imposed, like the prohibition of alcohol and marijuana, they are not obeyed."

She looked skeptical, this daughter of submissive Brazil, and she forced me to think, as she is wont to do. Aloud I thought, "It is the same with child-rearing. Authoritarian parents don't create law-abiding children. The children may be submissive while the parent is around; but rules are not internalized, so they aren't obeyed when no one is looking. That makes sense for both Brazil and the U.S."

Brazil has created a sticky bureaucratic spider web. This bureaucracy raises interesting questions about Brazil. First, is the government there to serve people, or is it like the doctor who pretended to be checking on a patient but really was covering up his malpractice? Second, why does the populace put up with this inefficient, expensive bureaucracy? Third, do the people actually have power to do anything about it?

In Chapter 2 I asked why Brazilians honor Tiradentes as their national hero. Now the interviews have placed a second question on the table: Is a country with such a bureaucracy able to function as a country of the people, for the people, and by the people, or is Brazil something quite different?

Before launching headlong into its problems, however, I must report that on a day-to-day basis, the interviewees live in a beautiful country, which they love. To illustrate why they do not live miserable lives, constantly angry about the problems which will be discussed further on, I must first bear witness to some of what Brazilians love about their country.

---

[15] Paraphrasing Groom, Winston, *Patriotic Fire*, New York: Alfred A. Knopf, 2006, 292 pp
[16] Gladwell, *Op. Cit.*

The greatness of a country is not the result of destiny, of luck, and even less of populist leadership but, rather, the result of hard work, constant study, and the patriotism of its sons.

Mario de Oliveira, Filho, 2009

Minutes of terror changed the way Graziele do Carmo de Oliveira, 24, looked at life . . .

Estado de Minas, October 9, 2009

Chapter 4: Inhotim--"A beautiful country"

My interview with Mario took place in the lobby of an apartment building. He worked there as a *porteiro*, usually translated into English as *doorman*. He didn't open doors, though. He functioned primarily as security for the building in which I was living. For twelve hours a day every other day, he made sure no unwanted visitor got past him. He watched the cars entering the gated parking garage, monitored deliveries and repairmen. To make extra money, Mario came in on Sundays to wash the residents' cars.

"What do you like about your country?" I asked. We heard the answer in chapter one:

"What do I like about Brazil? It is a beautiful country. I like soccer, Carnival, the music (especially Jobim), the culture, the theaters, the healthcare system, particularly for my kids, and the beaches."

"Belo Horizonte doesn't have any beaches."

"No, but on vacation I go to the beach at Marataizes in Espirito Santo."

Belo Horizonte doesn't have any beaches because it lies in the mountains above and to the north of both Rio de Janeiro and São Paulo. Brazil's culture can be found all around the place. One such cultural center is called the Inhotim Institute. I first visited in 2008. To get there one drives south from Belo Horizonte on BR-381 to the little town of Brumadinho. Then he takes a back road to Inhotim.

In addition to Tatiana, my guides included a computer expert and his lady friend, Elisa, an architect by training who eschewed her profession to teach ballroom dancing. I did not understand the meaning of this phrase, *ballroom dancing*, until I watched a video of her demonstrating a tango:

For a while, she and her partner danced beautifully, as one might expect from two professionals—complicated steps and maneuvers, perfect posture, perfect rhythm. For the finale, they took turns spinning each other faster and faster, more and more urgently, with Elisa finally landing on her left leg, the right leg straightened to her partner's shoulder. He lifted her by the outstretched leg and left underarm and swung her in a circle. She landed and began to lean backwards and extend the other leg, at which point he swung her in the other direction. Upon landing, she twirled first out one direction and then back in the other. As she spun toward him, he dropped to one knee, with the other foot and his left hand on the dance floor. He swung his right arm up, catching her at the waist, and swept her backwards, arching her onto his back.

Then they stood up without any help from paramedics. This was not the white-gloved Arthur Murray ballroom dancing teacher of my youth. At that point, however, I knew only that Elisa taught dance. I knew little about Brazil either.

The Inhotim attendants waved us to overflow parking. We walked through thirty-foot palm trees toward the ticket counter, paid a pittance, and proceeded to the exhibits. Along the way, we passed some of my favorite artwork the place had to offer: tree trunks hollowed out to make benches--some rounded, some flat.

For the most part, the institute supports conceptual art, art which is interesting for the ideas it conveys, as opposed to art which is beautiful for esthetic reasons. The businessman behind the museum, Bernardo Paz, told *Estado de Minas* (September 20, 2009) that through the vanguard of the art world, they discuss the reality of their world and hope to transform it for the better.

To enter one exhibit we passed through a turnstile. Each entry turned a gear that pushed out against the walls. In time the walls would collapse, as if the purpose of art were dialectic, to create something new that would lead to its own destruction. When I returned the following year, the exhibit had disappeared, but all the buildings remained standing. The institute had given each one to an artist to do with as he or she pleased.

We had returned to tour with two São Paulo architects and a filmmaker who had come to Belo Horizonte for the Chagall and Rodin exhibits. We interrupted the introductions to enter the first exhibit and take seats inside a circle of speakers. From each came one voice. Together they formed a choir. As well as conveying a message about how things are created through collaboration, this exhibit possessed esthetic beauty.

All were interesting: Containers of blood-like liquid strung together like a demented Christmas tree above a floor red with spills; a darkened room which replicated what the artist, Grippo, saw when he closed his English studio window all but a crack; fine strands of orange copper wound into cables which looked like carbon and became a comb, or came from a comb, blurring the distinction between organic and inorganic; two dancers shown from the waist down, he naked, as if clothing were obscene.

Outside we found three sculptures by Edgard de Souza, apparently bronze: First a headless man bending at the waist, next a figure with its head disappearing into the sand, and finally two figures--one I imagined to be a man and the other a woman--morphing into each other, causing me to wonder about the boundaries of the self, the separateness of man from earth, and the role of the brain.

Back inside, we found a room in which a heavy wire mesh was plastered into the wall except in spots where it grew out from the wall, blurring inside and outside, structure and art, saying that art is a revelation of the structure or maybe an escape from it; under a cube we seemed able to walk on water and inside we confronted a broken wall, revealing organic innards; we walked toward a wall which appeared to be an opening but was really only a barrier. This last exhibit, the cube building, won an award, said the architect-wife.

Finally, a bus took us to an exhibit still under construction. An American artist had arranged steel girders sticking upright at different angles from the ground. Regardless of what the artist meant to say, I found myself marveling at the natural beauty of the landscape compared to the clumsy efforts of humans. Maybe the Institute would agree; after all, they had placed these thought-provoking creations in the middle of a carefully manicured, tropical paradise of plants and swans.

Along the way we talked to Tatiana's two friends. The husband-architect asked what I was writing; and when I told him the title, he took offense: "Your country isn't perfect, either," he said. "You had Vietnam, and now you are in Iraq because of oil."

I defended myself by telling him I was getting all my information from talking to Brazilians and reading what they had to say. Then I declared my neutrality by recalling a quote attributed to Oscar Wilde: "America is the only country that went from barbarism to decadence without civilization in between."

Even though I have assumed the role of interviewer, the Brazilian reader may have an urge to kill the messenger. One could argue that Brazilians don't need any help criticizing their government, not when someone like Sebastião Nunes can deliver political commentary in a voice combining James Joyce and T.S. Elliot. His voice, not mine, described Brazilian civil law by providing a scholarly definition of terms alongside a fable about two asses.

He began explaining the law by defining the terms *ass (asna)*, *drove of asses (asnada)*, *asinine (asneira)*, etc. (In the Brazilian language, the word, *ass,* has the same connotation as it does in English when used to describe humans. In the Brazilian government, laws are made by *assembléias*, by the way.) Meanwhile, two burros which were yoked together found their way to a field of beautiful grass, a feast for an ass or two. The asses could not both eat at the same time due to the way in which they were yoked.

Leaving them to *assess* the situation, Nunes took time to compare the Law to an "astonishing folly in our catatonic, socio-cultural meandering." He never insulted the readers by explaining this juxtaposition.

The asses could both eat if they would work together like the ministers of a state or the senators of a Republic, he told the reader. He then asked in a multi-layered vocabulary, "Is there more area of sand (or, degree of foolishness) in the beaches of our enormous coast . . . than fantastic foolishness dotting the empty landscape of the dreadfully asinine destiny that appears to have been sadistically reserved for us by the gods of irony and the ridiculous (or the revealing/unmasking police mug shot)."

He answered, "[Cooperate] . . . is not what they (the asses) did." The reader had to assign the definitions where they belonged.[17]

No, Brazil has no need for visiting critics. Any statement about Brazil must begin as Mario began, with homage to the beauty of the land and its culture. If one looks only for faults in Brazil, he will neither see its beauty nor understand its difficulty solving other problems.

One weekend shortly before the visit to Inhotim, we watched a quartet, Quarteto de Paris, sent from France as part of the cultural exchange taking place between the two countries over the past two years. Brazilian Lourival Silvestre selected the music (*Bonita* by Tom Jobim, *Bebe* by Hermeto Paschoal, *Varios Chorinhos* by Michel Legrand, the vocalist's own *Choro falido*, Nino Rota's *Mia Melancholia*, the theme of *Amarcord* by Felini, Gerschwind's *It's Wonderful*.) He also played the guitar and *cavaquinho*, accompanied by an electric counter bass, a piano, and virtuoso Francesca Perissinotto on the flute, guitar, and vocals.

After we returned to Belo Horizonte, we would hear a blues band, The Gamblers. I remained mystified that Brazilians could learn the blues on their own. With the standard complement of guitar, bass, harmonica, drums, and vocals, and more than the usual talent and

---

[17] Nunes, Sebastiao, "Introducao ao Direito Civil," *Historia do Brasil,* P. 126-128

enthusiasm, they treated us to plenty of standards as well as their own bluesified arrangements of "Kansas City," "Sweet Home Alabama," and the Stones' "Miss You." I loved it all, and I don't even like the Stones.

On the next night we watched an Afro-samba jazz collaboration between Felipe Powell, the son of Baden, and Marcio Adnet, plus his two daughters. Excellent musicians played 70's style jazz.

There is more to Brazil's culture than its music. Before touring Inhotim with the architects from São Paulo, we could feast our eyes at the Rodin and Chagall exhibits at the Fiat House of Culture. After Inhotim we joined our two architect friends at two buildings designed by Niemeyer. First, the Museum of Modern Art of Pampulha showed us another example of Brazil's commitment to the arts. Built by the same administration that erected Brasília (See Chapter 12), it has some of the same good intentions. Glass walls surround the building and provide a view of an artificial lake, which, unfortunately, is dying.

Across the lake stands Niemeyer's church--closed for awhile, but open now. Apparently the Church hierarchy didn't like the art. Instead of lambs, artist Portinari painted a dog at Christ's feet, a dog that had come faithfully every day to watch him paint and had earned his way into the heavenly scene. The Church leaders apparently also objected to the absence of angels and other traditional signs of bliss. Instead, the artist focused on the suffering of the people to whom Christ was attending.

The female architect explained that Niemeyer eschewed walls and columns and formed the church out of one sweeping curve because steel-reinforced concrete allowed the innovation. I found it historically interesting at best. I did like the paintings, though, especially Portinari's dog.

Months later, Tatiana and I would visit with one of the architects in São Paulo and receive a tour of a different house of worship. In an urban setting limited in space, he designed a building infinite in its visual expanse. Light and water interplayed to create images of purification and change, even in an environment honoring tradition. A ceiling curved by the mind of a Brazilian architect spread the word in all directions.

By now the Belo Horizonte International Jazz Festival was underway. In its seventh or eighth year, the festival sprung from the brain of a local businessman, the grandson of a Jewish, communist immigrant.

On a Sunday afternoon we heard the Jack Schantz Quartet out of Cleveland. Jack played the trumpet but often stepped aside for the piano player and drummer (Dan Murphy and Mark Gonder) to take the spotlight. The regular bassist didn't make the trip, so without any rehearsal Brazilian Pedro Santana stepped in. Jazz musicians amaze me. They can play and compose and cooperate all at the same time, as if Mozart had manners.

On the second night of the festival, we were treated to tickets for a dance troupe called *Grupo Corpo*. "There is nothing like them anywhere in the world," I was told. "They started here in Belo Horizonte, so they premier each year's show here and then go to Rio and Sao Paulo and Paris. They go all over the world. You'll see."

I did see, incredible things--unique movements, awkward movements made beautiful, statements, inspirations, celebrations, and incredible athleticism. She was right: I'd never seen choreography like this. Only in Brazil.

Mario said he appreciated the Brazilian culture, but also the healthcare system even if he did have to suffer long waits in the clinic lobby. Brazil has done things with healthcare that my poor country can barely imagine. I read an article titled, "Children will be Vaccinated Free against Pneumonia." The vaccine will be provided free of charge by the public health system and will also protect against meningitis and acute otitis.

When I voiced surprise, Tatiana said, "Let me tell you about our health system. We can get free vaccines against polio, rubella, yellow fever, and influenza. Once a year, usually between August and October, the government offers dog owners free vaccines against rabies for their pets. Everyone in the country can have health care. When the university pays me, they deduct money for the welfare system as well as my health care. When I pay [maid] Geralda's salary, I also pay for her health care and her retirement. I could go to the public health clinic, but I don't want to wait for hours for my X-rays, so I pay extra to a private insurance company. Maybe Obama should know about this."

I told her Obama was not the problem. Except for its uninsured poor, I saw no problem with U.S. medicine until some of my own health problems surfaced four months into one visit to Brazil. Then I discovered that my Brazilian doctors were not only well trained, often in the U.S., but treated me unpretentiously with surprising warmth and concern. When she heard this, one Harvard-trained radiologist said, "Yes, some American doctors are not very kind to their patients, and they often don't use the techniques they teach."

Brazil suffers no shortage of thinkers, artists, musicians, doctors, aeronautic engineers, soccer geniuses, etc., etc. It also suffers no shortage of generosity. I observed a scene of generosity and warmth while sitting in a hospital waiting room with my friend, his wife, and her two children. Her doctor had scheduled her for surgery to remove a malignant tumor from her breast. When we walked in, we saw two other friends who had already arrived before 9:00 on a Saturday morning. The male, a physician, accompanied the patient when she was called to surgery. He spent two hours observing the surgery and then reported on its outcome to the family waiting for news. He served no other function, and was paid nothing for four hours of his time.

Before the surgery had begun, the patient's own personal physician showed up to hold her hand and watch the removal of the tumor. As she went under anesthesia, the surgeon, himself, took her hand and chatted with her. The contrast between personal kindness and institutional predation will be discussed later on (see Chapter 9).

Moments before I interviewed Mario in the lobby where he worked, another young man praised Brazilians for being warm and generous. The chapters that follow describe a different face of Brazil--a selfish, shamelessly predatory face. As this visage is unmasked, I hope the reader will remember the portrait painted by the following story:

On the night of October 7, 2009, Belo Horizonte suffered a massive thunderstorm. "Only once every fifty years does so much rain fall in such a short time," said the paper two days later. Over thirty inches (80 mililiters) of rain fell in an hour. The winds reached 65 mph (40 km/hr) and toppled 138 trees.

For me it began with an explosion outside my window. The lightening hit so close, we heard the thunder at the same instant. Where my girlfriend attended a meeting, the rain began not with a few drops tapping at the window, but as if a dam had burst and dropped a reservoir onto the roof.

Nearby a young woman named Graziele found herself trapped alone in a luncheonette with the door locked and water flooding in and short-circuiting the electricity. Fleeing to the second floor to escape the flood and the danger of electrocution, Graziele thought she was going to die. From the second floor window she saw two young guys in the street, pulling people from their cars. She yelled to them and the men, Youri and Alexandre, swam across the street to the shop, climbed atop a car floating nearby, and tried to break the grate over the shop window. When that didn't work, Youri climbed a tree to the second floor, took a key from Graziele, used it to open the front door, and pulled her to safety. Then the two men resumed rescuing stranded motorists.

The Brazilian nation, impacted for decades by political practices contaminated by corruption, dishonesty, and the interests of the oligarchy . . .

Mario de Oliveira, Filho

Chapter 5: Paraty—a divided people

During my first visit to Brazil, I disembarked in Rio de Janeiro. Somehow, my enterprising friend, Nelson, had managed to sublet an apartment in the Ipanema district, just two blocks from the ocean. Naturally, I wanted to go to the famous beach before seeing any other sites. Everyone has seen the photographs--peaks of submerged mountains poking up from a still, blue sea. Surrounding the city, more peaks look out like parents watching their children swim in the bay.

For some reason one the world's most beautiful beaches was not crowded. Between the volleyball games and the wave-deprived surfers lay plenty of empty sand. Above and to the right stood the mountaintop shown in *City of Men*, but no armed gangs appeared to take over the beach. As I faced the ocean, the scene appeared other-worldly, but I thought, "If this place really exists, it is earth at its best."

After a swim, I turned and faced the city for the first time. A more famous visitor would compare the bay to a toothless mouth, alluding perhaps the poverty of the people whose self-made homes clung to the hillsides. Not as well informed as my predecessor, I had a purely esthetic reaction: The landscape was beautiful; even the reddish bricks of the *favelas* seemed picturesque from a distance, and I liked some of the buildings taken separately; but from a distance the view bothered me for some reason.

"You live here and love it," I said to Nelson. "What do you think of Rio's skyline?"

"I think I know what bothers you, being a Midwesterner. With eyes accustomed to Chicago, you see the competing styles and placement of the buildings as haphazard or maybe even selfish, as if the buildings don't concern themselves with the good of the whole."

I resolved to put my preconceptions aside and try to see Brazil from the perspective of a Brazilian. I would begin in a much smaller place. Nelson rented a car and drove us away from the city. He pointed us west toward São Paolo and stopped at the tourist haven of Paraty on the bay of Angra. There we found a city with a plan typical of Portuguese colonies.

A Catholic church, *Igreja Matriz de Nossa Senhora de Remédios* (Church of Our Lady of Medicine, or maybe Cures), anchored the city plaza. Considered the "new" church, it was begun in 1787. Two churches previously stood in the same spot. The first was begun in 1646, twenty-one years before Paraty was even recognized as a distinct municipality. It appeared that the current version was intended to be permanent. Massive brick columns stood at the corners of white masonry walls and seemed ready to support the weight of towers. However, a shortage of money had left the towers incomplete, permanently unfinished.

The presence of a Catholic church in this prominent spot did not surprise me, but I had to ask Nelson, "Why are there four churches? There weren't Protestants here, were there?"

Nelson smiled knowingly and suggested we explore. He told me about considerable interbreeding among ethnic groups in colonial Brazil. I knew that. "But," he went on, "the early Brazilians did not engage in inter-racial or inter-class worshipping."

Divisions by Class:

The *Igreja Matriz de Nossa Senhora de Remédios* was intended for white workers and fishermen. The *Igreja de Santa Rita* (Church of St. Rita) served freed people of mixed race. They were manual laborers too but had darker skin than the group going to the white church. The *Igreja de Nossa Senhora do Rosário e São Benedito* (Church of Our Lady and St. Benedict) was for "negroes," apparently slaves. Whom does that leave to go to the fourth church? Rich white people, of course—the *Igreja de Nossa Senhora das Dores* (Our Lady of Sorrows) was for the elite whites, who apparently did not engage in manual labor. One can only wonder about the nature of their sorrows. A Brazilian businessman told me, "There is a saying that Americans [from the U.S.] are ashamed not to work, while upper class Brazilians are ashamed *to* work."

A member of the current generation, especially one from a different culture, should not judge colonial Brazilians by today's standards. Times were different then, but how different? At this point in my travels, I couldn't remember seeing any black hands on the wheel of a car.

The rush of prospectors to Brazil in the 1690's opened the interior of the colony to exploration. On the south slope of the mineral-rich highlands where the sea came up against the craggy peaks of an escarpment, the city of Rio de Janeiro became a busy harbor and much later a capital city, and Paraty soon became one of the busiest ports for slave ships from Africa. Reasons included rapid access to São Paolo, the gold in adjacent Minas Gerais, and the nearby agricultural region in the valley of Paraíba. One trading boom followed another--first sugar, then gold, then coffee. Paraty served as the door through which passed the slaves to do the farm work and the mining. The city also provided services which one would expect—inspection, policing, military to fight off pirates, auctioneers—plus one which would come as a surprise, namely priests. By order of a Papal Bull, priests had to baptize slaves before they could be sold. These people all helped to populate a village of 10,000.

A cobblestone road circled the plaza before branching out in different directions. White masonry buildings followed the cobblestones in three directions from the square. The four churches stood apart but connected by this road, which brought commerce and slavery to Paraty. Close to the square, what once were homes had now become shops, restaurants, hotels, and *pousadas* (bed-and-breakfasts). But what became of the divisions within the society?

Mario de Oliveira, Filho gave an interview to the magazine, *VEJA,* concerning a book he had written, *Brazil—the Secret Burden of the Privileged Oligarchies.*[18] The title suggests that Brazil bears the burden of a privileged class of oligarchs. He argued that this excess baggage impeded the development of democracy in Brazil and had to be removed. The author attended Brazil's public high schools and went on to earn three academic degrees, but I suspected that not all he knew came from books. Like the doorman at our building, a man of more limited education, Oliveiro also saw the government as failing to invest in its powerless people:

"The government doesn't invest in things for the working man--education, health, culture. These days, if you don't study, you will have nothing. In my day, we had no cell phone

---

[18] Oliveira, Filho, Mario de, interview with *VEJA,* April 18, 2007.

and no internet, but I learned to write and type. As a kid, I was told I had to type to get a job. Now kids are told they have to be able to use the internet to get a job. Whoever doesn't get a chance at formal education will never get a better job and will retire and be poor like the farm workers. When a farm worker retires, his pension is less than minimum wage. That's why people leave the countryside. Sometimes it doesn't work and they return to their homes. We should be able to survive in this country with so many natural resources: iron, gold, the Amazon. We should be able to exploit the Amazon without destroying it. It should provide tourism because it is so beautiful, but tourists are afraid to come to Brazil because of violence. I imagine that a tourist would be robbed of his wallet on the street because he looks like a foreigner. Brazil should become a first world country."

A working man with no money for luxuries, Doorman Mario said that "thieving politicians" are stealing public money and endangering his daughters' health and education. He complained about the wait to see a doctor: "We don't have insurance, so we have to use the public clinics. It is good we have free healthcare, but when I take the kids, there are no doctors available. We wait for hours."

My girlfriend would explain, "The money gets sent to the clinics, but it is either not enough or it never arrives."

This interview with Mario revealed a crucial attitude: Because his access to health care had improved, Mario was relatively happy with it. I would encounter this attitude later on when a survey reported that the government had a 65.4% approval rating. To put this report to the test, I conducted a little survey in the kitchen. I asked Tatiana's housekeeper, Geralda, if she believed that most Brazilians were positive about the government. She said, "Yes, because they have made things a little bit better."

Secondly, Mario mentioned education. He explained that he likes to work and is proud to be an honest, hard-working person. He respects the people in the building he guards because they work too: "They aren't millionaires like some people think. The building is empty in the daytime because everyone is working." Then he makes the connection between income and education: "Everyone who lives in this building studied. A large number of Brazilians are illiterate. They can't write or read. For example, my aunt is fifty-five and can't write her own name. The government has a policy to provide education because there are so many illiterate people. It is not enough to encourage kids to play soccer; they must get an education, learn about the culture, learn the value of work, and learn how to talk to people. I have to transmit good things to my kids, not the bad things. I will show my daughters the right way. We have to have rules. The duty of parent is to teach that there are rules to follow: wake up, make the bed, go to school. Without rules, everything is a mess. My daughters must do their homework."

He did not complain about the quality of public schools, which I was told had declined considerably since the beginning of the dictatorship. According to older interviewees, he was too young to know how good the public schools were before the dictatorship.

When Mario complained politely about the lack of respect for the workingman, we heard his recognition that while his tenants all worked like he did, he made relatively little money. The statistics backed him up: In 1996 São Paulo's top 20% of income-earners had thirty times the income of the poorest 40%. On his website for a movement to elect an independent candidate for president, Oliveira reported that though Brazil is the fifth largest and fifth most-inhabited country in the world, with vast natural resources and the world's tenth largest economy, it was 169th in distribution of income. Thus, only eight countries had a greater concentration of wealth in the hands of a few.[19]

Seeing beyond his own family, Mario saw problems with Brazil's attaining its potential: "We are a rich country with many resources, but something goes wrong. We cannot develop those resources. We are going backwards. I think other countries are surpassing us." Like Tiradentes, he feared that resources were being siphoned off by the powerful. Said Mario, " . . . like the destruction of the Amazon. When we need those resources, they'll be gone."

Again, statistics back up the intuition of the doorman concerning investment in the future of the country: Among the countries of the world, the world's #10 economy is only 67th in health, 70th in human development, 81st in growth, 96th best in rate of inflation, 103rd in per capita income, 106th in literacy, 112th in life expectancy, and 123rd in investment.

The question at the opening of this chapter concerned divisions within the society. The answer speaks of a vast gulf between the rich and poor in terms of money, yes, but also healthcare, education, and living conditions. The reason for these divisions is not the poverty of the country. The *country* is not poor, just most of its people. The reason for this division has to do with Our Lady of Sorrows Church in Paraty.

According to Mario de Oliveira, Filho, "While all current democracies like England, France, Germany, Japan, and the U.S. evolved from some form of oligarchy--feudalism, monarchy, dictatorship, etc.--the most developed nations are now to a great extent meritocracies in which people are rewarded for their accomplishments, rather than being given power and wealth because of a privileged position." Of course, everyone knows that a great deal of wealth is inherited in these countries, that "the rich get richer" everywhere. If the U.S. were a completely successful meritocracy, how would one explain the election of George W. Bush, not to mention his re-election? If the original privileged class were the rich whites to whom much of Brazil was given by the King, who occupies that position now and how could they maintain control over a democracy?

To even begin giving the Brazilians' answer to this question, the concept of the *coronel* (colonel) needs an introduction. Briefly, a colonel represents a step in the evolution of the wealthy class which has held power in Brazil since the land was first given to those twelve Portuguese families. When Brazil finally became a republic rather than a monarchy (see Chapter 6), these so-called colonels made up an oligarchy that actually ran the internal affairs of the country.

"A *coronel* (colonel) in this context is not an army officer, but a wealthy landowner who can bribe, manipulate and pressure the local electorate to vote for the candidates he chooses." Landowners from less-populated states continue as powerful oligarchs, and the most prominent of these is José Sarney, President of the Senate, a name to remember.

Said author and literary critic Afonso Romano de Sant'Anna, "The high Chamber [the Senate] is "debating an interminable list of ethical infractions and financial seizures commanded by the current owner of the captaincy of Maranhão, José Sarney."[20] If the guy is such a crook, why did he get elected and re-elected and re-elected?

A jurist from Belo Horizonte explained, "Why was Sarney elected? He's been in the Senate all his life. He will be re-elected or, if not, his daughter or someone from his organization will be elected because they do favors for so many people. He has given jobs to generations of

[19] Gallant, Katheryn, www.brazil.com/cvrmar97.1977

[20] Sant'Anna, Affonso Romona de, "Sarney e as capitania hereditarias," *Estado de Minas*, 2/8/09

families. If you are uneducated and he gives you a job, you will be grateful forever. These people would give their lives for him."

"But," I asked, "where did his money come from originally?"

The third person in the room, the interviewee's professor, answered:

"He owns his state of Maranhão, literally owns the land and employs the people. They vote for him so they can keep their jobs and because he promises them improvements--a bridge here, a sewage system there. Senator Collor is another colonel from the northeast. He was impeached as President due to corruption, but he still got re-elected to the Senate."

So, one source of political clout is to be born a colonel. What do Brazilians think of their colonels? According to Sant'Anna, some Brazilians think they're just great: "Sarney and others say that it is this way and should remain so."

Sant'Anna's own opinion differs: "Well, strictly speaking, it is understood that the hereditary captaincy program was the most advanced that the Portuguese monarch could come up with at the time. Half the world was in Portuguese hands, and the King was counting on a small elite to administer half the land and seas." It was a system in which the land and everything on it belonged to the captain and his descendants after him. "Soon was established a fusion between what is public and what is private." Furthermore, he argued, "Nothing has changed [in the behavior of the colonel] since the time of Duarte Coelho, [the first captain of Pernambuco]."[21]

However, ethical standards have changed somewhat, and something called *democracy* has changed people's expectations. "We can agree that to maintain the same scheme today is to be not only historically backward, but indecently predatory toward public property . . . Circulating on the internet these past days is a surprising list of buildings, cities, day care centers, bridges, roads, avenues, dead ends, and plazas of Maranhão which bear the name of Sarney and his subordinates. It is the indelible mark of crime. The system of taking things by naming them after oneself is a glaring example of semantic pillaging. It is not enough to occupy the posts, to arrange the placement of protégés. It is necessary to leave ones mark, ones own name, like a medieval seal inscribed on the rural and urban landscape . . . This [hereditary captaincy system] was 500 years ago. In the 21st century will Brazil persist in this mistake?"

Unequal Treatment Under the Law

I doubted the Senate Ethics Committee would accuse Senator Sarney of name pollution. As the discussion proceeded in the Senate, Brazilians told me he wouldn't lose his job. The weekly magazine, *VEJA*, voiced this sentiment:

"If a renunciation of Sarney were confirmed, is anyone able to imagine that those nominated for the electrical sector would be fired? No, it will not happen. They will stay there, doing everything that they always do . . . In the end, it is this, and it is going to continue being this way for a long time, the most efficient and safest way to do politics: trading votes for jobs, changing money for support, employing relatives and friends—all with our money."[22]

I asked the jurist about the basis for disempowering the Brazilian people. This was like asking what lurks at the bottom of the Black Lagoon made famous by an early American horror movie. On his way down to the bottom, the jurist then gave us a tour of the political system at the lesser depths:

"In each city there are the chamber and the city councilmen. At the state level are the state legislators and the governor. At the federal level are the senator and federal deputy. Finally there is the

---

[21] *Ibid.,* Sant'Anna, Affonso Romano de.

[22] Cabral, Otavio; Escoteguy, Diego, "A rendicao do ultimo coronel," *VEJA,* edicao 2124, ano 42, #31, 5/8/09, p. 64.

president. You would probably think these levels of representation add up to a democracy. They don't. The problem is that at none of these levels are the people's needs represented. People seek these jobs to benefit themselves personally. These jobs are ways to get public money through collecting favors. A government job is a gold mine of favors. The entire government is involved in influence trafficking. There is a chain of favors: If a city councilman needs something, he gets in touch with state official, who gets touch with the federal congressman, who will get in touch with minister (who has no expertise but is there as a result of campaign promises). To grant a favor, each level charges either money or a favor in return."

The newspaper[23] backed up what the jurist was saying. A judge (Wagner de Abreu) recently ordered a cut in the salary of one of the state's highly paid mayors. The mayor (Nide Alves) was making $110,500 per year to run his little town. He did not accept the pay cut without a fight: "In an attempt to reverse the decision, the mayor is threatening to reduce the number of doctors in the municipal hospital with the argument that no employee can earn more than the chief executive."

The jurist went on, "Federal legislators receive $78-104,000 per year. People get upset with the salaries of federal legislators, but the actual pay they receive is incidental. The salary isn't the problem. It is high compared to the average Brazilian, but it doesn't stop there. The problem is that on top of their salaries, they get $975,000 per year for staff, office, and other expenses. Each deputy uses the money differently."

(To understand the following example, one must know that federal Deputy Edmar Moreira was accused of using public money to pay the cost of security for his private company. During the investigation someone noticed that the deputy lived in a castle--not a large house, more like a small village--which he'd built while a government employee. The lawyer went on:)

"For example, the deputy with the castle: He used the allowance to build his house and to benefit his own business. Though his use of public money was visible to all, he was found to have done nothing illegal."

That is because there is no law against using his office allowance for private purposes. Would legislators like the good Deputy Moreira be willing to pass such a law?

The interviewee's professor commented, "Who else found him free of guilt but his peers who do the same type of thing? All have their tails caught in the misuse of public money. They are all guilty, even though they don't feel guilty and aren't legally guilty of anything."

The jurist agreed, "And everyone knows it. The Public Ministry does nothing about corruption by the Congress. If the Public Ministry starts to investigate someone like Sarney, in retaliation he can make life miserable for the investigator. Before the 1988 Constitution, a Sarney would completely erase a nosey prosecutor.

"The ethics committee also does nothing. The public prosecutors can't do anything because of the laws restraining them. Each legislator gets $1,000,000 per year for four years. [Brazilians demonstrate against this corruption, wearing clown noses.] It's senseless to go into the streets wearing clown noses to ridicule them. We are the clowns. We should wear those noses every day."

The system gives public "servants" enormous monetary and legal privileges. Thus, unequal treatment under the law contributes to the divide between the citizen and his ruler, the politician. Not only academics and lawyers recognize the inequities. One morning, years after my visit to Paraty, I sat at the breakfast table, reading the paper about banker Daniel Dantas' being arrested for income tax

---

[23] *Estado de Minas*

evasion. Geralda took a look at the headline and said, "He will never go to jail. In Brazil the rich do not get convicted, only the poor." As Geralda predicted, a year had passed and the bank president still walked freely among us.

Months later, I heard the story of a politician's son who drove drunk and had a car accident in which a number of people died. A computer expert gave his account:

"He was not arrested. Later he killed a retiree, and he was still not arrested. Then he killed a child. He has still not been arrested. The family of the first victims sued him, but they have received no money because the lawyers are still 'negotiating.' It could take ten years to get through the courts. If you have money to pay bribes to the judges, then things move fast. If you have no money, nothing happens."

When I later asked the jurist about these two complaints, bribery and withholding awards, he acknowledged that some judges take bribes. Money and privilege intertwine in Brazil.

The need for information.

We have heard that the rich get special treatment by the courts, and the federal politicians have huge amounts of cash available to them in salary and expense accounts. Even at the local level politicians can make salaries that shock Brazilian citizens. For example, one day I learned that in the state of Minas Gerais, the yearly salary of Paracatu's mayor had during the worldwide financial crisis grown from $84,000 to $112,000. As a result, he earned more than the president of the country. A few days later, I found out he was not the only highly paid mayor.

On May 11, 2009 the headline in the *Estado de Minas* read, "Mayors of Minas Gerais Earn Salaries to Cause Envy." Further on, the paper said, "Administration of cities in the state of Minas can be lucrative. One small city had a mayor with a bigger salary than Governor Neves ($72,000) and more than President Lula ($80,000). It is Reinaldo Landulfo Teixeira, who earns $133,000 for running Capitão Eneas, a town of 14,000 inhabitants in the north of the state. In Nova Lima, in greater Belo Horizonte (BH), the mayor earns $153,000, more than the chief executive of the capital (BH). Irrespective of size, there are numerous other examples, cities such as Mariana, Itauna, Uberaba, Uberlândia, Curvelo Pirapora, Montes Claros, Abaeté, Sabinopolis, Itabirito, and Três Corações."

Five days later (May 17, 2009) the paper followed up with an article titled, "My Dear Mayor," making a pun on the word *dear*, which in Portuguese even more clearly means *expensive* than it does in English. We learned that the mayor of Tiradentes' Ouro Preto made $91,000 per year at the current exchange rate. We were also told, "While payments to the mayors rise, many cities in Minas suffer from a lack of health, education, and infrastructure. In Inhaúma in the center of the state, work stoppages threaten the water supply and waste treatment, and the mayor makes $71,500, [a lot by Brazilian standards]. In Dores do Indaiá, . . . where basic services are lacking, the mayor makes $104,000 at the same time teachers getting paid $6729, little more than minimum wage [$5200], try to survive by working two jobs. In Belo Horizonte, the mayor costs $.05 per person. There are places where the rate is 800 times larger."

The paper reported that the only limit on mayoral salaries is that they can't surpass the pay of the judges who sit on the Supreme Court. What about the voters who paid those salaries, those 14,000 people in Capitão Eneas who paid almost ten dollars per person, and for what? How hard can it be to run a city of 14,000 people? The city councils set these salaries, just as they do where I come from. I could not believe the voters would approve of such salaries. So, how could they be so high? Aren't those councilmen worried about getting voted out? Why aren't they getting recalled?

I asked the last question, and my girlfriend looked at me blankly. She showed no sign of responding, a behavior more and more frequent as my questions continued to trouble her. She was becoming increasingly annoyed with her country and with me.

Someone in Brazil had heard of the concept of recall elections. In 1988, or thereabouts, when Brazil was writing a new Constitution after its recent dictatorship, Domingos Leonelli proposed recall elections for governors, state legislators, and mayors, but not the national congress.

When the military gave up running the country, many of the same politicians who made laws under the dictatorship attended the Constitutional convention. The conservative politicians from this party, as well as others on the right, disagreed about many things; but apparently they agreed that, first and foremost, they wanted to maintain power, and power in Brazil could not be hogged. It had to be shared. Keeping power in the hands of the politician, rather than the voter, they opposed the idea of recall by six to one. Those from the left of the political spectrum supported the idea, though barely. Thus, the National Constitutional Assembly voted it down.

Robber-mayors need not fear recall. However, sometimes the press can shame politicians into giving back some of the public money they have taken. On May 12, 2009, the *Estado de Minas* reported that two mayors had cut their pay in half after the paper published their salaries. They must have cared about re-election.

In the same issue a separate article told how only five of seventeen city council-people in BH had actually kept campaign promises regarding transparency. Unlike the over-paid mayors, these people seemed to have no concern about getting re-elected.

No one could surpass congressman Sergio Moraes in his disregard for the nation's public opinion. Moraes was serving as head of the Ethics Committee investigating the use of public funds by his colleague, Edmar Moreira, the afore-mentioned castle builder who was accused of using public money to pay for security of his private companies. Before the investigation had even begun, Moraes advised the press that he was going to absolve the deputy on the charges: "Public opinion is garbage," he told reporters. "The public doesn't believe what you write. You beat us up, but they re-elect us."

Thanks to public pressure instigated by the press, the chairman of the Ethics Committee removed Moraes from the ethics investigation. Criticizing the move, Moraes said, "The chairman of the Ethics Committee is under the control of Antônio Carlos Magalhães' grandson, to whom he owes favors." As one Brazilian cynic said, "If you want to know what a Brazilian politician is doing wrong, listen to what he accuses others of doing," leading one to suspect that Moraes owed favors to the accused castle builder.

Moraes may have been forced to step down as head of the investigation, but he predicted well. At last report, Moreira, the castle owner, had gone unpunished. And why? President of the Camara (House) Michel Temer was quoted as saying there was no rule against using tax money for one's private businesses.

The details of each scandal are not important. There are so many scandals in Brazil, a virtual museum exists to honor them. One important point is that a great deal of tax money is siphoned into the bank accounts of elected officials because there are no actual laws, nor sometimes even internal rules, to stop them. More strangely still, they get re-elected; but even when they do not, and a new bunch of legislators arrives in Brasília, nothing changes.

Moraes did not fear losing his next election. The headline announcing his plan to defend his colleague against the taxpayer said, "Instead of the People, a Cigarette." When I heard he came from a tobacco-growing district and championed tobacco use, I thought I understood his confidence in being re-elected: His constituents probably liked him.

At this point in my acculturation to Brazil, I barely understood the questions. The answers lay far from reach. I didn't understand why my informants felt as though they had such limited power over their elected government. Public opinion could stop a particular behavior, such as Moraes chairing the ethics committee, but it could not affect the overall outcome: Moreira was still found innocent of breaking either a law or a rule of the House.

Organizations like TransparencyBrasil seemed to believe that the people simply needed information, as if people could change things if they knew what their politicians were doing. The local newspaper, *Estado de Minas*, seemed to be doing its part in the educational process. Its investigative reporting reminded an American of the *Washington Post* during the Nixon administration (but bore little resemblance to the laryngitic American press during Bush's follies).

For example, Ronaldo Scucato editorialized, "Democracy Needs a Facelift." He called on the people to restore democratic principles such as equality, responsibility, and solidarity. In support of his thesis, he dug up a four hundred year-old quote from a Cardinal De Gondi, which said, "People have to rid themselves of corrupt politicians by means of the vote." He also quoted Rousseau: "The secret ballot is sufficient remedy for corruption." A clergyman with whom I spoke voiced similar optimism:

"I see changes, reasons for optimism. The perception is that the rich are not punished; but they can lose powerful positions in government. President Collor was impeached. We are highly taxed, as you may know. We used to have something called a 'check tax.' Every time wrote a check, a tax was charged."

"So you were charged one tax when the money came in and a second tax when it went out?"

"Right. It was supposed to pay for healthcare and to last only two years, but it didn't go away. It lasted two more years and two more and finally eight years. The press got hold of the issue and got people angry; and when enough letters were sent to Congress, the tax was repealed even though President Lula wanted it. Of course, then the income tax went up." (And the government is currently attempting to resurrect the check tax.)

"Do you think the tax went away due to public pressure?"

"Sometimes the politicians listen, sometimes not. Of course, we don't know if pressure also came from powerful groups and companies. We don't know how much politicians listen to people."

As we know, in Oliveira's view the politicians of Brazil are part of an oligarchy which continues to control the country and milk it for personal gain, just as Portugal did during colonial times. In his interview with *VEJA* he said, "Well, the social inequality is clearly and simply the effect, multiplied and amplified, of the permanent existence over many decades of undeserving, privileged oligarchies sucking up the public resources."

Why, then, does public outrage sometimes register on the politician? Could a few honest politicians change things? If people learned how to identify and re-elect honest politicians, could honesty spread? Perhaps a few well-publicized, good apples could purify the bushel. "We should vote for ethical people," Scucato suggested.

Sounds good; but where I come from, politicians and pundits like to say, "People vote their pocketbooks." Ethics are pretty, but apparently only skin deep. If they are to be motivated to vote for "ethical people," voters need to understand that they pay for corruption through the price of goods. They must be made aware that future jobs depend on economic growth. It sounded as if the average citizen needed information.

Publisher Carlos Oliveira gave a speech in which he argued, "Corruption was one of Brazil's ten plagues." If I understood correctly, he said Brazil must improve productivity, improve wages (The minimum wage is low.), improve internal competition, which would force prices down, reduce bureaucracy, reduce the tax burden, make giveaway programs conditional upon incentives to work and get an education (Fourteen million people are on the Family Purse program.), increase preventative health care, including water purification and childhood vaccinations (It's cheaper than waiting.), and reduce corruption because "corruption retards development."

According to the journalist with whom I spoke, the key is "education, education, education." She maintained, "Brazil needs education in critical thinking as well as job skills. It needs ideas, education in the ability to assess and plan development and growth, . . . and in the ability to envision the future and develop strategies for economic development. We need statesmen who will think about the future, plan and invest in development, not just winning the next election." Perhaps the schools could train young minds.

Divisions in Access to Education

An architect told me about working in the architecture program at a federal university: "It was a federal job, so it was secure but paid little. My colleagues spent their energies fighting each other over a small amount of money. Operating under unfair rules, they began to attack each other to win favors from the administration, like in *No Exit* by Sartre . . . Now the Lula government is trying to starve the public university system. When we elected a man who had not finished high school, how could we expect him to understand the importance of education? An uneducated electorate can easily be lead by demagogues. By voting for him, we asked for our educational system to be dismantled."

His aunt, a college professor, responded, "The Lula administration considers the federal universities to be elitist. First the dictatorship [starting in the 1960's] ruined the public schools, so people began sending their children to private schools to get a good education. Of course the students who could get into the federal university turned out to be the children of parents who could afford private high schools. Now this administration wants to destroy the federal universities instead of improving the public high schools. The students from the public schools are not prepared. They can't do the work. I don't think I've ever passed one. When the public universities lose good professors, the best education will go to the kids who can afford private schools all the way through college."

I thought out loud, "At least this way the wealthy will be paying for their education."

The architect corrected me: "The goal is to save money, not harm education, but that is the result."

Thus, we have been told that before the dictatorship, the public schools were well funded and superior to the private primary and secondary schools. The situation has reversed itself since 1965. Now, the free high schools don't prepare many students for the best colleges, which are in the federal system and, oddly enough, are free. Thus, in Brazil college is free for the best students, who come from among the upper classes. The result is a very well educated elite, which contributes to continued concentration of wealth in the hands of a minority.

On May 26, 2009, the *Estado de Minas* headline read, "The quota system is suspended in Rio." The article said, "The action against quotas for negroes and students from public school was proposed by the state deputy, Flavio Bolsonaro." The paper reported no plan to improve the public schools, or to give bright public school graduates extra help to prepare for the work at the federal universities, or to institute a scholarship program based on ability to pay.

According to one economist, economic growth will not result in a redistribution of wealth unless jobs pay well; and that won't happen without the education of the workers. Education must become "democratized," he said.[24] What might one conclude about Brazil if educational quality were actually in decline?

According to Easterly, in a highly unequal society, the oligarchy will vote against the education of the masses; and except for the rich elite, the medium level of income will stay low. In a relatively egalitarian society, on the other hand, the elite will vote for the education of the masses, and everyone will benefit from their increased productivity.

Mario, the doorman, didn't specifically mention college as a goal for his daughters. However, he did complain about "the social imbalance" and "distribution of wealth." He understands that education is the answer for his daughters and that they will have trouble competing with wealthy children from the best schools.

Divisions in Access to Business

On a Sunday afternoon, Tatiana and I sat down with someone near the other end of the economic spectrum from Mario. The owner of several businesses, Ronaldo wore a reddish beard which masked his thoughts. I had no idea what he was going to say about Brazilian society. As it turned out, he said plenty:

"From the point of view of business, corruption in Brazil, as in the rest of the world, opposes the flow of traffic, swims against the current of business . . . Here, talent or education is not enough to succeed in business. You need money to get in the game. People without money do not have access to business like those in the privileged classes. For example, before companies can bid on a federal job, bribes must be paid. The best-prepared, most competent company with the greatest technical capacity will not win the bid unless it pays. That raises the cost of everything . . . " He concluded, "Liberty is not equivalent to democracy." (We return to this statement in Chapter 9.)

An article in the paper would provide some statistics to back him up. With interest rates down, many Brazilians with money to invest find that putting money into their own businesses generates more profit than putting it into the financial markets. Accordingly, business startups have risen. However, an entrepreneur said, "Instead of buying fixed-income bonds, we are going to invest $200,000 to set up two gourmet cafeterias." Further on (see Chapter 10), I discovered how few Brazilians had that kind of money.[25]

One of the costs of opening a business is the bureaucracy. For example, to open a practice, a psychologist must have the funds to pay for a license and the overhead involved in operating an office, such as phones, utilities, etc. He or she must also pay a business tax which is not graduated according to income. The psychologist will not have a full schedule immediately, but the taxes must be paid, and they are not cheap. One psychotherapist told me she netted no income the first year of practice, just enough to cover expenses and taxes. In short, the tax discouraged business start-up.

---

[24] Easterly, *Op. Cit,* {/ 337-338.

[25] *Estado de Minas,* Oct. 11, 2009

A second business cost is bribery. The elected politician is only the tip of the governmental iceberg. One mustn't forget the bureaucrat. Ronaldo told Tatiana and me, "Brazil is wasteful. It has one million public employees." Bureaucrats holding strategic positions at the local, state, and national level can provide permission to a project or refuse to permit it, depending on favors and bribes offered.

On 5/11/09, *Estado de Minas* said this about bribery: "Business pays bribes as a running account . . . , it was discovered by a Federal Police investigation . . . To obtain advantages in competition, the subcontractor made 99 monthly deposits between $2,500 and $37,500 over twelve years into the account of the government employee."

When I asked the computer expert about this practice, he said that his boss could not bid on various projects because he was not on the list of bidders. To get on the list, he would have to pay bribes, but he refused."

Are people letting their imaginations run wild with conspiracy theories? Apparently not: *VEJA* provided a vivid picture of bribery when it reported the existence of a 110-minute videotape showing former Post Office Chief Maurício Marinho during an alleged bribery negotiation with a businessman. In the tape, Marinho received and put in his pocket R$3,000 (then about $1,259) in cash. He insinuated that Deputy Roberto Jefferson commanded the scheme.

Divisions in the Marketplace of Ideas?

According to Oliveira, even the intelligentsia can enjoy a privileged position if they support the oligarchy. In exchange for money, positions, or other advantages, the professor or researcher can withhold criticism of the government. I decided to ask Carlos, an award-winning writer, if this were true. In an email he wrote the following answer:

The question of oligarchy "is in my mind one of the most complicated and controversial. In the first place, *oligarchy* is a very precise sociological concept, abundantly studied by specialists. There appears to be unanimity that we accept it as a good definition of past and present Brazilian social structure. The highest concentration of power (political, economic, cultural, etc.) is in the hands of the oligarchies--small groups which are almost always, but not only, familial." Though here have been improvements since the middle of the twentieth century, "None of this has been sufficient to correct the inequalities of what is one of most unjust societies on the planet . . . I don't know the meaning Mario de Oliveira, Filho attributed to the word . . . It appears that he refers to Thought-Policing, that is, a strategy of persecuting and silencing adversaries . . . to eliminate the competition in whatever area would be in question: theater, film, art, literature, and everything else. Since the sixties, it has been a practice as common from the left as the right. Today the practice continues at full speed, and no one worries any longer if it's on the left or the right. It's all the same. One must recognize this as the result of pressure groups . . . that are formed naturally in all areas by people eager for advancement at any price. But this doesn't have a direct relationship to our oligarchic [social] system. Those [artistic] groups only can be called oligarchies in a figurative sense, not in the literal sense. But it is clear that an affinity exists [between the political oligarchy and those seeking cultural hegemony]. Thought-policing feeds off the system and *vice versa*. The idea that writers and artists are 'obligated' to criticize the system and to propose a 'better' vision of the world, or otherwise they will be accused of adhering to an 'oligarchy' and banished, has a lot to do with policing thought, but not much to do with the oligarchic [social and political] system in itself."

I would take that to be a "no." Carlos saw pressure coming from both sides of the political spectrum, but he didn't see the artists as a group which catered to the rich and powerful. Though Carlos doubted that artists participate in the oligarchy, he did not dispute that an oligarchy controls Brazil.

Spatial Divisions:

The extent to which urban Brazilians live in fear behind walls has been amply described. The urban divisions that have resulted from slavery and poverty are described further on (Chapter 7). Another form of geographical division came to light in a Brazilian home.

A professional woman showed me around her apartment and apologized for the "maid's quarters," tiny rooms in which the maid could sleep and go to the bathroom. She explained, "They are the slave quarters left over from the days of slavery."

Tatiana chimed in, "You saw slave quarters at the museum in Ouro Preto. They were horrible places."

I did remember seeing them at the Casa Bandeirista, former home to the tax collectors who plagued the miners and prompted the Minas Conspiracy. The slave quarters were dank, dark places where people slept close together in windowless dormitories. Most would have been men since the colonists didn't want many females and found babies to be expensive. In Brazil the hardworking, poorly cared-for males died young and were replaced not through breeding, but through new purchases.

She went on, "These little maid's quarters are still built onto the apartments in Brazil. Why are they so small? Why should someone be treated like this? You don't have this in the States."

"Maybe we don't currently, but we did in the past. A little Texas town called Remington has a great steakhouse. A lifelong Texan drove me out, and we passed a narrow, windowless shack. I couldn't imagine humans staying there in the heat of central Texas and asked, 'What was that shack for?'

"'Slave quarters,' said John.

"'Slaves? Why did they need slaves here? They don't grow cotton out here. This is cattle country.'

"'Why, to do the work,' said John without editorializing by comment or inflection."

Brazil remains divided. It started in colonial times with a few wealthy families enriching themselves by using slaves and underpaid laborers. For some reason, the ability to ignore the welfare of others continues in business and government, placing the wealth of a major world economy in the hands of a relative few. I would learn more about how this came to be, but ultimately I wanted to know what kept this oligarchy alive in a democratic country.

Back in Paraty, Nelson and I turned to the fourth side of the city's square, the sea. A deck full of tourists, mostly from São Paolo, joined us on a sailboat, and we divided into our own separate groups. Nelson went scuba diving. I chose to snorkel. In calm waters I watched a barracuda float motionless among a school of oblivious, tropical fish, like a privileged shepherd guarding his flock, his prey, his lunch.

Pedro, the Just, . . . The odious crime, of which he was the victim, hallucinated an infant and caused him to take up arms against his father.[26]

Sebastião Nunes

Chapter 6: Petrópolis Via the Highway of Death-- A Country without a Hero

Nelson and I dried off and set out for the city of Petrópolis. Our route took us north from the coast on pockmarked BR-040. The road skirted the terraced hillside. As long as our car drove on the inside lane, I enjoyed the ride. On the way around one of these hairpins, Nelson said, "I think one of the heirs to Brazilian throne died in an airplane crash. Third in line."

"What!" I blurted. "Brazil has a throne?"

"Oh, yeah. As a matter of fact, two branches of the family have guys vying for recognition as the current non-reigning King of Brazil, Prince Pedro Carlos from Petrópolis and Prince Luis from the Vassouras branch. Luis' son, Pedro Luis de Orleans e Bragança, went down with that Air France flight. On the Vassouras branch, he was third in line after his father. There is a lot of competition for that job."

"What job? Brazil doesn't have a king, does it? Did it ever? Why would Brazil have a king?"

(I was pretty ignorant on the subject.)

"Not any more or not yet, depending on how you look at it. It has everything to do with Petrópolis."

Upon our arrival at the summit, we found a small city full of dignified, institutional buildings, including of all things a former palace, now a museum. Nelson explained that the city had been the brainchild of Pedro I, Brazil's first king, an explanation which opened a whole new can of Brazilian worms.

"I still don't know why Brazil had a king, let alone why he would need a summer home in the mountains."

"Well, I'll tell you," said Nelson.

Nelson had an encyclopedic memory. At the age of fourteen, he could recite every nation in the world and its capital. Once he described the entirety of *Naked Lunch*--the incomprehensible, drug-induced film written by William Burroughs--his recitation taking as long as the movie, itself. Just to be sure, though, I checked on his historical facts concerning the building of metropolis.

Touring the city, he explained: "At the beginning of the nineteenth century, Dona Maria I [1734-1816] reigned in Portugal. Because she was half nuts, her son, Dom João VI [1769-1826] became Prince Regent of the Portuguese Empire. However, in 1808 Napoleon Bonaparte closed in on Lisbon, causing Dom João to flee to Brazil in a large fleet escorted by British men-of-war,

---

[26] Nunes, *Op. Cit.*, P. 92

temporarily establishing Rio de Janeiro as the official capital of the Portuguese Empire. From Rio, the Portuguese king ruled his huge empire for 13 years, and there he would have remained for the rest of his life if it were not for the fact that Portugal fell into turmoil without a king to keep people in line. In 1821 Dom João returned to Lisbon, leaving his twenty-two year-old son, Dom Pedro, in charge of Brazil. After a year in the homeland, the king attempted to return Brazil; but his son, Dom Pedro flourished his sword and declared Brazil's independence from Portugal and independence from his father. On October 12, 1822, Pedro wrote up his reasons for Brazil's secession from Portugal and established a Constitutional monarchy, assuming the title of King Pedro I of Brazil."

An informant told me, "Portugal didn't put up much of a fight, but some battles did take place in Bahia." Most famously, Mother Joana Angélica, a nun, martyred herself on a bayonet when Portuguese troops invaded her convent. Troops loyal to Portugal drove the Bahian rebels into the countryside, but guerilla war continued. Hostilities ended in 1825 when Portugal recognized Brazil's independence.

So, in 1821, almost thirty years after Tiradentes' martyrdom, Brazil got its own king but not self-rule in the sense of democratic elections. With Tiradentes scattered all over Minas Gerais, there was no hero to stand up to the King. I asked Nelson if anyone had taken up Tiradentes' fight for independence and self-determination.

He laughed and told me, "Brazil has a hero, but a very different kind of hero. Their cultural icon is a 'hero with no character.'"

"Who is that?" I asked him.

"His name is Macunaíma and he is the brainchild of Mario de Andrade. In 1928 Andrade wrote that his 'hero' dropped fully grown from the womb of his aged mother and didn't speak until he reached six years of age. Macunaíma traveled from the countryside to São Paulo with no goal other than *finding* 'lots of money,' as opposed to *earning* lots of money. Sometimes Brazilians, like Andrade, attribute Brazil's woes to a defect in the national character. Whereas Tiradentes was a workingman who wished to take responsibility for the governance and development of Minas Gerais, Macunaíma sought only comfort. He was content to scam wealth away from those who had it. Work and responsibility were abhorrent concepts. He was lazy but not ashamed about it. He unapologetically told people, 'I'm lazy.' His only goal was to make money. And he was dishonest. Once, in the film version, he said, "I didn't mean to lie. As soon as I had started talking, I was already lying." He was also not particularly sympathetic to fellow victims. After watching a man get cheated out of almost all his money, he chastised him and then stole his last dollar. Brazil has no other hero."

"Why would Macunaíma become a symbol of Brazil?" I wondered. I soon discovered that this view of the Brazilian character didn't begin in 1928. It had been around since Brazil's beginnings. When an interviewer asked Jadir Barroso[27] "how did corruption begin to conquer and destroy the country?" Barroso responded, "Pero Vaz de Caminha tells us that the oldest ancestors of the Brazilian people were two thieves and evildoers who during the time of exploration, or invasion, by the Portuguese, were called 'the degraded ones.' When Pedro Álvares Cabral returned to Portugal, he left these two 'degraded ones' here as exiles from Portugal. . . From their interaction with the indigenous people, they certainly left many offspring. They are the two patriarchs of the Brazilian civilization, two exiled criminals, the fathers of corruption in the country."

---

[27] Barrosa, Jadir, "impunidade causa principal do aumento da corrupcao no pais." P. 73-74.

Coming from a country with heroes like "honest Abe," "I-cannot-tell-a-lie" George Washington, and "Be-sure-you're-right-then-go-ahead" Davy Crockett, I found Brazil's cultural heritage hard to swallow. When I next met with the journalist, I told her, "When I ask Brazilians what they like and don't like about their country, they tell me they don't like the level of corruption. How would you explain Brazil's lack of success in curbing corrupt practices?"

I heard the same refrain: "Corruption is in the Brazilian DNA, not literally, of course, but it dates back to colonial times and is endemic to the culture."

I asked about Tiradentes, and she responded, "Tiradentes is more of a cautionary tale than a blueprint for how to be Brazilian. AFter all, he did not succeed in making Brazil democratic."

At this point, Tatiana muttered, "What do we worship on the anniversary of his death? We are still slaves, only now we are enslaved by our own system."

Between trips to Brazil, I sought tutoring from a Brazilian living in my home town, a young student named Carla. As my return trip approached and the classes were winding down, I asked Carla if she planned to return to Brazil.
"Not to live," she confessed.
"Why not?" I asked.
"In the United States there are rules, and people follow them. The Brazilian way isn't to change the rule if it is bad, certainly not to follow the rule, but to find a way around the rule."

All Brazilians know the phrase that describes this cornerstone of the culture, the *jeitinho brasileiro* was Carmen Miranda sang a song by the name, but she didn't exactly celebrate the trait. She sang from the perspective of the victim and advised the listener, "To always smell a rat" ("*Viver com a pulga atrás da orelha*"). The rat in this case was a man who watched his fiancée's sister undress in the garden while thinking about having both women.

Brazil even invented a law to cover such sins. In the pursuit of self-interest, a Brazilian can invoke the Law of Gérson. They say Gérson was a famous soccer player who always found a way to gain advantage over his opponent. If one gains advantage, the means employed are not considered important. It appears that politicians are skillful adherents to the law of Gérson and that voters expect and support such behavior. No one writing about Brazilian politics fails to mention the famous campaign slogan used by Adhemar de Barros, who served as mayor and governor of São Paulo during the 1950s and '60s. Forthright about his profiteering from public works projects, Adhemar allowed his supporters to successfully defend him with the motto, "He steals, but he gets things done." Lying and stealing are permissible under the Law of Gérson.

Macunaíma had no future as a political activist. He felt no responsibility for what went wrong. According to his analysis, what ailed Brazil was beyond his control: Brazil has "too little health, too many ants." His only solution to life's problems was to steal a magic stone which would bring riches to whomever possessed it--wealth without work or any other merit, an imitation of the Portuguese royalty.

If this was intended to be a metaphor for the evolution of a culture, it suggested that the Brazilian citizen did not feel responsible for the country, nor had he developed the skills necessary for self-rule. I wondered, "How did Brazil get from a monarchy to a democracy?"

In 1823 an assembly drafted a Constitution which reduced the powers of the King. At first Pedro I dissolved the assembly; but by 1824 he accepted the Constitution, which provided Brazil's model for a constitutional monarchy until 1889.

The rebellious son, Dom Pedro I, had a royal home in Rio, but the city was hot in the summer. (It still is.) His European guests didn't like the muggy tropical heat. Plus, some say

Dom Pedro was embarrassed because his house wasn't as big as some of the rich Rio dwellers, so he decided to build a palace in the mountains.

There weren't many amenities up there at the time. The Star Mountains stand over three thousand feet, and they weren't easy to climb, especially when the Coroado tribe was active. Nevertheless, Dom Pedro I liked its climate and in 1830 bought the Córrego Seco Farm, which was part of one Father Correia's estate. He planned to build a palace, but buying the land was as far as he got on the project.

One year later, Pedro wrote a paper (not so well known as his alleged proclamation — "Independence or Death") to state the reasons for the secession of Brazil from Portugal and bequeathed a constitution instituting a constitutional monarchy in Brazil, assuming its head as Emperor Pedro I of Brazil, also known as "Dom Pedro I" or "Dom Pedro Primeiro". He was liked by the common people, but displeased both the landed elites, who thought him too liberal, and the intellectuals, who felt he was not liberal enough.

To keep the monarchy intact, he abdicated in 1831, returned to Europe, and left his five-year-old son behind as Emperor Pedro II. Three years later, Dom Pedro I died, and Dom Pedro II inherited his father's estate, including the farmland in the mountains, which was leased. Some time later, a member of the child King's staff, Paulo Barbosa da Silva, decided to resurrect Dom Pedro I's plans to build a summer palace. He must have liked the mountains. Certainly little Pedro II didn't care one way or another.

As Dom Pedro II approached majority, cathedrals, museums, and other government buildings joined the summer Palace. They were built as the country seethed with civil unrest for the first nine years of Pedro II's reign. In 1840 both houses of parliament declared the young regent had reached majority, and he would rule Brazil for 49 years. As emperor, Dom Pedro II would spend up to six months per year in Petrópolis, the city that bore his name.

The summer season on the Star Range would last up to six months, from November to May, and during that whole time the Emperor remained in Petrópolis. In 1835, the Malê Revolt, perhaps the most significant slave rebellion in Brazil, took place in the city of Salvador da Bahia.[2] After a period of nine years of regencies, Pedro II was declared of age in 1840 and assumed his full prerogatives. Pedro II started a more-or-less parliamentary reign which lasted until 1889, when he was ousted by a coup d'état which instituted the republic. At that point Brazilian citizens still enslaved roughly 700,000 Africans.

At the end of his reign, he presided over the abolition of slavery in 1888. Technically, he was still King; but according to one version of the story, his daughter, Princess Isabel, actually made the decision for "her thoughtful and once astute, but now elderly and infirm father, the Emperor Dom Pedro II, who was . . . [by then] known around Rio as Pedro Bananas."[28]

After the Proclamation of the Brazilian Republic in 1889, when the Imperial Family was banished into exile in Europe.

Angry that the monarchy did not compensate the landowners for their slave labor, the large landowners, who held the rank of colonel in the military, staged the coup led by General Deodoro da Fonseca that ended the Brazilian Empire, and Pedro II was deposed on November 15, 1889. General Deodoro da Fonseca became the country's first president, and Dom Pedro II and his family were exiled to Europe, or in the words of Nunes, " . . . deported and desolated, Dom Pedro II took the monarchy into eternal exile (the country abandoned to the republicans, the military, and the opportunists) . . ."[29]

---

[28] www.historyworld.net/wrldhis/PlainTextHistories.asp?historyid=aa88.

Brazil had first freed itself from the control of one Portuguese king; then from his son, a Brazilian king. It was finally free to rule itself, but who would do the ruling? Not the majority of adults. In 1874 Dom Pedro II's Constitutional monarchy allowed one million of its ten million population to vote (10%). By 1910, the population had risen to 22 million. Of these, 627,000 could vote, or not quite 3%, but another 21,373,000 people lacked a voice. Thus, the Republic was less democratic than the monarchy.

Who made up this 97% that could not vote?

It is easier to say who weren't excluded from power. The army officers didn't put themselves among the powerless. That's for sure. Until 1930, a military junta served as only national institution in the country, but it didn't meddle in internal affairs. The military junta left administration of the nation to local oligarchies, those wealthy landowners called colonels.

The three percent who actually got to set domestic policy included these landowners and other wealthy people. The colonels ran their local areas and chose the state governors, who in turn chose the president. Thus, in this system the power remained clearly in the hands of the oligarchy regardless of what was written in the Constitution.

In the 120 years since deposing Pedro II, Brazil became a democracy with universal suffrage. Nevertheless, men like Senator Sarney were still being described as colonels. According to a report written in 1999, "This form of oligarchy still exists the poorer areas of Brazil, . . . including much of Brazil's rural North and Northeast, but also poor agricultural areas of the Southeast and South . . . The influence of the . . . colonels is based on two pillars: land and getting out the vote."[30]

The story of the Peixoto family illustrates the phenomenon. In 1890, the year after the coup, three Peixoto brothers arrived in the Jequitinhonha Valley, a Portugal-sized area in the northeastern corner of Minas Gerais. They found a dense forest, which they soon cut down and made a fortune selling the wood. Within a decade of their arrival, one of the brothers already owned 125,000 acres. The Peixoto family has remained one of the most powerful families in the valley. In 1999, the head of the family was "millionaire rancher Pedro Emílio Almeida Peixoto . . . . Peixoto is part of a close-knit and powerful group of twelve families that maintain an economic empire in the Jequitinhonha Valley."

These families are not as powerful as they once were. "It would be naïve, however, to assume that the reign of the colonels is nearing its end. Most city council elections, campaign financing, and even the selection of candidates remain under their control." It was as if the original captains had broken with the throne and found a way to continue running the country as they saw fit.

The story had taken us as far as the end to monarchy and the extension of suffrage to 3% of the wealthiest men. After taking a look at Pedro II's second home, Nelson and I returned to highway 040, which that year was Brazil's unofficial Highway of Death. (The honor would pass to BR-381 in the future.) The highway connected Rio with Brazil's third largest city, the unpublicized Belo Horizonte.

I would drive a stretch of the highway on another day when, having secured my Brazilian driver's license from a sad man in a small office at the department of traffic, I volunteered to

---

[29] Nunes, *Op.Cit.,* P. 88.

[30] Holston, James, "Democracy and Violence in Brazil," Comparative Studies in Society and History, vol. 41, no. 4 (1999): 691-729. (reprinted in: Mexico, Central, and South America: New Perspectives, Vol 2: Democracy, ed. Jorge I. Dominguez (New York: Routledge, 2001): 43-81.

drive round-trip from Belo Horizonte to the city of Tiradentes. On the very day of our tip, someone took the time to count the potholes on one side of BR-040 between the last Belo Horizonte exit and the next exit down the road. The number surpassed one thousand.

I could not match the speed of the native drivers, but unfortunately I tried. Everyone understood that lanes had no meaning on this road. Each driver needed access to both lanes to avoid the biggest holes and settle for the smaller ones. At times the shoulder provided the best route.

Six people died on that stretch of BR-040 over the weekend, and not all in one wreck. There were many wrecks. One woman approached a truck at such a narrows and like me stopped just in time, but the truck behind her did not stop and she was sandwiched to death.

Why is a major road in such bad repair? Remember Brazil is not a poor country. According to Tatiana, the state governor said it was a federal road. The federal government said the road had been sold to a Spanish company, and it was their responsibility. Do the Brazilians not care what happens to their compatriots? On this day they did. President Lula is generally liked, but occasionally even he can become the target of outrage. Residents along the highway appeared with banners declaring, "Lula, every pothole is a life!"

This all took place before Obama announced in a press conference, "Lula is the Man. He's the most popular politician on the planet." Obama's declaration received much hype in the Brazilian press, but no one mentioned how it came about:

Obama stood smiling beside Gordon Brown at a press conference as the G-20 met in London on April 1, 2009. Brown laughingly quoted Lula as saying something like, "When I was a unionist, I blamed industrialists. When I was the opposition, I blamed the government. Now that I am the government, I blame the Americans and the Europeans for the financial crisis."

Brown seemed not to notice he had betrayed and ridiculed a fellow head of State. Obama's smile froze. I gulped. It appeared to me that Obama was covering for Brown, or distancing himself from him, when he praised Lula.

I asked a local religious leader what the Brazilians like about their President, and he said, "He's a guy from the people, from humble beginnings, not much formal education. He fought to be President till he won. People respect that. The beginning of his presidency was a period of worldwide economic boom, which benefited him. The conservatives were relieved that Brazil did not become communist. He put good economists in the Central Bank."

The list of accomplishments was growing long, but he hadn't yet gotten to the crux of things: "When he took office, the minimum wage was about eighty reals a month, slave labor. Now minimum wage is not only higher, but is pegged to growth and inflation, so it grew twelve per cent in the last year, and it's growing three to four per cent above inflation every year. With the Family Purse Program, poor people get money not just to eat, but to buy other things, to be consumers. They also get money if they send their kids to school."

"Lula's the man." But BR-040 kills people. Banners flow in protest, but do banners address the problem?

Tiradentes and Macunaíma provide two competing models for Brazilian citizenry, the responsible versus the self-absorbed and passive. I mentioned the demonstration on BR-040 to the clergyman and asked if this were the exception that proved the rule:

"Are Brazilians passive and complacent about dishonest policemen, murderous highways, and government corruption?"

He conveyed his view of the Brazilian social conscience with this example: "Volunteerism doesn't work in Brazil. If I get someone to go visit an invalid, they might go once or twice, but then they stop. They don't stick with a cause unless, for example, cancer has hit a family member, and then they might campaign for money for cancer research."

I asked, "What does it take to motivate people?"

"People get really mad after the media exposes corruption. They write letters, and something might be done. But this bothers me about Brazil in all classes. There is a culture of stealing. We are not ethical about money and property."

I commented, "If kids are harmed, Brazilians seem to become outraged."

"Over children, yes. Brazilians are very affectionate and caring. Children and family are very important. They get very upset about things like that."

I also gained some insights into the Brazilian social conscience from the red-bearded businessman. We were talking about soccer.

I asked about performance of the Brazilian soccer team in a World Cup final against France. I wondered if they had been bribed to throw the game.

"That isn't it. Their performance shows a cultural difference from the U.S. In the U.S. you are raised to try your best in school, in sports, in work, to put forth effort. But in Brazil it is not that way. We have the best players, but not the best effort. The Brazilian player is happy to be in the final, but victory is a team thing. In such a situation, the Brazilian player does not give his maximum effort. In the U.S., hard work and talent can lead to success and wealth, but in Brazil there is no guarantee that effort will bring rewards. In the U.S. people are proud of working hard; in Brazil, is shameful to work . . . From colonial times, Brazil had no program for homesteading. The entire country was owned by a dozen families. Others worked while the rich got richer. They were not building a country, but raping a land . . . The U.S. culture was different from the start. Immigrants to the U.S. were building a country. They took ownership, financially as well as having a sense of responsibility. In Brazil the Japanese, the Chinese, and the Jews have retained a culture in which the family is invested in education and the child tries and excels, but it isn't part of the Portuguese culture . . . "

Do the Brazilian people not feel a sense of responsibility for their country? A little while after this conversation, Lula invited anti-Semitic Iranian President Ahmadinejad to Brazil. In São Paulo a crowd of thousands demonstrated; and a law was proposed making it a crime against humanity to deny the holocaust ever took place, as Ahmadinejad had done. The Iranian decided he was too busy in his re-election campaign to make the trip. Months later, the holocaust denier quietly made an unannounced trip to Brasilia.

The grandeur of the Law is in its total impartiality. The law punishes equally whatever citizen--rich or poor, powerful or humble--who bathes in public places, sleeps on park benches, and robs passers by.

Millor Fernandes

The Brazilian nation, impacted for decades by political practices contaminated by corruption, dishonesty, and the interests of the oligarchy . . .

Mario de Oliveira, Filho

Chapter 7: Rio de Janeiro—Is Brazil as Violent as they say?

On this day, Nelson and I were taking the road in the other direction from Belo Horizonte. We coasted downhill into Rio during the spring, so we were spared the sauna which once drove the Brazilian kings to Petrópolis. On a mild, breezy night, Nelson insisted I have some typical food and drink. Not wanting to freeload on my friend, I had to make a stop at the ATM. He suggested I not linger at the money machine after making my withdrawal.

"There haven't been many kidnappings lately," he said, "and you don't dress like a rich guy, but you still have to be careful."

I scored a few hundred reals and disappeared into a crowd with the money in my front pocket. Then, to hold us over until dinner, we grabbed a snack at a popular sandwich shop in Ipanema, where Nelson helped a famous American clothing designer read the menu. It was interesting in a strange way to watching the celebrity wink and smile at him.

The dinner menu would have to include *churrasco*, varieties of meat cooked on a grill and brought to the customer until he ate himself into a state of unconsciousness. It was okay. I'd had barbecue before, but never *cachaça*. They make it from sugar cane, and some varieties are very good. My least favorite came with a snake in the bottle. Like the worm at the bottom of a mescal bottle, the snake had given up its innards, including its poison, to the drink. It tasted like kerosene and made my lips numb. Nelson discouraged my sampling this one. He said it was only for dumb tourists, but I couldn't pass up a drink with its own snake.

Over dinner, Nelson insisted I take the trip up to the huge crucifix overlooking the city. I refused. It looked just fine from my seat on the beach. I did take him up on the tour of a *favela*, though. I knew practically nothing about *favelas*, except they were considered slums and hosted gang wars.

I would read that an estimated fifty-one million Brazilians live without water, sewer, and trash collection, though probably not all in *favelas*. The *favelas* were also reproducing: The census in 1991 counted 384 *favelas* in the city of Rio; in 2000, they found 513, an increase of over 30%. In the state of Rio de Janeiro the number of impoverished neighborhoods grew from 661 to 811, up 22.7%. The rate of population growth in São Paulo's slums is five times the growth of rest of the city. As for the living conditions, I knew only that they were considered dangerous.

"Don't worry," he said. "You're probably safer up there than you are down here it the city. The tours have an agreement with the drug lords that you will not be harmed during a tour."

"What about police?"

"There are squads that raid the *favelas* from time to time, but they don't dare conduct regular patrols. The *favelas* police themselves. You'll see."

An American expat got the same story when he first moved to Brazil. He told a Brazilian friend he intended to take a walk up the hill.

"Into the *favela*?" screeched the friend.

"Yeah, why not? The people seem friendly."

"You have to have permission from the drug dealers. Police don't even go in there."

I would later learn that years ago police rid one of Rio's *favelas* of its drug business and set up a station there. Now that *favela* has a small hotel for tourists. Being high up, the hotel provides a great view of the city, or so I was told. However, a policed *favela* is the exception.

Urban Brazilians believe that crime originates from impoverished neighborhoods, both *favelas* and *cortiços*, where the people are considered to exist on "the fringes of society, humanity, and the polity." (*Cortiços* are subdivided houses that lack the spaces, installations, and separations that designate a home.)

A tall Scandinavian-looking woman, the guide talked passionately about the *favelas* while driving a van-load of tourists up the mountainside. First she told us the reason the van contained only foreigners: Few Brazilians ever visit the slums overlooking their major cities.

Then she explained their history: The military used promises of land to induce slaves freed in 1888 to fight against Pedro II. The deeds must have been lost in the mail because the unemployed, former slaves descended upon Rio and had no place to live.

According to another source, many of the original *favela* builders migrated from the northeast where much of the population had slaved on sugar plantations. After the end of slavery, the northeast had many unemployed former slaves, driving the wages of labor down. According to the British consul in Recife, labor was cheaper in sugar-producing Pernambuco than anyplace in the world outside of Asia. Not surprisingly, poverty led to property crimes. The unemployed stole livestock, food, tools, guns, money, and anything else they could sell. Many then moved south to the industrial cities in search of jobs.

When the former slaves reached Rio, they didn't find the existing slums appealing. The authorities didn't find the newcomers very appealing either and demolished some of the existing slums to force them out into the streets. Then they decided to move to the high, vacant ground on the hillsides in and around the city. No one, no landowners or representatives of the government, appeared to dispute their presence, and they began to build structures. The first *favela* dwellers built their houses out of wood and garbage. Later, when they had the money or access to free building materials, they upgraded to a concrete home. The first *favela*, said the guide, was built on Providência Hill, now in the center of Rio de Janeiro, but we had by then arrived at another.

Stepping out onto paved streets lined with the brownish brick buildings, someone asked, "Where do the building materials come from?"

"They are appropriated from construction sites--the bricks, the pipe for plumbing, the wiring--it all comes from down below."

"Appropriated? Not bought?"

"Not bought. They generally don't have money to buy these things."

Those who found no employment resumed their previous occupations as thieves. Drugs came later.

"Drugs are trafficked in these *favelas*," she said, "but don't ask the residents about it. You are being allowed to visit their homes. They would consider it rude to bring up the topic. Most of the residents have nothing to do with drug trade."

None of them spoke Portuguese, so the problem would not arise.

"Does the city provide them with water, sewer, and electricity?"

"No, officially, this community does not exist. These houses have no addresses. They splice into the power supply with something called a cat hook. The residents have learned how to take water from the public supply and return sewage to the city system."

"All unofficially?"

"Yes."

"So, how many people live in these nonexistent communities?"

There is no way to know for sure. If you were born here and died here, the government might never know you existed. But, as you will see, in many ways it is very much a part of the city's life."

Strolling through the streets, we saw the works of local artists on display--paintings, jewelry, clothes, toys. In one building we heard the sounds of a radio station broadcasting live. We found people sitting at computers and surfing the net. Motorcycles made deliveries just as they did in the city below. Buses ran. People did their banking. We were told that the city even collected the trash.

Certain residents had contracted with the tour to allow visitors. The rooms we walked through were clean and uncluttered, but sunlight passing through small windows left them dark. I didn't breathe fresh air until we got outside, grateful we toured in the relative cool of spring.

When we passed the poster of a famous soccer player, the guide explained, "He is very popular here. He comes from this *favela*."

"What kind of work do these people do?" someone asked.

"Those who don't have a CPF number aren't eligible for many jobs, and lots of them don't want the government questioning their income. So, they are limited to cleaning, babysitting, performing on the streets for tips, prostitution, and drug dealing. But others do all sorts of jobs. Construction workers, teachers, some policemen who keep their professions secret, and at least one doctor live here."

"The policeman wouldn't want them to know he was a cop?"

"No, the traffickers would be paranoid, so he'd be killed. The police are afraid to come up here on patrol, but they have to sometimes, and they come up shooting. Because of this, the traffickers are very strict. Residents can't do anything which will invite a visit from the police— no stealing from one another, no wounding a family member or neighbor who might need medical attention."

"If you do these things?"

"You disappear."

"How do they know what is happening?"

"Their informants and look-outs are everywhere. If you hear a few firecrackers at night, the lookouts are signaling that the police have been spotted. If you hear a lot of firecrackers, that means the local soccer team has won."

"Why would a professional choose to live up here?"

"I don't know about a doctor, but the military police and teachers don't make much money. Up here there is no rent, no utility bill, no property tax, and it might be safer."

"If the people with good jobs have more money, do they buy more stuff?"

"Sure. You'll see TV's and computers. They take the same precautions as anyone—locks on the doors, grates on the windows. Even here it isn't completely crime-free."

One tourist asked, "I've heard the government has built housing for the *favela* dwellers. Do they like moving out?"

"They like to be given a new apartment, but lots of times they don't stay in them, not if they can't afford the rent and taxes. Some of the people from the *favela* move in, remove whatever they can carry, and then rent the place to someone else. They get an income that way."

Another questioner changed the subject. "How does it work that different families build on top of each other?"

"Mostly, people 'own' only the floors they build. It would be dangerous if they let the buildings get too high, so there is a limit on the number of floors. Each builder of the first . . . [several] stories finishes off the roof with footings for the next story."

I left the tour with questions. To begin with, if these places breed crime, does the government plan alternative living arrangements for the poor? On May 20, 2009, the mayor of Rio de Janeiro told *VEJA*, "In campaigns, to enter the *favelas* it was normal to meet men armed to the teeth. Today I have a chance to contribute so my kids don't live in a similar situation . . . There is no plan to remove *favelas*. There is a need to improve the quality of life, and there are situations in which removal ought to be discussed. There are 1000 *favelas* in the city. Most are very small; and in this universe, yes, there are cases in which removal is a solution."

So, his government would like to see the *favelas* replaced by safer, cleaner, crime-free neighborhoods. Meanwhile, Belo Horizonte is building fifty-four apartments to replace bulldozed homes in Pedreira Prado Lopes, the oldest *favela* in the city. Those eligible want the health benefits of more garbage collection, less population density, and increased security. One former resident said he was reluctant to leave his lifelong, eight-room home for a two-bedroom apartment; but once moved, he appreciated the reduction of violence. It sounded as though the drug gangs in Belo Horizonte weren't keeping the peace as well as those in Rio.

Favelas can be thought of as a real estate problem. They occupy potentially valuable land, but the residents are not benefiting from its appreciation. On a flight back to the U.S., I sat beside a Brazilian computer engineer who lived permanently in San Diego and talked about the process of increasing wealth.

"Why did you emigrate?" I asked.

"I am financially better off in the U.S. I can use my home to build wealth. First, I can get a thirty-year mortgage. That's unheard of in Brazil. A twenty-year mortgage is very rare. [It had become less rare in the several years since he and I talked.] In the States you can resell your house at a profit and reinvest in a new home."

Obviously slums exist because of poverty. One must not forget that Brazil has the ninth worst distribution of income on the planet, meaning millions of people have hardly any money. People can live in better housing either when they find jobs and have sufficient income to move out of a slum or if the government were to build them homes which are practically-speaking free of rent, taxes, and utility costs.

Why do so many Brazilians live in such poverty? Where did the millions of urban poor come from? Different people give different answers. My first answers came from the tour of a *favela* in Rio.

After the tour of the *favela*, I didn't really understand the nature of drug trafficking in Brazil. I turned to academic research, to a retired policeman who wrote a book which has since been made into a movie, to a social psychologist, to two films well-known in the U.S., to a recent (2009) autobiographical film by a convicted cocaine user and dealer, and to the press.

The social psychologist spoke to me in her parents' home. Her paintings adorned their walls and told of her ability to capture a complicated scene. In explaining her view of the problems facing the *favela*, she painted a disturbing picture.

In her view, people continue to migrate to the cities looking for work. They come from different cultures, with little education, with no knowledge of city life, and with few skills for work in factories and offices. "It is similar to France," she said, "where the immigrants from Moslem countries create cultural clashes, and violence rises. Here people come from the countryside, desperate and poor, and find themselves crowded into small quarters, often without basic conveniences like a shower. As they run out of money, they have no job and no family to help them. Nearby, people live in relative luxury, as if in a different world. The proximity to rich neighborhoods stimulates both the drug trade and the burglary and car-theft businesses. Young children become involved because they cannot be arrested. It becomes a dangerous and explosive situation and very complicated to resolve."

She talked about the movement of the drug trade from the campuses of the sixties to the *favelas*. "Drugs were introduced by foreign students from the surrounding countries, including Colombia. During the seventies there was an anti-dictatorship, hippy counterculture. Marijuana and cocaine were common and not considered criminal by people of this group. The government which created the drug laws was not considered legitimate, so drug users didn't think they were doing anything wrong. The people in the *favelas* had nothing to do with it at that point."

A dramatization of this transition took place in the award-winning film, *City of God*, which got its name from one of Rio de Janeiro's *favelas*. The story began in the 1960's and depicted the *favela* as a Levittown of small, free-standing brick homes along dirt roads. Most of the residents were African-Brazilians who had come "to find paradise," thus the settlement's name. Apparently, heaven was not equipped with hot water; when one of the characters took a hot shower in an apartment outside the *favela*, it was the first of his life.

Early on, the film focused on "the tender trio," three young "amateur" hoodlums who carried handguns and stole for a living. They were shown stealing money for themselves as well as canisters of gas for their neighbors. The implication was that the older generation attempted to work for a living, but their male children were growing dissatisfied with their poverty.

Crime reached a higher level when a younger boy called L'il Z started giving the three older guys ideas for making more money. He suggested they rob a motel full of prostitutes and johns. Not till the end of the film does the viewer learn that L'il Z returned to the scene of the crime after the tender trio left and killed everyone there just for the fun of it. In a few years, L'il Z would become the kingpin of cocaine traffic in the City of God.

In other words, serious crime came into being when the male sociopath realized he could have money and power by selling drugs to the rich people in the city. Whether this particular individual was fact or fiction, his character depicted the makeup of the young men who turned the *favelas* into the center of a profitable and violent trade in cocaine.

During his interview, doorman Mario told me, "The worker who struggles to feed his family and doesn't do anything wrong is not worth anything. The drug dealer in *favela* is the guy who is looked up to."

In the film this happened after L'il Z killed other dealers and was awash in money. Adults who didn't consider L'il Z "respectable" nevertheless out of fear treated the murderer with respect; but to the younger males, he became a role model.

By this point the film depicted the *favela* more like the one I visited. Along with free-standing shacks, taller buildings appeared, creating a much higher population density. Perhaps as a result, the Runts appeared, little boys smoking pot and running the streets. As they got older, the boys were recruited to deliver cocaine. Later they graduated to the job of lookout, which in those days involved sending up a kite when they spotted police.

The movie showed how drug dealers discouraged crime within the *favela*. The Runts were stealing from *favela* residents. The boss, L'il Z, didn't like the practice because it invited police attention, so he forced one of the children to kill another. Then he sent them off to tell their friends to stop stealing in the neighborhood.

The film showed how this violence created an escalating cycle. Z sadistically raped a young woman, which made an enemy of her boyfriend. The boyfriend became a central figure in a year-long war like that which preceded my visit to the real *favela*. Each violent act brought violent retribution. Did the movie end apocalyptically with the violence breeding so much violence and revenge that the whole system imploded and destroyed itself?

Of course not. The ending predicted Brazil's terrifying present. Z was killed, not by the police, not even by his rival drug lords. Li'l Z had armed the runts, and then they killed him.

Did they say, "He was a bad man. Now, let's go to school"?

No, they yelled, "The business is ours!"

In the final scene the Runts walked away from L'il Z's corpse, one preschooler tripping on his flip-flops and pulling up his pants trying to keep up with the big boys. Waving their guns as if they were harmless toys, the kids made plans to kill other children whom they didn't like.

One asked, "Can anyone write?"

Another answered, "I can a little."

"Let's make a blacklist," said the first.

Armed, illiterate children who killed happily—no wonder Brazil has a problem with violence.

The movie claimed to be based on a real story about a *favela*'s resident called Rocket who took pictures of the war and became a journalist named Wilson Rodrigues. (It also might have been based on a novel by Paulo Lins, who did rise from the *favela*.) One of Rocket's pictures showed police selling guns to Z. Another showed the cops releasing Z after taking his money. In other words, the police armed these gangs and helped maintain the drug trade as a moneymaking proposition, a claim made by others.

No one with whom I spoke complained about drug use, itself. The complaints focused on its bi-product, the violence. I interviewed Leonardo, aged 23, with his mother and a friend over lunch. He explained one of the forces driving the drug trade.

Leonardo: "What I like and don't like about Brazil? I don't like the violence. I like the generosity of the Brazilian people, but it was better when I was young. Now people are more frightened. They will not start up a conversation with a stranger because he might demand their money."

I told him, "I read that in 1996 Brazil had twenty-five homicides per 100,000 people. At that rate, it would be 750 killings a year in greater Belo Horizonte."

"It's higher than that now," he told me.

Compared to Rio and São Paulo, Belo Horizonte has little crime or drugs, but that isn't saying much. To put things in perspective, crime, especially violent crime, has been rising steadily since the end of the dictatorship in the 1980's. In São Paulo, for example, an armed assailant robbed an estimated one of every twenty inhabitants in 2002. That's 1,704 robberies per day, an impressive rate. Between 1980 and 2001, homicides rose 130% to 27.8 in 100,000 inhabitants per year. In comparison, the homicide rate in the U.S., a relatively heavily armed and violent country, is usually five to six per 100,000, a fifth as high. In and on the periphery of *favelas*, the death rate often exceeds 100 per 100,000 people, one of highest in the world.

And which people are dying? In Rio the murder rate of young males between the ages of 15 and 28 was a staggering 239 in 1999. At its current size (almost twelve million in 2008), if Rio consisted entirely of young men, 28,000 would be murdered per year. A high proportion were hunted down by police and attacked like enemies in a war. I didn't witness any young men being killed by police, so what's the basis for saying they were killed "like enemies in a war?"

During a five-year span in São Paulo, police killed 1500 people, 111 of them in an infamous prison massacre. Were these killings the result of the police needing to defend themselves against heavily armed Brazilian criminals, or were Brazilian police more often trying to kill rather than arrest the suspect?

Recently in New York City for every person killed by police, four were wounded. This would lead one to believe that the NYC police weren't usually shooting to kill. On the other hand, in 1992 São Paulo police killed 4.6 people for each one they wounded. So, in São Paulo a person who was shot by a police officer was eighteen times more likely to die of his wounds than a New Yorker.

One writer claimed that "the killing rate in Brazil, tens of thousands of violent deaths a year, falls within the parameters of the United Nations' definition of a low-intensity civil war." Roughly ten years of war in Vietnam produced 58,256 American names on the war memorial, around 6,000 per year of shooting. At the rate cited above, São Paulo police, alone, could kill that many suspects in a mere four years.

So, Brazil is violent. Back at the interview with Leonardo, I asked. "What do you think is the reason there is more violence?"

"I think it is because of materialism. They watch TV and see the ads, and then they want things they can't afford. People want more, but they are poorer now."

The friend disagreed: "People aren't poorer now, but appetites have been created. They want more, and they don't have the education or the means to get these things without dealing drugs or stealing."

Leonardo's mother added some doubt about poverty being directly related to violence: "In Bahia people are poorer, but it is not as violent as here in Belo Horizonte."

"And Belo Horizonte is not as violent as Rio?" I asked.

Leonardo: "No, Rio is worse."

Leonardo's mother picked up the paper (*Estado de Minas*, March 14, 2009) and opened it to a picture of young men who had been arrested for drug trafficking. Lined up against a wall with heads bowed, all were in their early twenties or younger. One looked no more than twelve. The charges included dealing cocaine and marijuana, possession of firearms, and murder. The scene was being repeated daily in the major cities of the country. "They are just children," she said. I was pretty sure none could read or write very well.

As a consequence of the robbery and constant threat of violence, the rich and even the middle class live behind walls. The wealthy hire security and install electronic surveillance for their apartment buildings. Such a building might claim among its very wealthy tenants a businessman (gem dealer), a doctor (plastic surgeon), a politician (a senator), and a member of the legal profession (a judge), to give but one example of who accumulates wealth in Brazil.

Someone with considerable money but a lower profile might be content with a guard sitting behind bulletproof glass and unlocking the gate only for residents and invited guests. His neighbors would likely include professionals and businesspeople.

The freestanding homes of those who can afford them hide behind high walls. To gain access to one such home, I have to call as I pull up. If the sidewalk is empty, the gate is unlocked electronically from the inside and closed immediately after I pass through.

I have visited another type of freestanding home. One has an open view of the mountains and valleys an hour outside of town, but even this remote site requires an invitation or a bribe to get past the guard. A professional woman with a medical husband has such a second home in a gated community. They built it with double the needed materials. The first load was stolen the weekend after being delivered. Someone drove up with an empty truck and somehow convinced the guard that he should be allowed in. Then he managed to sneak out unnoticed past the guard's station with a truckload of bricks and lumber.

To recover the cost of the loss, the victims must sue their own homeowner's association, which will take years to get through the courts. The police haven't managed to locate the truck driver or the guard.

This kind of robbery is pedestrian by Brazilian standards. A major university recently lost much of its computer hardware when stealthy thieves sneaked unnoticed past the guards and electronic surveillance with a ton of computers. Apparently the guards didn want to die for a universitýs computers and didn´t have the firepower to match the thieves´.

I also visited Leonardo's home in a less affluent part of town. The bottom floor is not open to the street, but a burglar could easily enter by the back. The three pit bulls have so far dissuaded them.

As he was growing up, Leonardo and his family lived in a different home, one owned by his father's employer. They thought they were building equity in the home. After Leonardo's father died, his mother assumed they would be allowed to stay as long as they continued to make payments, but the owner said they had to vacate. Among his other duties, Leonardo's father helped his employer hide money. On paper his father owned lots of things, including their house. Unfortunately, the home did not really belong to the family.

They would have lost the house if his mother's employer, Tatiana, did not have enough money to hire an attorney and threaten to sue the dead husband's boss. Fortunately, the company didn't want its crooked books opened by the court, so they offered Leonardo's family a cash settlement for the house. It was enough for her to buy her current home.

The new house is stucco and open to the tropical air. When I saw it the previous winter, it had a solid, permanent feel. The following fall, the picture had changed. It had rained a lot over the summer, almost every day for months on end. The neighbor's house sits on a hill above theirs. The water is supposed to flow along a retaining wall and down the hill. Unhappily for Leonardo, the neighbor, without benefit of either a permit from the city or the advice of an expert, has begun building a two-story addition for his daughter and her kids. This building abuts the retaining wall which holds the hill in place and protects Leonardo's home from a mudslide. The addition prevents rainwater from flowing off the hill as it should. Instead, the rain seeps into the ground, forces itself through two holes it has created in the wall, and gushes into Leonardo's living room.

When I arrived, Leonardo and a handyman were laying pipe from the hole to a floor drain. This would prevent the water from flooding the living room, but it would not prevent the water from washing the soil out from behind the retaining wall. Since this dirt supports the house which sits above them on the hill, in time this house will begin to sink and lean into the wall.

I suggested they get someone from the city to inspect his addition, but there were three problems standing in the way: (1) The neighbor would be angry and seek revenge, (2) their repairs were also not up to code, and (3) Leonardo's mother had a parrot. Seven years ago she found an injured parrot which had lost its jungle home to urban sprawl. She took care of it, but Brazilian law forbids someone from keeping a parrot at home. If someone from the city came to inspect the neighbor's construction, he would also look in Leonardo's house and see the parrot; and they would not only lose the bird, but would be fined $2,500, $2,500 which they don't have and never can have.

From Monday through Saturday, Leonardo's mother gets up at 4:00 a.m. to take two buses across town. It takes an hour in good traffic, but she often sits on buses for two hours. She cleans, cooks, conducts business for the household (deliveries, repairs, shopping), and does laundry.

For ten years she used the same washer--a small, rickety model, which had since been discontinued. After ten years, her employer bought a new one and gave Leonardo's mother the old one. She was ecstatic because when she finished cooking, cleaning, and doing laundry for her employer, she went home and did the same thing there, except she had always done her own laundry by hand.

Leonardo and his two adult sisters attended public schools. At this point in the story they owned no car, but Leonardo had paid to take drivers' education and secured a chauffeur's license. Then he got a job driving and making deliveries for a restaurateur.

Leonardo's oldest sister paid tuition to attend a professional school. Being smart, thorough, and hard-working, she found a good job. I asked her mother's employer a stray question about the young woman's upward mobility:

"Where I come from, women in her position sometimes marry the boss. Could that happen here? Will Leonardo's sister marry a wealthy, young business owner?"

"Never."

"Why not?"

"He would take her home to meet his mother, and the mother would ask her, 'Where does your family live.' She'd tell her the neighborhood where they live. The mother would ask what her parents do for a living. When she said, 'My mother is a maid,' the relationship would be over."

The youngest daughter works as a clerk in a store. Like her mother, she must take the bus to work because the family has no car. Not too long ago, she was robbed on the bus. Recently, she earned her driveŕs license.

Surprised to hear about her driver's license, I asked if she had a car.

The young woman's eyes glistened with tears as she said, "No, we can only dream of such things. We have to work very long to buy them."

The restaurant owned by Leonardo's employer serves small portions at European or New York prices, but the food is delicious, and the restaurant has been packed since it opened. On a Friday as the owner was leaving with the night's earnings, several men robbed and beat him. The thieves said they were keeping him alive so he could continue to work for their money. The owner said he would hire security. I asked Leonardo's mother if she thought the security would be sufficient.

"It will help, but it isn't enough. The thieves drove a car. Two got out but others were inside. If he doesn't give them money, they will kill him. If he gives them money, they will beat him because it is not enough. This is Brazil."

Four days after the robbery, the restaurant owner had not hired security. Did he think the thieves will not strike again? The robbery was his second *of the day*. His safe had been robbed of gold that morning. Leonardo sometimes closed the restaurant at night or opened it in the evening. He also carried cash to and from the bank, sometimes as much as $20,000. He became so afraid of being assaulted and robbed, this professional driver accidentally caused a fender bender shortly after the robbery.

If the police were investigating, the robbers would not be hard to find. They mentioned the name of a former employee who probably told them about the gold in the safe.

"Will the police pick them up?" I asked.

This is the answer I received: "There is an ex-policeman who is now retired and has become a gangster. He gets arrested and then released, and he starts his business again. He owns slot machines, sells drugs, runs a gambling operation, and now he is prison again for dealing coke. He is controlling his business from inside prison with his cell phone. So prison isn't enough."

"Do you think Leonardo is in danger," I asked.

I was no longer getting "yes" and "no" answers. I got this: "At 7:00 one night two years ago, a professor at the university was walking to his car with his teenaged son. Thieves with a gun took his car, his money, his cell phone, and were about to drive off. As they were getting in the car, one of the thieves turned and shot the man in the heart in front of his kid."

Thus, in relatively quiet Belo Horizonte, Leonardo says people are afraid to talk to strangers. Mario agrees: "I don't like the violence. You can go out onto the street and get robbed; and when you ask for help, it won't solve the problem. No one provides help. Police take hours to get there. The thief won't be arrested. The police are weak. Laws are flexible. They open and close according to someone's interest. If it is in the policeman's financial interest to arrest someone, he will try. If not, he won't. Police are corrupt. They receive bribes from the criminals. In my neighborhood it happens a lot. I've seen lots of cases where the drug dealers bribe someone in charge of security." On cue, the paper reported that as the residents were moving into their condominium in a new high-rise with state-of-the-art security, thieves somehow managed to remove all of their valuables despite cameras and guards.[31]

The frequency of crime has created another problem for Mario: "There is prejudice against the working man. In this wealthy neighborhood, people have seen me working in this place; but when I go down the street dressed like this [white shirt and tie] to go home, they still turn away thinking I may be a thief. [Mario, who is mixed race like many Brazilians but relatively few of the upper class, is politely suggesting the presence of racial stereotyping, i.e., even if he is well-dressed, people in the neighborhood assume he is poor and therefore dangerous

---

[31] A thorough explanation of Brazils Judicial system is described by Marcelo Cunha de Araujo in *The Rich Don't do Time in Brazil*, available in English on Amazon.

because of his dark skin.] I like to work, so on my days off I come in to wash cars. I'm dressed in shorts, and I can see people are scared of me. People who dress like that work for criminals, and that's why the people are afraid."

Businessman Ronaldo was less likely to be the victim of robbery on the street than someone from a less secure neighborhood. Still, he concurred that police are corrupt: "The police in São Paulo and Rio de Janeiro are completely corrupt. If you are stopped and you don't have your documents, you will pay $25 to the police so they don't take your car. Is not ethical. The impunity of those in power is left over from colonial days before the dictatorship. The citizen accepts the schema, whether large, medium, or small."

My girlfriend suggested, "The individual should start to become ethical."

Ronaldo countered, "Or, the law should be enforced at all levels. There is a lot of white-collar crime . . . " Then he went on, "These cities [Rio and São Paulo] lack security and are more violent than Belo Horizonte. Most places aren't as bad as these two."

The press occasionally mentions police corruption, even suggesting that police confiscate drugs and then resell them to the traffickers. Research supports the common belief that police corruption is at the heart of Brazil's crime:

"[There exist] criminal activities which are so pervasive that they could not exist without police cooperation or complicity: The rise of drug trafficking; the sale of not only guns, but heavy artillery like anti-aircraft missiles and landmines; theft and robbery of vehicles; the frequent escape of prisoners . . . are all testament, in their own ways, to the involvement of police in organized crime. More troubling for democracy, however, is serious corruption, which is evident in criminal activities so pervasive that they could not exist without police cooperation or complicity."

I asked a young man, "What does it do to a man to live with such impotence, such helplessness to protect his family? Leonardo complained of the violence but without suggesting that he could do anything about it."

The man answered, "There is nothing we can do except move away." His best friend had just immigrated to New Zealand.

"It can't be that bad, mate," I thought in New Zealandese. Alas, while I transcribed my interviews, my girlfriend was at work. A phone call interrupted her. Her daughter, a realtor, had been robbed.

The young woman told her mother, "I was with a client, a pregnant lady, and we were looking at an apartment across from the hospital. It was well lit, and there were people around and a guard watching over things. I put my purse in the back seat when I got in. Before I could start the car, I heard this explosion. Two guys, just teenagers maybe 16 or 17, had thrown a rock through my window. There was glass everywhere. They took my purse. It had all of my I.D.'s showing where I work and live, a spare key for the apartment, cash, credit cards, the documents for my car, and the check you wrote me to pay for my licensing class. It was blank and you had signed it. My client said she doesn't think she will buy in this neighborhood."

The worried mother immediately had to cancel her appointments and come home because her cell phone would not allow a 900 call to ask the bank how she could stop payment on a stolen check. She came home and found out she had to go to a branch and perform the operation on one of two computers that print checks. Fortunately, her bank had recently instituted evening lobby hours.

The first computer would not recognize her card. The other one believed who she was; but when she followed the instructions given to her by the 900 man, the machine would not let her cancel the check. It wouldn't let her "exclude" the check, so she decided to "include" it, and the ATM accepted the transaction.

Of course, that was not all. She performed this transaction on a Friday night, but her request would expire in 48 hours. She would have to hope the thief did not sign his name to the check and cash it on Sunday night. Then on Monday morning she had to drive across town to speak to someone who could make the cancellation permanent.

After that, it would take 96 hours for the police report to be available. In the meantime the daughter, who needed her car for work, had to get her window repaired and all new I.D.'s and driver's license. Her mother and I would go to the hardware store to buy a new deadbolt for the apartment door.

Monday and Tuesday were spent getting new documents. Finally the victim would have a new driver's license at 6:00 p.m. on the second day. Without it she would not be able to work.

The police report was thorough, a little too thorough: They even fabricated one detail: "We pursued the perpetrators but were unable to apprehend."

The victim explained the next development: "Some of my documents were found in a nearby dumpster. The workers find many left there by thieves, and they called to tell me. I picked them up and discovered that the robbers kept my license and car documents. As soon as my brother heard, he said, 'They plan to steal your car. They know where you live and where you work. You cannot drive that car again. We must sell it tomorrow.'

"We spent the evening on the internet looking at car prices, and I've arranged to take my car into the dealer where I bought it, but I cannot drive it in by myself. We need a man or maybe two to drive it in. My mother will take me in another car."

"Is it risky in broad daylight?" I asked.

It was a dumb question. Whenever we are stopped at an intersection, Tatiana askes me to roll up my tinted window. The windows are tinted because on her way to work one morning, some kid looked through the then-untinted window, saw a woman alone in the car with a purse on the seat next to her, and used a rock to break the window. Then he extracted her purse and sauntered in the direction of the nearby *favela*, twirling the bag happily.

Without stopping to think about the consequences, she got out and ran after him. Fellow motorists drove on. Pedestrians laughed at her. Weeks later, after replacing all of her stolen documents, she got tinted windows.

Tinted windows didn't help the guy parked outside her building last year while his wife ran upstairs to fetch something. Around the corner in her nice, safe neighborhood lay a little police station to provide rapid service to the residents. The nearby cop shop didn't deter the thieves who spotted the man in his car at noon, waiting for his wife. They got in and made him drive them away. Then they kicked him out of the car and drove it into the *favela* where no policeman dared follow for something as trivial as a stolen car.

Leonardo's sister was robbed on a full bus. No one did anything.

"Why not?" I asked when I heard this.

"A policeman stopped a robbery and has been charged with a crime."

"What crime?"

"The thief got hurt during the arrest, and he was a minor."

"Gimme a break!"

I wondered how much danger my girlfriend's daughter had been in while being robbed.

I was told, "Last month a businessman was robbed right at the same spot by the hospital. After he gave the kid all his money, the kid shot him and killed him." Then Tatiana asked me, "Is this the consequences of a fatherless society?"

"What do you mean by *fatherless*?"

She answered, "I mean the role of the father, not necessarily fathers, themselves. The father role is filled by whoever has authority in the culture, whoever establishes the values and makes the rules and enforces them. Without the society providing this function, we return to barbarism. In civilization everyone must give up something for people to live together. If there is no shared authority that people accept, the children will run wild. And no person can be above the law--no king, ayatollah, or elected senator. When someone is above the law, we have tyranny. I don't know which is worse tyranny or barbarism."[32]

I thought about what I'd been hearing and wondered if a country could have both tyranny and barbarism, but instead I asked, "What effect does it have on the husbands and fathers if they cannot protect their families? What happens to people if they cannot count on the police and courts for protection, if the children are armed and running wild?"

"Is that a rhetorical question?" she asked warily.

"It would be, except I am going to write down your answer."

"My answer: Barbarism! And there are no longer any innocent children. It is *Lord of the Flies*. Anyone who is unarmed becomes a victim."

"Reminds me of the U.S. during the 70's when Charles Bronson made all of those vigilante movies."

"Jody Foster just made one about a female vigilante."

"I am feeling like Charles Bronson."

"We all are. It spreads like evil. [Others have used this term to describe the spread of crime in Brazil.] I don't know what would happen to me if someone were going to hurt my children. I don't know if I could become a monster who would kill that person."

"This has already turned me into a Charles Bronson, but you are being turned into Meryl Streep in *Sophie's Choice*. You cannot act to save your children, and you are already feeling guilty."

Despite being warned not to visit the park when there were few people around, I wanted to work out at the track, and I thought I'd take my recorder in case I found someone to interview. Once past the grocery story and the little plaza, the road ran downhill to the park. A lavender building sat conspicuously near the entrance. Grassy mountain peaks framed the park; and part way up the slope, a *favela* sprouted from the mountainside. On the left of the *favela* sat large houses; on the right, more homes for the rich—hundreds stacked in splendid, condominiumized apartment buildings.

The crowded public schools had both morning and afternoon sessions, so the boys who were "guarding" the cars in the parking lot in the early afternoon may have been legitimately out of school. The patrons were glad to pay them to prevent vandalism to their cars. They didn't even think it odd that vandalism might take place in broad daylight while they were only steps away. The boys were small. How could they protect a car from a vandal? Who would damage the cars if they were not paid to be there? *They* would, of course. Their customers didn't bristle at

---

[32] Freud, S. "Totem and Taboo."

this protection racket. They were not outraged. They were just glad to be spared the cost of fixing their cars.

Though the neighborhood was wealthy, the residents worked during the day, as Mario pointed out. Retirees and babies brought there by nannies occupied the park, but the noon and after-work crowds were busy at this time of day, so the park was practically empty. School-aged children used the track to get from school to the *favela*. I was invisible to most. But a group of young teenaged boys saw my recorder and looked at me as if I were prey. I was practicing karate on the asphalt, so the brazen, fearless stares surprised me. Then I remembered that I couldn't use much karate against these kids if they decided to jump me for my recorder. Brazil passed a law against doing any physical harm to a minor even if assaulted. For this reason, children made many of the drug deliveries.

As I worked out under the watch of the teenaged boys, I recalled this conversation with a computer guy:

"I've heard it is illegal to defend yourself against a minor who might attack you. If a group of big 17 year-olds attacked you, would you defend yourself."

Computer guy: "How many?"

"Seven"

"Too many."

"Two."

"Are they hitting me?"

"Yes."

"I am allowed to defend myself then, and I would. Videos on TV show people defending themselves, pushing the attackers away, blocking their blows. These are okay. You cannot attack them back."

When I told about my trip to the park, my lady friend chastised me for going there in the middle of the afternoon. "It's too dangerous," she said. "Never go there except at noon or after five when the crowds are heavy and the police are there to watch."

So imagine her reaction when I decided to walk forty-five minutes through town after dark on my way home from an interview. The housekeeper shook her head at my carelessness. I was not yet convinced.

I typed away on my computer in the doctor's waiting while my girlfriend had an appointment. First, her doctor came running out and down the stairs. Then she followed close behind, but not running.

"Are you done already," I asked.

"No. Didn't you hear the car alarm?"

"Yeah, those things go off all the time."

"My doctor's car was just stolen. Would you check on my car?" she asked, so I did.

Her car still sat where we had left it. As I watched over it, a police car raced by the building, then came back around the block, this time spying the address, and pulled in. Soon, the doctor appeared, a passenger in someone else's car. He had chased the thieves as far as a *favela* but didn't dare follow any farther. He'd lost his vehicle and his computer. The police took a report but did not even pretend they would recover the car.

Young men committed all of these crimes. A psychologist who supervised the treatment of young criminals said that minors who committed crimes should participate in the process of setting up consequences for their crimes. It sounded like a good idea. Kids should learn something from consequences. "Unfortunately," she told me, "the youthful offenders do not honestly feel sorry for their crimes and rarely follow through on the agreed-upon consequences."

Apparently the young criminals have not internalized the ideals laid out in Brazilian Constitution by the nation's father figures. Tatiana said that they could not identify with the politicians who run the country like oligarchs in a feudal society or maybe a Portuguese colony. In my girlfriend's view, civilization begins when society institutes a rule of law which requires that both the ruled and rulers accept limits to their power. She does not see Brazil as a society in which the institutions of government—such as the lawmakers, the judiciary, and the police—are occupied by people who both enforce the law and obey it, people who thereby embody the country's ideals.

Trying to understand Tatiana's view of Brazil as a figuratively fatherless society, I read an article which psychologist Guilherme Massara Rocha co-wrote concerning the father role in society.[33] After viewing both *No Country for Old Men* and *Elite Squad*, he argued that in both stories, one set in Brazil and the other in the United States, people in authority fail to uphold moral standards and to maintain order. Each film depicted a deficiency of the societal father.

In *No Country for Old Men,* murderous Anton Chigurh, the agent of drug dealers in the U.S., was pursued by a sheriff named Ed, played by Tommy Lee Jones. However, Good did not conquer Evil in this Cormac McCarthy film. (Cormac McCarthy likes to write about evil incarnate.) Ed tried to defend the law, but he could not match Chigurh's singleness of purpose and amoral focus. Ed simply got tired. The principled father figure (Ed), so necessary to a civilized society, lost the battle with barbarism. He retired without capturing the murderous criminal.[34]

Though evil, Anton Chigurh followed a code, not a moral code, exactly. It was personal: He did whatever he has said he would do. He killed a woman simply because he told her husband he would. This was not the kind of code that would have a civilizing effect on society, quite the opposite.

In contrast to Ed, The protagonist in *Elite Squad* was a cop named Captain Nascimento. A military policeman in Rio de Janeiro, he stood on the opposite side of the law from Chigurh, but their behavior was indistinguishable in its cruelty. Rocha saw more similarities between the ruthless Nascimento and the evil Chigurh than between the two police officers.

This autobiographical film, *Elite Squad*, painted an ugly picture of police activity in urban Brazil, particularly the police involvement in drug traffic. To begin with, the ordinary Military Police of Rio were immersed in a continuous process of bribery. The film showed what one student of Brazilian police described in the following words: "Petty forms of corruption include small bribes, shirking, and passive corruption (e.g., turning a blind eye) are common."

In the film, the police culture centered around payment and negotiation: When an officer asked for vacation time, his superior opened a drawer full of money and said it would be difficult to arrange. The officer said he had a right to his vacation. The boss replied that he could help the officer if the officer helped him in return.

The film began with two recruits learning the ropes. In the motor pool the recruits learned that new police cars arrived with old engines. The originals had been removed and sold. An honest recruit tried to report bribery concerning car parts, but his superior tore up his report, and

---

[33] *Estado de MInas,* 19/4/08: "A Nostalgia do Pai," Douglas Garcia Alves, Jr., and Guilherme Massara Rocha.

[34] McCarthy, Cormack, *Blood Meridian.*

another officer warned him not to "step out alone" against the system. He was also told, "To steal for the [military police] battalion is to steal for ones family."

It appeared the system's first duty was to protect itself. When a murder victim's body was found in one precinct, the system did not seek justice for the victim. It did not spring into action to find the murderer and prevent another killing, thereby protecting the citizenry. It did not even consider how to best help the policeman to do his job. The goals came from the top; and those at the top did not want to report crimes in their precinct. Dead bodies made them look bad and interfered with promotions. In the film's most cynical scene, police moved the corpses to a different precinct.

These officers also took money to permit drug traffic, something confirmed by *Don't Call Me Johnny,* an autobiographical film that told about the cocaine trade from the dealer's point of view. *Don't Call me Johnny* showed how João, the protagonist and dealer, was apprehended by a couple of military police officers and had to borrow money totaling five figures to reclaim and sell his product.

Unlike the rest of the military police, the Elite Squad treated the fight against drug trade as war. In other words, " . . . corruption and brutality have allowed some areas of Brazil to develop into zones where drug-trafficking, organized crime, and police violence run rampant . . . the reprisals and friction between police and gangs have produced pockets that resemble war zones." According to the *The Elite Squad,* peace in Rio de Janeiro depended on "a fragile balance between the munitions of the criminals and the corruption of the police."

Since the traffickers were so heavily armed, the members of this unit entered the *favela* at night, carrying automatic weapons equipped with night scopes. Suspects were tortured or assassinated. (Said a researcher, "police corruption is frequently connected to torture, the excessive use of force, and brutality.") If a resident of the *favela* gave information to the police rather than have them insert a broomstick into his body, the gang would then kill him for violating the "code of honor" among the traffickers.

Is the film exaggerating to attract audiences? According to one report, different police have different approaches: In São Paulo, the civil police torture suspects, but the military police execute them. A professional who worked nights in Belo Horizonte explained, "My office is near the police station. On a hot night, I cannot open the windows because I hear the screams of the prisoners being tortured. It is horrible. Even with the windows closed, I sometimes hear them."

Rocha described Capt. Nascimento as a *justiceiro*, a word which connotes both righteousness and inflexibility. His war against drug dealing is not exactly a war against crime. He is more than willing to break the law to enforce one law. Under his command, a police sniper was shown murdering a drug dealer. Could this actually happen in Rio? In 2003 one thousand, one hundred, and ninety-five (1195) civilians were killed by police. That's 3.2 per day.

Elite Squad also exposed the other side of drug traffic, the buyer. It showed law students breaking the law to buy marijuana. In *The Elite Squad* Matias, an undercover cop, told his law school classmates, "Trafficking is trafficking," and marijuana is just as criminal as cocaine. In other words, those who violate the law attack the fabric of the society, even the college students who buy and openly smoke pot. Because the customers for cocaine and marijuana are wealthy, upstanding citizens and their children, Matias lamented, "There is no social contract."

Until being sent to prison, João of *Don't Call me Johnny* showed no sign of suffering as a result of his constant use of cocaine or his dealing, no sign of internal conflict about the dissolute, pleasure-dominated, illegal way he had led his life. Neither did anyone in his family. He dealt and used cocaine out of his father's apartment, but his dying father never complained or advised a change in lifestyle. His mother was tearful during the trial, but in every scene she continued to wear the expensive necklace given to her by João and paid for by his illegal activities. No one in João's life found anything wrong with his lifestyle except the Judge, who said he showed "complete lack of respect for the laws of the country."

Rocha's article on the father figure makes the distinction between civilized and uncivilized execution of power, between exercise of power and maintenance of the social contract. Nascimento is not a policeman enforcing the law to protect fellow citizens. He is a soldier at war with an enemy over *one* law, the drug law, and his Elite Squad is above the law. No one, certainly not the drug traffickers, but also not the police, nor even the law students and their professor, respects *the* law. Brazil does not appear to meet my girlfriend's definition of a civilized society.

According to Rousseau, the law is impotent against the wealth of the rich and the misery of the poor. If Brazil is not ruled by law, what rules the country? Is it the drug lords? I heard this story more than once:

"A drug lord in Rio was arrested, found guilty, and imprisoned as the World Cup of soccer approached. When Brazil made it into the finals, he sent two demands to the warden of the prison. He wanted a cell phone in order to conduct business from prison, and he wanted a TV to watch the finals. The warden reminded the young man that he was a prisoner and not entitled to such favors. 'You will wish you said yes,' replied the crime boss. Soon thereafter, carloads of gang members descended on the business districts of Rio. Stores were shut down, and policemen were shot."

The interviewee told me, "I think that was the time the drug dealers closed the major tunnels into the city. The military was called in, but the residents of Rio objected to the presence of the soldiers. Apparently it reminded them of the dictatorship (1964-1985). Then the government pulled the army out and sent lawyers to the prison to negotiate with the leader of the gang. When they finished discussing matters, he had his TV and his cell phone, and he reminded them, 'Don't forget who runs this city.'"

A few years later, a former student of mine received a phone call in the middle of the night. He heard screams of a young woman and feared his daughter had been kidnapped.

The woman had not yet said her name; but, unthinking, he asked, "Antônia, is that you."

Then the woman screamed, "Daddy, it's Antônia. I've been kidnapped. Please pay them the money."

Fortunately, he then checked the number of the caller, hung up, and called his daughter. She was at home in bed.

I was told that this ransom call and others like it were probably made from jail. Thus, the kidnapping business has fathered a child, the false kidnapping. With the availability of cell phones to prisoners, the incarcerated can continue to make money even as they serve out their sentences.

I don't know what to make of this report by an interviewee: "The veterinarian just told me the latest fashion in crimes these days is the kidnapping of dogs in our neighborhood. Thieves go to the park and kidnap the dogs that are playing alone while their owners are distracted. The thieves contact the owners by phone and tell them the dogs will only be returned if money is paid."

This is a new animal game. Brazil has had another for more than a hundred years. The Brazilian equivalent of America's numbers racket goes by the name of *jogo do bicho*, the animal game. The head of Rio's zoo started it in 1892; and though Rio's penal codes 369 and 370 declared it illegal within two weeks of its birth, it never went away. It eventually became illegal in every state except Paraíba, but Brazilians take pride in their defiance of efforts to stop them from playing.

Since the game violates the law, its survival spreads disrespect for the law and both creates and attracts criminals. For example, because it is illegal, the civil police can make money protecting it. Like the illegal drug trade, it is run by people who are by definition criminals, often the same people with the same violent results, the same police cooperation, and the same needs for money laundering as any other illegal business activity. Police investigations have shown that the runners of the *jogo do bicho* pay bribes, ally themselves with drug traffickers, deal in arms, evade taxes, and even infect Brazil's two favorite institutions: soccer and the samba schools that produce Carnival from the *favelas*.

The federal police reported that the Beija-Flor samba school won the 2007 Carnival contest through bribes and death threats. One of those implicated had strong ties with Brazil's 1996 championship soccer team.

Criminals need friends in high places. Jose Carlos Gratz reportedly used funds from operating the *jogo* to gain control of the state government of Espírito Santo. "By early 2003, Gratz was president of the State Legislative Assembly, controlled the machinery for electing assemblymen, and had appointed allies as judges and prosecutors."

An interviewee summarized all of this when he said, "*Jogo do Bicho* was originally run by samba schools. Then the guys who run it took over the samba schools and teamed up with drug dealers. So now drug dealers from the *favelas* control the samba schools. The city awards a cash prize to the best float, and this money supposedly pays for next year's float and costumes. The making of Carnival is a yearlong industry, and who pays for all the other floats? It's a facade, an hypocrisy. It's paid for by drug money and everyone in Brazil knows it."

So, a simple game designed to make money for a zoo was outlawed and eventually became a source of corruption which has infected Brazil's most cherished cultural events, its protectors of public safety, and its government. The animal game is a symptom.[35]

Araújo explained the underlying disease in these words: "The fight against organized crime in Brazil is almost totally limited to the most visible . . . of the organized criminals, such as the trafficking of drugs and arms, illegal lotteries, prostitution, urban violence, and actions taken by groups of convicts. For an effective fight against organized crime, however, there is a . . . need to tackle, not only the obvious manifestations, but also the secret relationships of crime with the institutions of the State . . . To move millions of dollars or to participate in the power plays and financial dealings requires relationships at the highest levels of the State."

According to the experts, not only would changes in certain policies and procedures be advised--such as putting a police presence in the *favelas*, blocking cell phones in prisons, and increasing the penalties for drug use and dealing--but the legislature and judiciary would have to start prosecuting and punishing white-collar crime, such as money laundering and administrative impropriety.

Araújo maintains that the problem of crime in Brazil is related to the social condition of the least favored, but most of the money designated for Brazil's social problems never reaches its goal. Many times public officials pocket it. If this is true, Brazilians working for the State and wearing white-collared shirts are stealing money from those who wear blue collars or no collars

---

[35] Benatte, Antonio Paulo, Ë bicho na cabeca," *Historia Viva,* #54, Editora Duetto, April, 2008, P. 66-70

at all. This, he says, is the heart of the problem of crime in Brazil. To fix it, Brazil must alter the structure of the state.

Yikes! To decrease the level of violence in Brazil, corruption has to be addressed, and to do that "the structure of the state must be altered." Is that really necessary? Is Brazil's corruption really so bad?

A shocking robbery without precedent is only the precedent to a bigger, shocking robbery.

Millor Fernandes

Society has become an inert receptacle for the daily denunciation of misdeeds.

Mario de Oliveira, Filho

Chapter 8: Lavras Novas—Is Brazil as corrupt as they say?

South out of Belo Horizonte, a traveler on his way to Lavras Novas doesn't have to stay on the treacherous BR-040 very long. By April of 2009 the road crews had laid down enough asphalt to get us to the Ouro Preto exit. Only one pothole lay in our way. We dodged it.

Mountains stood between Lavras Novas and Belo Horizonte. On the way up, pine trees and palm trees grew side by side. In time the palm trees sensed the cold and disappeared. At Itabirito people approached on horseback and continued on their way down the mountain. On a downward slope the air became tropical again, and on the left we passed a tree which appeared to have the leaves of a fern and round, tangerine flowers. Soon we turned off the road to Ouro Preto where a sign should have been but wasn't and drove along a dirt washboard road to the cobblestones of Lavras Novas, where slaves once worked the mines at 1600 meters above sea level.

Elaine Lucchesi--the smiling, charming innkeeper--greeted us, replenished the dining room with a buffet full of breakfast food, and gave us our keys. As we ate, husband Sergio entered, wearing long grey hair and a ski vest. He looked to be someone of my vintage who had survived the 1960's but still said, "Man" a lot. I asked a few questions about the place and learned that both had been teachers; she, of Portuguese and math; he, of history.

The history of Lavras Novas tells of some cannibalistic, indigenous people who saw no purpose in digging for rocks, not the kind of colleague one would want in a dark mine shaft at lunch time. Consequently, the Portuguese imported some short but strong Africans who together with the indigenous people bore responsibility for the stature and skin color of the current inhabitants, not including the business owners and restaurateurs who moved in more recently to build a cult tourist haven. Our teacher reported that a history of slavery failed to produce a culture of community responsibility. I did not find this surprising.

The surprise came when Sergio escorted us to our lodgings. We would be housed in a bright, yellow bungalow with a red tile leprechaun's roof which swept up to a point. We should have expected as much. All of the chalets bore the names of one gnome or another: gnome of secrets, gnome of winter, and so forth, all surrounded by toadstools and adorned with gnome memorabilia. To reach ours, we would have to traverse a shallow ravine by means of a swaying, plank-and-cable bridge, the kind that breaks as the hero of the movie is trying to escape the villain and then dangles far above the rushing torrent. I went first, carrying the luggage.

In rural Texas a new building which has been built to look old goes by the name "shabby chic." Our gnome home could have been called "shabby quaint." The gnomes had built the floor of old wood and decorated the walls with their gnome art. In addition to a refrigerator in the sitting room and fireplace in the bedroom, the cabin had one signature detail, a viewing window from the bed into the shower. You had to watch fast, though, because the window steamed up in the cool, fall mountain air.

That night we would open some wine and build a fire. We remember it as a romantic evening even though the fire had a ridiculous beginning: We needed toilet paper to light the kindling under the logs. To create an updraft, a tower of wet branches wrapped in toilet paper like a soggy teepee stood above hissing logs. Finally the logs dried out enough to catch fire, and we sipped our wine with a sense of accomplishment.

In the morning new adventures would begin, and one would soon end. Tatiana's son had stayed the night with his girlfriend and another couple in a two-bedroom home for younger gnomes. It overlooked a valley of rolling mountains which spread as far as the horizon. We approached their chalet along a path lined by living toadstools, stepped up the natural rock stairway, entered a small living room dominated by a rough-timber staircase, took a seat, and waited to join them for a hike.

Lavras Novas advertised a waterfall at a higher elevation. We fully intended to accompany the younger travelers up the mountain; however, not a hundred yards into the trek, my girlfriend and I paused on an anthill, not the best decision. Soon thereafter, we commenced to jump around while swatting at our legs and ultimately decided to explore safer ground. By the time the young people returned, we had planned the rest of the day.

Not all plans are created equal. The plans for lunch landed us on a lawn full of dogs. Our unstable table had an umbrella which almost prevented the rain from falling on us and our food. The rain didn't spoil the food, though; the cook had already taken care of that in the kitchen. Later, we would find better food down the road at a spacious, roofed, cafeteria-style chalet overlooking the valley.

But it would be difficult to find better entertainment anywhere than we found that night in Lavras Novas. Somehow, in the mountains of Minas Gerais at the end of a washboard dirt road, a Brazilian named Rodrigo Nezio played the guitar like a virtuoso and sang the blues. He asked for requests, and he and his drummer could play anything that didn't require a bass, anything—Eric Clapton, Robert Cray, some Stones, some Beatles, even "The Sky is Crying" by Stevie Ray Vaughn. He sang it all in English and wrote his own songs in English but claimed he didn't speak English. I wasn't sure how that worked.

After breakfast the next morning, we were treated to a conversation with a local entrepreneur. I began with a question about business in this busy, little tourist town.

Arriving by way of a swinging bridge, I expected him to tell us how adventuresome and innovative his fellow entrepreneurs were, but our informant complained of their passivity and resistance to change. He explained that they were interested only in their businesses: "They don't care about community issues, in the development of the town in which they work. They care only about making money."

Apparently they weren't even very forward thinking about promoting tourism there: "They think small. I suggested starting a website for tourism in the city, so someone did, but he charged us to advertise. He explained he was charged for the site, so I told him to make it *.org*.

He did but still charged us, which made him a little money in the beginning but discouraged people from using the site."

Heavily influenced by recently teaching a course in perversion in the cinema, Tatiana said, "It is perverted to make money off an effort intended to help the businesses."

I'd seen signs for the city of Ouro Preto on the way into town, but to me it seemed as though Lavras Novas sat in the middle of nowhere. I wasn't exactly sure what a community organization would address, but our interviewee explained, "Lavras Novas is really a neighborhood of Ouro Preto. We don't have our own government. We don't even have our own city councilman on the Ouro Preto city council. There is no sense of community here or anyplace in Brazil, for that matter."

I asked what he thought Tiradentes accomplished, and he answered, "Portugal didn't allow any development in the country. The people from São Paulo were competent and wanted to develop the area, but the Portuguese gave it to two families to exploit. They had no interest in development. When visited Portugal, we found it was a poor country. Where did all that tax money go?"

I didn't know.

He explained, "It went to Britain to pay Portugal's debts and finance the Industrial Revolution. It also went to the Vatican. The people here still don't think about the future and don't plan. We still accept masters. We are passive and take what is given to us. What else can serfs and slaves do? We have not really achieved self-government."

"What is needed for self-government to be achieved?"

"One thing is transparency."

One man's transparency is another's indictment. I told them, "I read in *VEJA* that Michel Temer [the president of the House of Deputies] complained that gathering personal information on suspects creates a weapon for stool pigeons."

Our stool pigeon went on, "The resources of Brazil are still being used to enrich a few, except it is now a few Brazilians, rather than the royalty of Portugal. A lot of it is done in secret; and if we hear about it at all, it is too late. Have you heard of Eike Batista?"

I hadn't. My girlfriend had.

"He is one of the richest men in Brazil. His father, Eliezer, was Minister of Mines and Energy during much of the dictatorship and had maps showing the location of valuable resources all over Brazil. Eike got a hold of the maps and applied for, and was given, much of the mineral rights in Brazil without paying for them. This is how things get done in Brazil."

(This was contradicted by an article which accused Eike Batista of using privileged information, secured from his father, during his negotiations with mining companies. This suggested that he knew what to buy but did have to pay something.)[36]

"Another thing we need is local control over spending projects. You see, 80% of politicians are thieves."

The estimate might be low. A contributor to the paper said, "The press . . . is interested in the future of the country. It only seeks to contribute by offering some criticism to save the institution [of Congress by] purging it of the bandits, which, unfortunately, occupy 90% of the seats."[37]

Sounds like an auction: "We have 80. We have 90. Do I hear 95?"

---

[36] wikipedia.org/w/index.php?title=Eike_Batista&action=edit&section=3

[37] *Estado de Minas,* May 29, 2009

In 2006 Brazil had the distinction of falling eight positions to rank 70th out of 163 countries in its perceived level of corruption among politicians and public authorities. This places Brazil "right in the middle of the pack. This is not necessarily something to be complacent about, since the company included the likes of Peru, Poland, Bulgaria, Croatia and the Czech Republic. As for the citizenry, Brazilians may be less sanguine since . . . on a daily basis, the media have no trouble in finding dozens of stories of corrupt practices, ranging from high-level bureaucrats who accept bribes to award contracts or cut red tape, to political hacks who are paid for no-show government jobs, to minor functionaries who can expedite license and visa applications, to traffic policemen who can ignore traffic violations for a [bribe] . . ." [38]

In 2002 a survey collected data from "nine major cities (Belo Horizonte, Brasília, Curitiba, Fortaleza, Porto Alegre, Recife, Rio de Janeiro, Salvador, São Paulo) as well as the interior of São Paulo. It asked for responses to this statement: "The first thing that the government needs to do is end corruption . . . " Eighty-two per cent said that they "completely agreed" and 12% said they "somewhat agreed." No other issue--not employment, education, or national security--garnered as much support.

Apparently, the citizens are upset partly because the scandals are endless. Renato Scapolatempore quoted the oft-said statement, "The recent scandal makes us forget the one before." Stories of Brazil's corruption could fill libraries. They have already filled a museum. I am grateful to a neighbor for sending me the address of a website for the virtual Museum of Corruption in Brazil.

The public is also upset because bribes and profit taking are pervasive throughout their government: The headline stated, "Mafia planned the Bribe." The article quoted Luiz Antonio adventuresome, one of the planners of a fraudulent scheme to skim money from a project's budget, as he told how legislators, businessmen, and bureaucrats all received a piece of the pie according to a pre-established payment schedule.

By this point in my tenure as a tourist, I had concluded that the press makes the government corruption quite transparent. The President of the House of Deputies even gives interviews explaining why embezzlement happens, goes unpunished, and will only improve through slow, gradual, step-by-step change.

In a scandal that occupied the headlines in the fall of 2009, federal deputies were found to have spent $2.25 million on airplane tickets between January, 2007 and October, 2008. The law allowed them airplane fare back and forth from Brasília to their home districts, but this money was spent on travel out of the country. In the month of December, 2008, alone, congressmen spent $40,000 traveling abroad.

One federal deputy, Fabio Faria, was accused of buying tickets for "artists" . . . Sâmara Felippo, Sthefany Brito, and Kayky Brito, as well as his girlfriend and her mother. He denied the charge but repaid the Treasury $10,500, the value of the tickets. Deputy Temer was asked about this deputy in particular. It is worth listening to parts of his interview with *VEJA*:

The interviewer asked Deputy Temer whether he thought Deputy Fabio Faria should be punished for taking his girlfriend and her mother to Miami on public money.

(I must interrupt the interview for a question about the question. As I read about the embezzlement, I had the same question; but, I hate to admit, that doesn't make it a good question. A better question would have been, "The press and the readers are outraged, but did the Deputy do

---

[38] Zonalatina.com, Political Corruption in Brazil.

anything illegal, and if not, why not?" That would be two questions. Even though neither was asked, Temer hinted at the answer to the both.)

Temer said that they couldn't punish Deputy Farias because he didn't break any law, not even any rule. The rules stated only that the deputy had money in his account. It never specified how the money had to be used. Thus, if a foreign visitor thought someone should go to jail for embezzlement, he would be completely ignorant. He could even be accused of arrogance. Someone familiar with a U.S. politics might point out that when James Traficante from Ohio was sentenced, he was only the second U.S. Congressman to go to jail since the Civil War.[39]

More knowledgeable than this, the questioner did not call for legal sanctions. He used the word "punish." Any punishment for going overboard in spending tax dollars would be decided by the House, itself, not by the judicial system because there was no law to break.

Secondly, Temer pointed out a "lack of control" in the system and said these cases would be solved "little by little." His reaction was considerably calmer than that of commentator Luiz Carlos Prates, who said, among other things (see Chapter 9), "[Politicians] are disgusting and have no respect for the people . . . It is time to react. Put them out of power. Crooks!"

In Temer's analysis, there was no question of criminality, just a glitch in the system. And it was not something one should rush to fix. He suggested it would take time. There was no indication that all of these glitches should be addressed in a major reform of the institution.

After the press had ranted for months, a committee decided to change the rules about travel allowances. A deputy present in the meeting admitted, "Politicians are not very sensitive to public pressure. But when the campaign financiers began to attack us, we felt it was the time to react."

Temer's interviewer reported that a Senator Cristovam Buarque "proposed a plebiscite to decide if Congress should be closed . . . [saying that] thirty-seven per cent of Brazilians now think Congress is somewhere between bad and horrible."

Temer answered, " . . . in the entire history of Brazil, the people only praise the legislature after emerging from an authoritarian regime."

The interviewer persisted on the question of Brazil's history, asking whether Congress always seemed to function like a corporation, its members exchanging favors in pursuit of their own interests, creating the general impression that no one is punished in Congress. Then came a very interesting response:

"In the political process, everything is based on the principle of expediency. I gave a classical theoretical example of a president who was being judged for a crime . . . It was verified that he committed the crime, but it was also shown that if he lost his position, this would propel the country into a civil war. What would one do in this case? In my view, it would be expedient to avoid institutional chaos even if this required interrupting the case against the president."

The question was whether the legislature was doing more harm than good, particularly while the country watched the spectacle of elected officials using tax dollars to take vacations abroad. Temer's answer proposed that these practices should go unpunished because the country would be thrown into a civil war if politicians were held accountable for crimes and stripped of their jobs.

What an interesting answer. A reader is inclined to nod in agreement: "Of course, clemency is better than civil war." Only later, he or she might ask, "Wait, why would a civil war erupt if some congressmen lost their jobs for using public money on their vacation travel?" Perhaps Temer's statement suggests Nunes was correct when he described this government:

---

[39] "E preciso reagir agora," *VEJA,* April 22, 20009, P. 17-21.

"PhiloSophistry . . . , angered by scorpions biting its own substance, ravenous and casual, insatiable and merciless, like Calígula."[40]

Would it be "philoSophistry" for the brilliant rhetorician, Temer, to say the nation would be in peril if the institution of the House were challenged and altered? If the argument does not reflect real dangers, what is its purpose?

Does it not invite the reader to agree, "Yes, civil war is bad"? Furthermore, when Mr. Temer alludes to a president, one does not think of the impeached Collor, but of the beloved Lula. "It would be a disaster to impeach Lula. Yes. Yes," we agree, frightened by such a horrible prospect. But in truth, no one was talking about impeaching President Lula. He had nothing to do with vacation travel to Miami. Why did Mr. Temer raise this specter?

One cannot know his intention, but one can see the effect: The listener is encouraged to agree that institutions should be protected to prevent chaos. In other words, fear of chaos is used to win support for the House continuing as it is. One is distracted from asking, "Why is it a good idea to give the House so much freedom to spend the public money?" Nevertheless, recovering ones senses, one asks, "Why is this access to the Treasury such a sacred building block of the Congress? What would crumble without it?"

A more general question rises to the surface as well. While Mr. Temer shows great concern for the institution of the House, Anastasi and Santana voice a different priority. They suggest that one of the hallmarks of a well-functioning representative democracy is "the capacity of the citizens to vocalize their demands as part of the public [political] agenda." Further on, the issue of immunity from prosecution will surface, and the public's opinion will be sampled by a newsmagazine (see Chapter 11). At that point, we will question whether the public demands are (1) heard by Mr. Temer or (2) are represented by the Constitution, itself. The interviewer anticipates this issue and suggests that perhaps the current system threatens the democratic process:

"Do you see a real threat to the democratic process now?"

"No, no way. The institutions are as solid as never before."

The visiting observer becomes confused. The institutions may be strong, but does that mean they are responsive to the wishes of the people?

Deputy Silvio Costa fought for his travel privileges, saying that limiting his travel allowance " . . . will cause me to have to separate from my wife."

Just as I was feeling sorry for Deputy Costa, *Estado de Minas* (May 4, 2009) reminded it readers that after denouncing the personal use of public money, Congress tends to grant amnesty to all the legislators who have committed abuses. Sure enough, the leadership decided to grant amnesty but bar future partying on public money. After he was assured he would receive no censure, Deputy Costa changed his tune and took the high road, saying, "I see that taking our wives is small compared to the importance of this House." He said nothing about the ethics of entertaining his family on public money.

Apparently, the worst possible consequence of embezzlement of public funds is loss of ones job, even though that needn't be permanent. Even deposed President Collor has made his way back to the Senate, re-elected by his home state because, in the words of one informant, "He owns the state. He's a colonel."

The end game of a scandal can involve a pretense of disgrace. Senator Gérson Camata was "in his third term, lives in Brasília with his wife, Deputy Rita Camata, is owner of an

---

[40] Nunes, *Op. Cit.*, P. 178

apartment in the city, but the couple didn't let go of the housing allowance of $3400 per month. Confronted, he said he was the victim of slander. Tearfully, he lamented, 'It is easy to destroy forty-two years of public life, of work, of dedication, with integrity, without any proof . . . '"[41]

(I interrupt this performance to ask, "For whom is Senator Camata crying?" I am reminded of an interview taped between Focus on the Family guru James Dobson with convicted mass-murderer Ted Bundy on the night before the latter's execution. At one point in the interview Bundy appeared to be crying. A little tear glistened upon his cheek. I rewound the tape to see what had brought the condemned man to tears. He was not weeping for his victims or their families. He was crying about all of the poor killers on death row who were the victims of corruption by violent pornography. Apparently, some people feel like the victim regardless of their crimes. This analogy is not intended to equate embezzlers with mass murders. However, further on the jurist will argue that white-collar crimes, though not as horrific as violent crimes, have their victims too, and the perpetrators should be considered enemies of the state.)

Senator Camata went on, "At least 261 of the 513 deputies, which is 51% of the House, paid for tourism outside the country with public money . . . [Temer] is responsible for judging the ethical deviations of his colleagues.'"

Ah ha, Temer is the judge and dispenser of punishment. I think he neglected to mention that in his interview, and not every Brazilians knows this.

As the scandal over airline tickets was disappearing from the headlines to be replaced by another, the first British president of the House of Commons to renounce his position in 314 years did so over the improper, but not necessarily illegal, expenses of at least 170 members. None will be allowed to run for re-election according to both Prime Minister Brown and the leader of the Conservative party. The magazine pointed out that in Brasília everyone got amnesty and no one has criticized the leadership.

Is the money public or private? In the minds of many government officials, the distinction is irrelevant. "Parliament: Is public, is private," said an article which gives the views of a constellation of experts. The article quoted Sergio Buarque de Holanda saying, "The Brazilian in public life was incapable of distinguishing his personal interests from the interests to the people." To sociologist Francisco de Oliveira it attributes the statement, " . . . Although the use of airline tickets in the manner of Roseana, Jereissati, and Maia was not illegal, they were clearly immoral and lie on the border between corruption and the inheritance of patronage, the curse that remains in Brazilian society."[42]

According to Cláudio Weber Abramo, "Patronage is at the base of corruption . . . The capture of the state by partisan interests is the definition of corruption . . . Corruption is more than what is illegal." (See also, "A doença tem cura," *PensarBrasil*, Oct. 10, 2009.)

President Lula is the face of Brazil abroad and ran on an anti-corruption platform. He remains as popular as ever despite all of the corruption scandals. What did Lula think about the paid holidays in Miami?

According to Guzzo, Lula defended the free vacations, thereby showing that he understands how things work in Brazil and doesn't want to change it. Guzzo also blamed the scandals on the quality of the politician who run for office, something which will receive attention further on.

[41] Cabral, Otavio, ¨Chore, pör nos, senador¨ (*VEJA*, #42, #17, 29/4/9.

[42] Magalhaes, Luiz Antonio, Parlamento:"E publico, e privado, *Valor*, ano 9, #444, 19/4/09, P. 10;

In a book on the legal system, Marcelo Cunha de Araújo coined a new term for the government of Brazil: "In other words, the exercise of fundamental rights cannot be abused to the point of hiding criminal acts committed to the detriment of others' fundamental rights or of the relevant Constitutional values. But it is so. Fundamentally, it is a cleptocracy!"[43]

In saying this, he was neither being cute nor was he using the term as an analogy. The author spoke with a scholar's precision. In his view the government was built to steal public money. Could this legalized theft continue if the majority of government officials believed in the difference between public and private money? Why was this distinction unclear to the Brazilian politician?

One man's answer connects its colonial past to its corrupted present: "We have a society with many privileges, which is the principle reason for our low growth rate. Privilege is a negation of the concepts of a republic and a democracy. The elites . . . are dominant classes that are seen to be part of the country and understand the importance of prioritizing the national interests above all others. On the other hand, the oligarchs are the dominant classes that have no national feeling, no sense of belonging to a country, and who put their interests above any other . . . This organization of society prevents the full realization of a meritocracy [and] blocks the free competition that is the motor of the capitalistic system. Here is the reason for the delay in the development of Brazil. This rubbish [or encumbrance] of privileged oligarchs' is the great impediment to the civic, moral, and economic development of Brazil, because it (a) weakens . . . the sense that the citizen owes something to the country when he sees on a daily basis the laws being disrespected and the oligarchs are relishing unearned privileges, (b) consumes the resources necessary for investment, [and] (c) . . . interferes with the passage of better moral and civic values to the children . . . In his children's eyes a father appears naïve or worse, an idiot . . ."[44]

Back in Lavras Novas, when I asked two entrepreneurs if they had hope for the country, one said, "Yes," and the other said, "No."

(The businessman in Lavras Novas wasn't the only person losing hope. Shortly after we returned home, Geralda saw that the Regional Labor Tribunal's President's wife was receiving a salary of more than $65,000. She shook her head and said, "There is so much wrong in Brazil. You have other places you can go. You have another home. I have no other way." Unlike her congressman, she couldn't afford the airline tickets.)

The Lavras Novas entrepreneur went on, "The state says they help us by sponsoring ecotourism, but ecotourism is wrong here. A TV journalist covered a site which claimed to be ecotourism but was actually polluted. The reporter was told this but aired the piece anyway. Minas Gerais says it invests millions in tourism, but is doesn't provide infrastructure—roads, sewers in the city, pavement on the road to Lavras Novas, a safe highway . . . Problems just aren't solved. Ouro Preto is poorly cared for. We still have Chagas disease [which is associated with impoverished living conditions] nearby."

Tatiana said, "It is the same as when the Portuguese were in charge, only now it is our elected officials who bleed us for their own personal gain."

---

[43] Araujo, *Op. Cit.,* P. 56.

[44] Oliveira, Filho, Mario de, interview with *VEJA,* April 18, 2007

"Exactly. Where does the money go? There is no local control, so we don't know where the money goes. When they paved the road, they never did the sewer. They did 40% of the project and kept 100% of the money."

Another person at the table said, "My boss told me that there is a law which protects a company from being sued if it completes just a quarter of a project."

This is not just the whining of a few malcontents in a dining room off the beaten path. Others have complained long and hard about the fatal effects of Brazil's corruption: In addition to having a new highway of death every year, Minas Gerais also has its own Bridge of Death. For some reason, engineers in 1957 thought it would be a good idea to build a bridge which curves sharply on kilometer 592 of BR-040 between Rio and Belo. On a daily basis between ten and twelve thousand vehicles cross 150 feet in the air. Why would that be a problem? Lots of heavy trucks soar off the side, often taking small, innocent cars with them. No one has kept track of the deaths, but the total is estimated to be over 200.

In 1998 different engineers decided to put a curveless bridge across another section. The first half of the new bridge looks good. I saw it. It's too short though. It stops in the middle of the ravine and has for years. While trucks plunge off the Bridge of Death, the Bridge to Nowhere stands watch a few hundred yards away, suffering from erectile dysfunction. On March 23, 2009, the State of Minas told us, "Government delays work [on the new bridge] and keeps the Bridge of Death alive."

One might ask why the straight bridge couldn't have been built first. Mistakes happen. On the day the State of Minas tentatively predicted the new bridge would finally be completed after eleven years, one informant saw more in this than bad engineering followed by bureaucratic delays:

"The Bridge of Death was considered an engineering marvel when they built it in the 50's. But it is typical of how things are done here, like the design of Brasília without any consideration for people. They built a curve on a narrow bridge and left it up to drivers to anticipate the danger. So people died. Then it took more than eleven years to build a replacement."

I asked, "Why so long?"

"If the priority were people's lives, it would have been done long ago. If the government and contractors were spending their own money, maybe one safe bridge would have been built in the first place. But in Brazil money is spent and projects are done poorly or never finished. Since this is the norm, it is safe to say that the people's tax money is going exactly where the government wants it to go, into their hands and the hands of their friends."

"Why is the new bridge being finished now?"

"Maybe the fact that the governor of the state is running for president has something to do with it."

Was she being paranoid to suspect that politics had something to do with life-saving projects being completed? The journalists didn't think so. A few months before (April 19, 2009), the *Estado de Minas* ran the headline, "Votes in the Ballot Box. Work Stops."

Is there any hard evidence that money for government projects gets diverted into the pockets of interested parties? On August 9, 2009, the *Estado de Minas* described on how tax dollars find their way to the hands of criminals:

Every deputy (513) and senator (78) has the right to offer amendments to the federal budget. During the most recent budget year, each had the right to suggest $5 million in spending, so the total amount would be almost $3 billion. In the majority of cases, the legislator directed the money to their constituents for construction of health centers, roads, schools, day care centers, and the promotion of festivals. Following fraudulent bidding, sometimes by fake businesses, government money is spent to pay inflated prices, often for substandard materials. In some cases legislators, themselves, receive bribes from the city halls. In some cases government employees participate in the fraud by failing to account for the money or by finalizing the agreements without enforcing the contract's minimal requirements. With a portion of the money going into the pockets of participants in the scheme, the works never get completed or are done with inferior quality materials. Closing the cycle, in some cases the businesses that participate in the fraud repay the legislator by contributing to the next election campaign.

Therefore, commentators like Abramo complain, "It is very common for the State to buy one thing, and the business delivers else. It ought not to be this way. There needs to be a careful adherence to all contracts."[45]

Brazilians have frequently told me and written that the corruption in Brazil interferes with the development of the country. Is that much money really being diverted through fraud? How much money are we talking about? The paper ran a story saying that these four fraudulent schemes, alone, cost the taxpayers $425,000,000 from 2006 to 9/2009.

My embarrassed girlfriend suggested I write, "Dear Reader, you do the math. I am too disgusted." These things about her country embarrass her.

In fact, the dear reader need not do the math. The enterprising *Estado de Minas* (8/10/09) found someone who had, Paulo Ziulkoskil, president of the National Confederation of Cities. By his calculations fraud eats up 20% of city contracts, a *quinto*, Tiradentes' fifth of the way to hell. (Another author suggested a much higher rate of theft.)

The journalist in Belo Horizonte described the system in this way: "The State controls the coffers. The State writes the checks. The fox is in charge of the henhouse. Again, because justice is slow and self-enriching, the system works for the government. The three powers are accomplices in corruption, and it's the only game in town."

If they run the "only game in town," why would they want to change anything? The Constitution talks as though the government exists for the common good, but we have heard many examples of public money being diverted into private hands. What do the leaders want to change about the system? When Flavio Penna asked Michel Temer that very question, the President of the House did not say he would change the level of corruption, just "the public image of political activity."

When Brazilian politicians do start to make changes, they seem to have trouble finishing the job. For example, in 1996 Senator Roberto Freire introduced a bill that would have prohibited the hiring of relatives in all three branches of the federal government. After passing in the Senate, the bill was shelved by the Chamber of Deputies and replaced with another bill, which vowed to end nepotism "at an unknown date in the future." This date continues to exist only in some hypothetical location in the fourth dimension.

A more recent 2006 law, written after some scandal or another, says politicians have to declare their property. It gave the appearance of making them accountable for their incomes. However, the law never stated that they have to reveal the *value* of the property, so they don't. As a result, no one can evaluate the extent of their fortunes.

---

[45] *Ibid.*, P. 64

How is this affecting the relationship between the citizen and his government? The usual view is this: "Corruption breeds distrust of public institutions, undermines ethical principles by rewarding those willing and able to pay bribes, and perpetuates inequality . . . Individuals who wish to conduct their affairs fairly and honestly are demoralized and lose faith in the rule of law . . ." Even one expert who performed a cost-benefit analysis and found potential benefits of corruption concluded that corruption becomes a liability when it leads to the deterioration of legitimacy.

I wondered if this were happening in Brazil. While sitting in the living room with my girlfriend and the bearded businessman, I asked, "Why hasn't corruption eroded public trust in the government?"

He answered, "It *is* eroded! Everyone is paying for the inefficiency and corruption of the federal government." Then he connected the loss of legitimacy to a loss of trust in the criminal justice system and a diminished sense of safety: "The police in São Paulo and Rio are completely corrupt. Those cities are much more violent that Belo Horizonte. Even here, the average citizen lacks security."

An article echoed his sentiments: "In our country a serious system of justice does not exist. It is clear that some honest people live in Brazil, but there are also a greater number of people without ethics and respect for others, who think only of themselves . . . The system of corruption is so strong--the lack of obedience to the law, the lack of human values and ethics-- resulting in few people thinking about the future of Brazil, resulting in Brazil becoming a country that looks bad to others. In other words, Brazil will become more hellish to live in, which is already happening in some places in the country." [46]

The insightful Mario summed it up for us: "I don't like what I see in news--the politicians that steal, social inequalities in wealth, services in municipal health centers. People who can't afford private care have to rely on public health clinics, and that's where I take kids. Is free. If I take my kid to the doctor, we wait hours and hours. No doctors are available."

(Tatiana later explained, "It is this way because they are so poorly paid and work so many places, and so little money is sent to public health centers. The public health centers were a nice idea but money is not being sent or it does not arrive.)"

Mario continued, "We lack many things. We are a rich country with many resources, but something happens that stops us from cultivating our resources. Take the destruction of the Amazon, for example. We'll need those resources, and they'll be gone."

"Why doesn't it change?"

"Lula is trying, but he is not accomplishing much. Politicians don't allow progress. They may have nice plans to change conditions in the *favela*, but it will never be done. There is so much income tax. We pay too much tax, and it doesn't go where it should. Look at health, education. The money isn't getting there. If a mother needs to work, she needs to take the kids to daycare, and she will have to pay with her own money. If she gets minimum wage which is $400 or less, she won't have money for good daycare and will have to rely on daycare with no regulation of conditions. I just heard that a child died in daycare because of mistreatment. Changes that matter aren't happening because Congress doesn't allow them. It is because of corruption. When politicians get caught, nothing will happen to them. But Brazil is a beautiful country. Other countries have problems too."

---

[46] Preto, *Zonalatina*,com, "Political Corruption in Brazil."

The professional woman unable to retire because of her tax bill was less sanguine: "I have no problem working to provide taxes for the new welfare system that provides people with food or for the healthcare system, but when money goes to rich politicians and crooked businessmen to build castles and fly to Miami for vacation and I can't retire, I get furious."

The original question was, "Is Brazil as corrupt as they say?"

By one definition, "Corruption is a form of behavior which departs from ethics, morality, tradition, law, and civic virtue . . . The United Nation's Global Program Against Corruption defines corruption as the 'abuse of power for private gain' and includes both the public and private sectors. Although perceived differently from country to country, corruption tends to include the following behaviors: conflict of interest, embezzlement, fraud, bribery, nepotism, sectarianism, and extortion."[47] By this definition, the short answer is, "Yes." More corrupt than Bulgaria, Brazil is now only the world's 70th least corrupt country.

Where Brazil is concerned, the answer is not so simple; but for now this will have to do. In the next two chapters we turn our attention to some of the obstacles that stand in the way of eliminating corruption in Brazil.

---

[47] Filgueiras, Fernando, "Marcos Teoricos da Corrupcao," *Corrupcao--Ensaios e Criticas,* editoraufmg, 2008, P. 355-358.

On the contrary, we are in a responsible, pragmatic democracy where all are equal under the law . . . Since I don't pay taxes and my neighbor pays, the law is very wise. This is the beauty of a true democracy.[48]

Millor Fernandes

Basically, among Brazilians there grows a feeling of impotence, of humiliation, and even shame that they do nothing to change things.

Mario de Olveira Filho

Chapter 9: Belo Horizonte—National Identity: "We Are Nobody"

Tiradentes opposed the *quinto* from his hometown of Vila Rica, now called Ouro Preto. For his trouble, executioners hung him by the neck until dead and tossed his body parts all over the state of Minas Gerais. Since then the state capital has been moved to Belo Horizonte, Brazil's third largest city.

Belo Horizonte sits in the mountains above the cities of Rio and São Paulo. The mountains give the city its horizon and its name. The minerals in those mountains have attracted four million people to the metropolitan area. Now, at the center of the city, tall buildings create canyons which make it impossible to see the beautiful horizon from the street. In many, many ways, however, the people of Belo Horizonte keep their eyes on what is beautiful. (Recall Chapter 4.)

Tiradentes would be happy to see the mining companies and their offspring, the factories, making profits for private citizens; but I don't know what he'd think of the wages of the laborers. He wanted his state to have universities, and it does, including UFMG, the state's main branch of the Federal University. An eighteenth century man, he might be shocked that the university charges no tuition, but I doubt he would be surprised to learn that the children of the poor rarely gain entrance. A man killed for disagreeing with the Portuguese Crown, Tiradentes might regret the century of his birth after a glance at the city's courageous newspaper, *Estado de Minas*, which criticizes the government on a daily basis.

Since the beachless residents of Belo Horizonte need some place to congregate, he would find himself among the country's highest concentration of bars, but there would be many other things for him to do. Roman Simovic, the Montenegran violinist, would astound him when performing Mendelssohn's Concerto for Violin op. 64 with the Minas Gerais Symphony. Tiradentes would not know what to make of the stride piano played by American Judy Carmichael or the rock 'n roll sung in English by the ancient Johnny Rivers to the vocal accompaniment of his equally aged, Portuguese-speaking fans. Since Belo lacks beaches, he would be "spared" the display of skin one witnesses in Rio. But if he'd attend a

---

[48] Fernandes, Millor, *VEJA,* 9/9/9, P. 36.

play based *The Immoral Soul* by Nilton Bonder, he would learn about the physical and feminine side of human nature during the one-often-naked-woman performance by Clarice Niskier.[49]

I don't think the level of violence perpetrated by citizen upon citizen after slavery's end would shock Tiradentes. Slave owners always had reservations about giving freedom to those whom they'd abused. He certainly would be appalled at the increase in taxes, though. Brazil has many taxes. He thought a 20% tax interfered with development. What would he think of the current tax rate?

We heard a businessman complain, "The tax rate is abusive and absurd . . . [Despite spending on welfare and bureaucracy], this government has not spent money on building infrastructure or job creation, costing the country more money in the long run. The U.S. invests much more on research."

This was not just one guy's point of view. Another critic said, "Forty per cent of what is produced goes to feed the bureaus of the government and pays the price for our heavy and unproductive bureaucracy."[50] The journalist I later interviewed concurred, "Yes, our tax rate on business has doubled and is headed toward 50%. We are almost halfway to hell."

Tiradentes might feel discouraged at this point. If he'd read the previous chapter of this book, he would believe the government of the Republic to be thoroughly corrupt and, like the Portuguese monarchy, unworthy of the money it receives in taxes. He might foresee that "multiple forms of corruption . . . will become a cancer that weakens the body politic and the Brazilian citizen's faith in the institutions that should serve him," and he might wonder how a democracy would let itself get so corrupt and what forces keep all of this corruption in place. Often the Brazilian citizen receives the blame.

National character—in search of a hero

At a family lunch I asked Pedrinho, an architect, who he thought Brazil's heroes were. Tiradentes took an active stand against the bleeding of Brazil by an oligarchy, so I thought he might be a candidate. Pedrinho did not consider Tiradentes a hero. He had some doubts that the man ever existed. He had more interest in the idea that "nations might invent the heroes to prove a point." He thought the government invented Tiradentes:

"I think he represents a liberation myth, to give people an identity as a free people. Having fought for something gives people an identity. It happens on an individual level but also on a national level. But Brazilians have never fought for anything. That defines our identity. By not having to fight for what we are, we are nobody. I don't mean that in a pejorative sense."

"So, was his dream realized when Brazil gained independence from Portugal?"

"It is tragic. When Pedro I stuck the flag in the ground and said, 'Liberty or death,' what was that?" (Actually, he didn't plant the flag. He unsheathed his sword and pointed it to the heavens.) "The people were not involved. It was between father and son, and there was no fight . . . Tiradentes didn't inspire that. He became a symbol in the 1880's and 90's at the beginning of the Republic, as if the Republic had something to do with the people's wish for freedom, which it didn't."

"By celebrating Tiradentes Day, the rulers wanted to convince the people they had self-rule?"

"They began to paint him as a Christ-like martyr who had delivered them to political heaven."

"Who would the Brazilian heroes be then?"

---

[49] Nilton Bonder, *A Alma Imoral,* Rocco LTDA, Rio de Janeiro: 1998, 135 pp. Adapted for stage by Clarice Niskier.
[50] Cicero, Paulino, *MercadoCommun,* ano XV, #192, 1/7/08, P. 20.

"I think the soccer players are very, very important. I don't really like soccer, myself. If you asked most people about their hero, they would name a soccer player."

"I was asking about how badly they played in the World Cup against France, and someone told me Brazilian soccer players don't always try very hard."

"Brazilians understand the vagaries of soccer because they all play it, and they forgive losses." He then gave an example of a player who missed an important penalty kick and Brazil lost. The fans forgave him.

"Are they heroes for their skill or their victories? In the U.S. to be a hero, you must win."

"Maybe we are more human about our heroes. In the U.S. people fly the flag every day. Brazil's flag flies only on the day of a big, international game. It is our only time of national pride."

Just when I'd been convinced Brazilians didn't care about winning, the headline on 8/2/09 said, "Finally, a hero," and it referred to a gold-medal-winning, world-record-tying sprint by a swimmer. Not only was he the best, but he was "proud to be Brazilian." His heroism derived from his victory, apparently, as well as his national pride.

For me, the important issue was not whether he was a hero for swimming well or for winning, but because he was an athlete waving the Brazilian flag, not a statesman waving the Constitution. Other nations have their Nelson Mandelas who spent two decades in prison rather than submit to racial discrimination, their Ghandis who passively defeated the power of the British Empire, their Judge Baos who upheld justice in the face of pressure from the Chinese Emperor, their Aung San Suu Kyis who has lived her life under house arrest in Myanmar because she would not surrender her democratic principles. Why has Tiradentes' martyrdom fallen on deaf ears?

National Character—A happy people

When I interviewed Mario, I asked what he liked about his country. He began by saying, "I like to go out to the bar for some beers with friends, watch soccer on TV, have some laughs, and look at the young women."

A young, married man with two daughters, he laughed in an embarrassed way. I assured him I understood.

"Brazilians are a happy people," he said. Even after he cited many problems in his country, he concluded optimistically, "The country will get better besides all problems. Other countries have problems too. The people are happy."

Oddly enough, the happiness of the Brazilian people may offer one obstacle to change, and there may actually be a scientifically identifiable basis for their happy mood. The BBC and the magazine *VEJA* reported there was a gene which may facilitate optimism through improved serotonin uptake.[51] The presence of genes which control the transport of serotonin and affect mood was not news, nor was the fact that one version of such a gene would lead to a brighter mood. But I was surprised to hear that only 16% of Brits had this version of the gene, while 40% of Brazilians had it. Maybe corruption, crime, and poverty are so high in Brazil because the people are not yet unhappy enough about it.

Malcolm Gladwell speculated about the effect of herders upon a society.[52] The argued that farmers didn't watch their crops the way herders watched their herds. He pointed out that if

---

[51] Beguoci, Leandro, "Ö gene de otimismo," *VEJA*, 6/5/9, #18, ano 42, p. 132-134.

[52] Gladwell, Malcolm, *The Outliers,* New York: Little, Brown, & Co., 2008, P. 161-176

you stole some corn from a farmer's field, you wouldn't put him out of business. Corn would grow back. But if you rustled the rancher's cattle, he was done for. Herding engendered irascibility, violence, even a little paranoia. Countries which had a lot of herders would include the U.S., Great Britain, much of the middle east, and Italy.

(Why Italy? In the Preface I warned the reader not to take Millor and Nunes literally. I now issue the same warning for the following paragraph. I had three choices: (1) Delete the exaggeration and play it straight, (2) put this warning in an endnote, or (3) use parentheses. I chose the latter because no one reads the Endnotes:

(In the past, the Vatican was very protective of its sheep. Ask the medieval Moslems. Following the crusading Popes' example, the Mafia currently lives off protection money paid by its flock. If they lose one payment from a business, it is a problem. If they begin to lose businesses, as they currently are in some cities, it's a disaster; and the mafia shepherd can become cantankerous.

Unfortunately for the U.S. and possibly Iraq as well, the more cantankerous states with lots of herders and a culture built by such folks were in control of the U.S. government on September 11, 2001. The U.S. response to the terrorist was irascible and not completely rational.

The Minas Conspiracy ended in 1789. In that year James Madison proposed to amend the Constitution of the brand new United States of America with ten changes called the Bill of Rights. Among those Rights, number two established "the right of the people to keep and bear Arms." Nowadays, people generally think of this as a measure to allow people to hunt for food and sport and to protect their homes against criminals; but the original intent was probably more accurately echoed by a modern-day Texan who told me, "I don't care about owning a hunting rifle. I want the right to own an automatic weapon, an M-16 or AK-47, and I don't want it to protect myself from criminals. I want it for protection against the government should it attempt to ignore the Constitution. If only the army is armed, you become subjects."

That's cantankerous. The point is that Brazil isn't a nation of herders.)

Rodrigo had said Brazilians were cordial. With an oligarchy watching the flock, the people would therefore be considered sheep. Can one teach sheep to lead?

According to the man of the cloth, the press may be solving this problem of excessive happiness: "The press is important. It's the fourth estate in a nation, but the papers emphasize the bad news. Brazilians used to be happy and optimistic. Now they are becoming more and more depressed and hopeless, and not just in the cities. Even in the countryside the intake of strong psychiatric medicine is on the rise. People are feeling too sad and are taking this medication a lot. Life was supposed to be healthier and less stressful in the country."

I don't know if he was correct that people are becoming more depressed and taking medication for it or if the increased reach of healthcare causes more people to be diagnosed and treated. At any rate, if people seem to be less happy with their lot in life, is there nothing they can do but take medication?

National character—Passivity, lack of social responsibility:

More than one Brazilian typifies his countrymen as selfish. For example, "In the case of Brazil, [it is] . . . a culture which sees a swindle in favor of oneself with lenient eyes and observes rules in the same fashion, and that probably expresses our heritage of slavery, elitism, and inequality . . . Selfishness and pursuit of self-interest are facts of life here . . ."

When I interviewed the clergyman about Brazil, he raised the issue of selfishness among his congregation. I had asked, "Can a senator or deputy be arrested for taking bribes?"

He started talking about selfishness and broadened the description to portray a general passivity:

"Brazil has a strong heritage of privilege for the rich and powerful, dating back to the colonial days of slavery. We've always had a few powerful, rich politicians and many poor, powerless people who are too easy-going and relaxed to object. Plus, they don't believe they can change the system. They try to enjoy their free time. There is not a long tradition of working for causes.

"For example, many middle-class Brazilians live in buildings which have meetings every three to six months to make decisions about repairs, employees, things which connected to people's basic needs. Even so, people don't come, maybe just three or four, plus the chairperson. This little group does all the work and makes all the decisions. The other residents relax, take it easy, and complain. If people don't work to improve their own building, can I expect them to help the . . . [larger] community, which is pretty far removed from their needs?

"I see it in my congregation in terms of volunteering. I studied in the U.S. and saw that Americans take volunteering seriously. They commit, and they follow through. Here, people commit and go few times and quit."

"And you think this is partly because the U.S. lacks tradition of being owned by crown?"

"The Portuguese came to exploit, not to construct a society. They wanted to get rich fast, so they took the riches, the gold and the precious stones. A few families owned all the land. I see the same thing now in countries with lots of oil. They are underdeveloped. A few people are rich and powerful, but they don't share the wealth with the rest of the country. As for the rest of the people, the ones who would do the work to make the rich richer, they don't benefit."

National Character—the *jeitinho brasileiro*

Many people to whom I've talked assert that Brazil's "national character" causes corruption. Corruption is in the cultural DNA, said the female journalist. Put differently, "Brazil would be inevitably and definitively corrupt owing to certain values and practices which, present since its origin, have become part of its character and way of existing."[53]

Comparing the Brazilian culture to a painting of one man cheating another in cards, a critic said, " . . . as Brazilian as the *jaboticaba* [a native fruit], corruption has neither borders nor dimensions. It can be seen as a huge hole in the public coffers or as a small cheat in a simple game of cards."[54]

A variety of experts have expounded on the *jeitinho brasileiro* as part of the national character. It reveals a cultural tendency to accept certain crimes as justifiable, or even creative, and justifies using public institutions to give and receive personal favors, benefits, and privileges. This "ambiguity" toward rules is seen positively as a window to flexibility and innovation. For example, as the product of an aristocratic social regime disguising itself as an egalitarian democracy, the *jeitinho* can be justified as a way of seeking equality. On the other hand, it can be seen as the opposite of ethical behavior.

The mayor of Rio has encountered an attitude different from the one my girlfriend considered necessary to create an ordered, civilized society where everyone makes sacrifices in

---

[53] Reis, Fabio Wanderley, "Corrupcao, Cultura e ideologia," in *Corrupcao--Ensaias e Criticas*, editoraufmg, 2008, P. 14.

[54] "Corrupcao--Crime ou Costume?" *Revista de Historia Biblioteca Nacional,* P. 18.

the name of law and order. Instead, the mayor said, "Someone might applaud the removal of a bar's tables from the sidewalk and then be furious if he's ticketed for parking on the same sidewalk."

The average Brazilian has remained powerless for more than 500 years. A half millennium can engrain passivity and pessimism. Being the victim (of slavery and other forms of inequality) contributes to the *jeitinho*, [defined as] "small survival strategies in a world where there is little chance for the poor . . . The Brazilian doesn't see corruption with the seriousness it deserves. He is accustomed to seeing elections manipulated, controlled, or bought; a bribe buys an advantage in the competition for public works . . . Corruption plays a part in the typically Brazilian way of doing business. And by laughing, we in Brazil join in and normalize our bad practices."

In Chapter 4 we observed a warm scene in a hospital while my friend's wife awaited breast surgery. The description omitted events taking place offstage. As she awaited emergency surgery, her health insurance company was doing everything it could to avoid paying. After previously denying payment for several tests and pre-op procedures, it now tried to argue that she had failed to demonstrate need for the surgery by sending copies of reports—something it had never requested and later said was unnecessary. Finally they agreed to authorize the surgery but sent the wrong procedure code, a delaying strategy they had used before. The physician-friend waiting with her said this was a strategy to induce the patient to give up in desperation and agree to pay out of pocket. In other words, this company was behaving in the oligarchic manner described by Oliveira, feeding off the country but showing no concern for either the nation or its people.

Such generous people, such predatory systems--how can one country produce such kindness on the one hand and such indifference to suffering on the other? It made more sense as I watched. When the hospital behaved humanely and said the cancer victim would receive surgery and the hospital would worry about procedure codes, the patient and her family breathed a sigh of relief, actually feeling happy. Like the man who beats his head against the wall because it feels so good when he stops, they felt exuberance at having won a battle against the vicious system, as dangerous as her cancer.

Clovis Melo, a newsstand vendor in Rio de Janeiro was quoted as saying, "The Brazilian public has habits that encourage corruption. Moreover, the people have a short memory when it comes to corruption scandals, which means that the most recent always seems like the worst ever." Since the oppression of a heartless system is omnipresent, my friend and his wife felt as though their only victories could come from success at outsmarting the enemy. Nothing seemed unusual about the life-threatening dishonesty of a large company, and it was accepted and put in the past.

The resurrection of President Collor provided an example of this acceptance of the status quo. After his impeachment, President Collor moved to Miami. In August of 1996, *VEJA*, interviewed him and asked if he was harassed by Brazilians whom he encountered in Miami. "On the contrary," Collor told the reporter. "'People go out of their way to greet me . . . ' When the Collors decide to spend a night on the town, their destination is frequently Prima Pasta. The restaurant's cozy atmosphere and moderate prices make it popular with paparazzi-fleeing celebrities such as Cindy Crawford, Madonna, Jean-Claude Van Damme, UB-40 and the Bee Gees. 'I only remember two important politicians coming here,'" Argentine-born Gerardo Gea, Prima Pasta's owner, told *VEJA*. "'One of them is Collor de Mello and the other is José Luis Manzano, an Argentine ex-Cabinet minister who was accused of corruption, run out of Buenos

Aires, and came to live here in Miami. But that one went back not too long ago.'" Gea saw the difference in how other diners treated the disgraced politicians. "'Whenever he came to the restaurant and ran across some Argentine, Manzano was persecuted. They pointed a finger at him and asked how I could allow a crook in my restaurant. With Collor, it's different. The Brazilians insist on greeting him.'"

This is the kind of reaction that causes Brazilians, themselves, to argue that the people in general have been corrupted. Though they may object to government corruption, they are complicit, forgiving, and forgetful. And, to make matters worse, they accuse themselves of dishonesty in their own lives. For example, *The Elite Squad* shows there is no way to function as a military policeman in Rio without being corrupt, either taking bribes or murdering and torturing fellow citizens.

After reading the views given by so many commentators on the Brazilian national character, I decided to ask two octogenarians, a retired electrical contractor and his wife, a retired translator. They gave very personal answers:

"Does the typical Brazilian want to prevent corruption? Would most people want to take advantage if they could?"

He answered, "Brazilians don't cooperate. They try to get advantage for themselves. They don't care if you succeed. As a matter of fact, they don't want see you succeed."

His wife agreed, "There is a lack of respect. They want to take advantage, for example, a lack of consideration in traffic or in the grocery store. They try to get ahead in line, get through the door first, roll through the stop sign and let pedestrians beware. Brazilian drivers are selfish and inconsiderate, always following the law of Gérson, always trying to gain an advantage over the other driver. They don't follow the rules or respect other people's rights."

I'd heard that before. If the citizen creates the problem, the citizen must change: "To change this picture, each of us in our daily life needs to act honestly, thinking of others, alerting ourselves to the evils of corruption and the true function of politics, worthy people working to be elected to exercise political mandates, denouncing all impropriety that comes to our attention, . . . becoming an agent of change for the end of corruption . . . "

After agreeing with the experts about the average Brazilian, the old folks offered themselves as exceptions. (I read someplace that 80% of Brazilians say they are honest and think the other 80% per cent are not to be trusted.)

He began, "Yes, there are many ways people try to take advantage of each other, but not everybody would like to take advantage. We worked for every single object in this house."

She answered, "I worked for three governors. I could have become rich through favoritism and had a private driver, but I drove to work in my own car every day."

The granddaughter of these folks saw dishonesty in a form relevant to her generation. I asked her, "What do you like about your country?"

"My family."

"What else?"

"When I was in Bahia, they were generous and welcoming. They like to serve, take care of people, be hospitable toward others."

I commented, "That's what Leonardo said."

She admitted, "I don't like my country very much. I don't like the corruption. We aren't honest. You cannot believe what people say. Even their agreeability is self-interested."

"Why are they so dishonest?"

"We have laws, but they are not respected."

"Can you trust the people at work?"

"Some."

"In relationships between men and women?"

"Brazilian men of my generation are dumb. They cannot tolerate the accomplishments of women. Machismo is not an issue for my generation, but the men are not interested in finding someone to love or in feelings. They want to go to the bar, not to a concert. If you ask what they want from a woman, they will lie. They are not honest. They will say they want a woman who can understand them, but they do not want to understand her; and if there is something wrong at work, they don't come home and discuss it with their wives. They sit at the bar and talk to their friends."

I asked a middle-aged professional woman about the young woman's comments. She answered, "There is no universal pattern about this, except that worldwide men probably have a more impoverished inner life. You'd have to ask men what they want from women and what they are looking for when they finally marry."

Over coffee, I did ask a male psychologist about the younger woman's comments, and he answered, "This is a typical complaint by Brazilian women at this age. Many times the man and the woman do not state clearly what they want from the relationship. I was talking to my friend in the States, and he said that there the expectations of the relationship are stated very clearly. He says in the U.S. on the first date, people make it clear whether are looking for a casual relationship or something serious. My friend also told me that people form groups in which characteristics are more clearly defined. Similar people come together with similar expectations. It is not like that in Brazil. A man or woman might be looking for entertainment or for a relationship."

His wife spoke up: "It would be better if people told each other these things. Really, people don't respond honestly. A man wants to get married and have a family but he doesn't say that right away. A woman too. If they were open, they could make a choice. It's crazy. But I'm not sure the people there [in the U.S.] behave differently than those who are starting a relationship here. They might be as unsure as we are. It is not something that be explained by culture or the times. It has to do with not knowing what to expect in a new relationship."

Her husband added, "I also hear the same complaints from men about women."

Once again, it became hard to pin a label of dishonesty on Brazilians alone, but my own girlfriend would not let her countrymen off the hook. She reminded us of my most recent landing in São Paulo. I stopped at a snack bar for an apple and a water and gave the clerk a R$50 bill ($25). She smiled in a friendly manner and gave me my change and a receipt. When I moved over to one of the little tables, I checked my change against the receipt. She'd given me $2.50 in change. I had trouble believing that an apple and a water cost $22.50 so I got back in line, politely pointed out the error, and expected her to argue that I had given her a ten ($5.00). Instead, she gave me my correct changed with no apology, and I moved on. I assumed she figured me to be a tourist who could neither read nor speak Portuguese and probably couldn't count, but Tatiana was embarrassed for her country and disapproving of her countrymen:

"That is the way Brazilians are," she said. "My father went to a very good hospital here in Belo Horizonte for his prostate biopsy and was instructed to put his valuables in a plastic bag, including $30 in cash. When he left he had $15, just enough for cab fare back. You can't trust anyone."

For example, after performing the surgery on my friend's wife, the surgeon asked the husband if he planned to stay with her.

"Yes," he said, "I'm not leaving until she does."

"Good. That will be safer," replied the doctor.

"How will it be safer?" I asked.

"From theft," said my friend.

A theologian took the defective-DNA argument to its logical conclusion. Lourenço Stelio saw four aspects of the society—(1) public indifference toward the citizen, (2) cheating, (3) corruption, and (4) impunity—all turning in a vicious circle around the axis of the *jeitinho*. "We theologians see in natural man a degree of natural perversion. We don't believe in Rousseau's idea of a completely good man. The person must be transformed by his spirituality and his education. It is what we would call a conversion. The *jeitinho* needs redemption. We believe in the transformation of the individual from the inside out."[55]

That is where this argument takes us. If the citizen is to blame, he must be saved one conscience at a time. Good luck. If dishonesty were indeed ingrained in the national character, I wondered what the psychologist would say about Tatiana's theory that Brazil lacked the civilizing effect of societal father figures.

I asked, "With so many immoral father figures, do you think Brazil suffers from an impaired identification process. Tatiana says that civilization needs a representative who insists upon everyone sacrificing his own interests on behalf of the common good. The Brazilian people have no such person with whom to identify. What prevents Brazil from returning to a barbaric state?"

Tatiana put a finer point on the problem: "We have aspects of civilization within a barbaric state. We live in isolated islands where we can still be civilized, follow the laws, and pay our taxes. Meanwhile, the State--the government, itself--is barbaric in the sense that it does not function for the common good. It is not restrained by law. And it rules by force, not because the people see it as legitimate. What keeps us hopeful and stops us from acting like outlaws? I'm not going to act like politicians such as Sarney. What prevents me?"

The psychologist showed no sign of answering, so I asked, "What happens to the children of Brazil if they do not feel they have a chance to take part in the world of the adult, meaning the circle of adults who have a say in the running of the country?"

That struck a nerve. He told about a teenaged boy who found some money in school. It looked like it had been hidden, not lost, but he took it anyway. Then the boy said, "We live in a country where everybody robs everybody. Look at what the politicians are doing. So, what's the problem if I take the money?"

"What kind of relationship does he have with his father?" I asked.

"His father works for the government as a watchdog over expenditures."

"He probably has immunity from prosecution and may be stealing too," I offered.

"Or maybe his father is honest, and the son thinks he is a fool," Tatiana suggested.

This sounded like Oliveira's previously quoted statement about the corrupting influence of the oligarchy: "It . . . interferes with the passage of better moral and civic values to the children. A father looks to his children as naïve or worse, an idiot.

---

[55] Stelio, Lorenco, ***Op. Cit.,*** P. 35.

Every Brazilian with whom I spoke decried the level of dishonesty in his government, and many complained about generalized dishonesty in the culture. But, judging from the people who spoke with me, no one likes this level of dishonesty. Why are some countries honest?

Long ago I read about a study of national honesty. The experiment involved leaving a wallet with money and I.D. on the street. Three nations had an almost 100% return rate for the wallet and the money. One was China before capitalism. The others lay on the Baltic, Norway and Denmark. More recently, capitalistic China didn't fare as well. So I suspect the high rate of return had to do with a national cohesiveness, something which no one thinks Brazil possesses except during important, international soccer games.

Brazilians insist their countrymen are dishonest. If Brazilians say the *jeitinho brasileiro* is alive and active in their country, so be it. Who am I to argue? However, I can tell where I *don't* see it. I don't see it within the families I've encountered. I don't see it in the treatment I received from the Brazilians who have hosted me in their homes and offices. I don't see it among the circle of people who are becoming my friends. I am not unique in this view: The first thing out of Leonardo's mouth was that he liked the generosity and warmth of the Brazilian people. I told the psychologist that I did not think Brazil's culture had rendered the Brazilian incapable of generosity or honesty. I asked if it were a matter of national identity, not national character.

He answered, "Psychoanalysis has encouraged us to look at the individual. It is a mistake to generalize from Madoff that all Americans or all Jews are dishonest. It is fascist. It is also ludicrous to say all Brazilians are dishonest."

Then I asked, "The dishonest politician pockets money a Brazilian has paid in taxes and keeps it rather than building sewers for Lavras Novas. Why does the taxpayer then turn around and play this game, this *jeitinho brasileiro*, with his countrymen: 'You steal a little from me; I steal a little from you; we all get along.' What is the psychological gain from such behavior?"

"It's like kids playing. If they don't like how powerful adults treat them, and they don't dare act aggressively toward the adults, they take it out on their toys or their playmates. If the Brazilian taxpayer doesn't like how the powerful politicians treat him, they act out their anger by cheating other powerless people. It restores us narcissistically [i.e., restores our self-esteem] when we can turn the tables on someone even if it isn't the person who cheated us in the first place. And it even feels safer if we do it in this playful way. This doesn't happen only in Brazil. I think it happens with human beings in general."

While inquiring about large-scale corruption, I came upon a sad personal story, one which can be read either as evidence of personal dishonesty corrupting business or as an example of a society with vast discrepancies in wealth corrupting its people. It began eight years into a relationship between a woman and her domestic employee. We have heard about the employer who "loaned" money for her housekeeper to hire a lawyer so she could have a home after her husband died. Other gifts were called "loans," but the two women shared an understanding that the money could never be repaid. The employer helped with tuition money for her daughter to attend a professional school, money to make her new home livable, money for doctors, money for unexpected bills. Though the employer made room in her budget for such gifts, she had never needed a savings account because she never had any extra money. Then she retired from one of her jobs and opened an account to receive her pension checks.

The account came with a debit card, which she kept in a drawer. When she traveled, she wrote her password on a piece of paper and left it where the adult family members could find it. One day she noticed that her card had twice been used to buy groceries from the store near her home at the exact moment she was at the bank. When she reported this to the bank, they argued that her actual card had been used, not a clone. "If the card had been cloned," said the manager, "your account would have been emptied right away. It would not have been used for groceries. Someone knows your password."

She found it unlikely that anyone could have known her password without her maid's help, and no one except the housekeeper could have been sure when she would be busy and not buying groceries at that particular store. There was not enough proof to convict someone in a court of law, but everyone in the household felt 99% certain that their trusted employee had stolen the money.

To this point, the story sounds sad but not unique. In this situation, an American would likely say, "I'm sorry, but I can't trust you anymore. I feel betrayed. You're fired." However, if a Brazilian employer were to fire the housekeeper, she would find herself in court, being sued for slander and soon paying fees, fines, and back wages.

Instead, the theft was talked about openly in the home, allowing the housekeeper to overhear and become uncomfortable. Relations became strained. Without admitting the crime, the maid offered her tearful resignation, but the employer could not accept it because the cloud of suspicion would be perceived by the Judge of the Workers' Court to be evidence of an unjustified dismissal. Instead of accepting the resignation, the employer assured the housekeeper she was not under suspicion, but no one believed it to be true.

The employee began to redress the grievance by doing extra work for no extra pay, but relations remained strained. Neither could tell the truth for fear of the legal repercussions. The employee could not admit what she had done because she would then be unemployable and doomed to poverty. The woman who had enough money to hire a housekeeper did not have enough money to fire her. They coexisted behind a strained façade of cordiality, emotionally and verbally dishonest with each other, a situation created by the reality of the housekeeper's poverty and an illusion of the employer's vast wealth.

Ironically, at the time of the theft, the differences in the two women's incomes had grown smaller than ever. After years of supporting her children, the housekeeper finally had three other wage earners in the household. By this point, her son could even afford a car. Nevertheless, she remained one of the roughly 30% of Brazilians who cannot save more than $50 (see Chapter 10).

The employer, on the other hand, had retired from one of her three jobs. The sight of money flowing into a savings account might have seemed like unimaginable wealth to the housekeeper, but in fact the boss's income had fallen.

Were inherently dishonest Brazilians corrupting a relationship, or was poverty inducing dishonest behavior in ordinary people? Ribeiro has complained about the latter: "There is a third corruption, called post-modern. This is corruption committed by honest people."[56] Perhaps Brazil's distribution of wealth turns citizens into criminals and countrymen into foes, just as Leonardo, himself, had said when explaining the increasing crime rate. The prosecution of the Brazilian character rests its case. Is there any defense?

Through his creation, Macunaíma, Andrade portrayed his countrymen as essentially dishonest, selfish, and passive. I can't dispute this character analysis, but a higher authority can. The Brazilian film, *The Elite Squad* (*Tropa de Elite*), starts with a quote from the American psychologist, Stanley Milgram. According to my English translation of the filmmaker's Portuguese translation, in 1974 Milgram said, "Usually it isn't the character of a person which determines how he will act, but the situation in which he finds himself." Apparently, neither rampant and violent drug trafficking nor police brutality can be

---

[56] Ribeiro, Renato, *PensarBrasil*, Oct. 10, 2009, P. 10

blamed on character. If the Brazilian DNA does not carry a gene for dishonesty, then what explains the corruption of the government?

People operate within systems, environments, cultures, societies. Perhaps something is wrong with Brazil's system. A Brazilian activist wrote that governments with a high level of ethical behavior encourage honesty in employees by scrutinizing their behavior on the job. If this were true, politicians would act the same wherever they could get away with it.

I received a joke by email from the U.S., which I consider to be irrefutable proof that "power corrupts." In defense of the Brazilian national character, I offer this American joke:

One day a florist went to a barber for a haircut.

After the cut, he asked about his bill, and the barber replied, 'I cannot accept money from you, I'm doing community service this week.' The florist was pleased and left the shop.

When the barber went to open his shop the next morning, there was a 'thank you' card and a dozen roses waiting for him at his door.

Later, a cop came in for a haircut, and when he tried to pay his bill, the barber again replied, 'I cannot accept money from you, I'm doing community service this week.' The cop was happy and left the shop.

The next morning when the barber went to open up, there was a 'thank you' card and a dozen donuts waiting for him at his door.

Then a Congressman came in for a haircut, and when he went to pay his bill, the barber again replied, 'I cannot accept money from you. I'm doing community service this week.' The Congressman was very happy and left the shop.

The next morning, when the barber went to open up, there were a dozen Congressmen lined up waiting for a free haircut.

And that, my friends, illustrates the fundamental difference between the citizens of our country (U.S.A.) and the politicians who run it.

No one in any country likes corrupt politicians, except other corrupt politicians. On April 20, 2009, probably right after computing his income tax, Luiz Carlos Prates, appeared as anchorman on RBS TV in Santa Catarina and in his final two minutes of commentary ranted about the scandal over travel allowances to federal legislators: "The tickets were intended to pay for congressmen to go to and from Brasília . . . Shamelessly they used them to leave the country. One said that his family is sacred and for this reason he must use the money to take his family to Europe. Businessmen, staff, fools shamelessly take their pals to Rome, Miami, Paris, wherever they want. Nothing will happen because the people are stupid and won't react. They are your guests in Brasília. They are responsible for the security of the country. We pay taxes. They are disgusting and have no respect for the people . . . It is time to react. Put them out of power. Crooks!"

The viewers beside me sang out, "Yes, that's right. That's how we all feel." Yet nothing changes. What are they waiting for?"

Yearning for a Strong Leader

Mario said, "If you go to soccer stadium, you will notice there are fights. Fans are there to watch game, but gangs will infiltrate and mess things up. When gangs fight, innocent bystanders will get hit. The common workman is not interested in violence. He just wants to go home, have a nice weekend, and go to work on Monday. Sure, in the *favelas* or agglomerations there are honest workingmen. Because of a few drug dealers everything gets messed up. We need an Obama. I was very happy when he was elected. I hope a serious man will be put there to make it improve. Till then it will be worse."

The President is the head of government and would be a prime suspect as the source of corruption. Mario hoped for a great leader who would appear on the scene and make everything right. It is not unheard of in Brazil.

Juscelino Kubitschek (JK) has been praised for vision and leadership in leading Brazil to "fifty years of progress in five years." A recent publication contrasted impeached President Collor with revered former president, JK. Focusing on the men who fill the posts of government, not the system, itself, the contributors tell how JK accomplished so much, while Collor "caused decades of regression in only two years . . . But these two years were enough for him to start criminally to dismantle the Brazilian political machine, the closing of various public bodies, the elimination of more than two million jobs . . . beyond confiscating the people's savings on the first day of his government. And more, he implanted . . . a shameful system of corruption, . . . and the collection of bribes to fill his pockets and those of his group."

Collor was impeached. After chief aid P.C. Farias was mysteriously murdered, he fled to Miami. The system looked healthy as it expelled the virulent Collor, but the eventual president, Lula, was described in these words: "After being elected, Lula abandoned the changes he'd promised and proceeded to transform the agencies of the federal administration into dens even more corrupt than the government before."

Those who see the president as the head of the government blame whoever is president for the corruption. Plato would be surprised at nothing less. He didn't trust the unwashed masses to elect leaders, thinking they'd be easily fooled by demagogues and preferred the idea of wise, just, unselfish philosopher kings like JK. Brazil searches for another such leader.

Meanwhile, some of the press excoriates the current leader for the lack of ethics in government, as if he had created the problem. When Lula states that the country has common and uncommon people (see Chapter 11), it is called a triumph of cynicism that advances the decline of good political practice. Meanwhile, Roberto Romano is reported as saying that the leader is being turned into a messiah; and anyone who criticizes him, a blasphemer.

I told my girlfriend, "Mario said Brazil needs a strong, honest leader. He likes Lula but he is disappointed in him."

"One man can't stop a giant machine built to steal," she countered. Then she voiced a fear for her country:

"That is when dictatorships come to power. People get discouraged and hopeless and become nostalgic for strong leadership. That is when people will go along with a dictator," as if a new oligarch could solve the problems inherent in an oligarchy.

Ronaldo, the businessman, commented, "We need a revolution. But the military dictatorship here was horrible. Brazilians are much happier with corrupt democracy than the dictatorship. We endured a mountain of corruption which was intended to prevent communism. Now we allow corruption to prevent dictatorship." Thus, we've heard fears of dictatorship arising if Brazilians voice their objections to the current corrupt system or if they don't.

If it relies on an honest president, wouldn't a healthy system identify and then expel its dishonest chief executives? A Brazilian political scientist said, "The big problem isn't identifying corruption, but punishing it." President Collor was "punished," to the extent that impeachment, alone, could be considered punishment. In December 1994 Collor was acquitted of corruption by the Supreme Court on the grounds of insufficient evidence. Convicted of no crimes, he is now back in the Senate. If a system cannot really be cured of a disease, and the infection returns over and over again, the disease must be called chronic. Perhaps there is something wrong with the system's immune functions, with its capacity to expel a virulent infection.

It is difficult to imagine anyone from inside the system initiating reform. A jurist said, "To rise to the top of the system, you have to be corrupt." Perhaps this is the key. How do people get elected in Brazil?

Elected representation:

Tiradentes died for lower taxes and self-rule. Since then, taxes have doubled, and the descendents of Tiradentes say Brasília houses a den of thieves. If "that is how we all feel," why can't they vote the crooks out?

In theory, Brazilians could reduce corruption by the vote. In reality, this doesn't appear to be happening. People complain that their politicians are mediocre. One of Plato´s philosopher kings is a lot to ask for. Findings hundreds to gain control of the Presidency, the House, the Senate, and the Supreme Court would be a lot to ask, too much, apparently. If not platonic philosopher-kings, who are the voters electing? Do the voters knowingly elect candidates who steal, but "get things done?"

Fabio Portela would vote "yes." He is one of many who point out that in Brazil there is a fine line between the game or joke and the swindle or fraud. The verb, *burlar*, has both meanings. In English, too, to play someone is to deceive him. This suggests that Brazilians have a perversely high tolerance for being robbed of their tax money.[57]

Maybe they vote them in and then vote them out. According to Samuels, there is "a relatively high level of circulation into and out of the legislature (over 50% with each election) but relatively little change in the 'social' composition of the legislature itself, which continues to be dominated by members of Brazil's economic and social elites . . . This elite also remains largely male . . . "[58]

One possibility is that the new office-holders are already convicted criminals. A petition drive to propose a law that would prevent convicted felons from running for office has gained the 1,300,000 signatures needed to require the congress to consider it. It seems like a good idea. It was the brainchild of the Catholic University and the churches of Belo Horizonte.

However, Federal University of Brasília political scientist David Fleischer said the legislation, if passed, would surely be found to violate the Constitution. According to him, an amendment, rather than a law, should be proposed.

Oddly, a subsequent article in the paper (August 31, 2009) described the petition as an attempt to "insert *into the Constitution* a prohibition of candidates involved in corruption to run for office." Thus, it is not clear (1) whether the petition drive is for a law or an amendment, or (2) whether the Congress will respond by approving it. This much is very clear, though: Some Brazilians (a previously cited study said upwards of 80%) very much want to rid their government of corruption.

For example, writer and commentator, Alcione Araújo, thought it "Irrational that a law violator could represent the people and make laws that he didn't have to obey! . . . Enough of these dishonest deviants without character, it's absurd to give power to someone who breaks the law!"[59]

---

[57] Portela, P. 73, *VEJA, 20/5/9, edition, 2113, ano 42, #29.*

[58] Samuels, *Op. Cit.,* P. 14

I suspected that even an amendment would make no difference in the criminality of the legislature since most things the congressmen do aren't illegal because they haven't made laws against taking public money. But I was wrong. The paper said that 228 (of 594) legislators in Congress would be prevented from running if the new law could go into effect before the 2010 election. Araújo opined, "Many take refuge in politics to escape prison through parliamentary immunity."

That came as a surprise. I wondered what kinds of crimes these 228 legislators had committed. The paper told, "For things like formation of a *quadrilha* (a group conspiring to break the law, such as a racket or cartel), embezzlement, passive corruption, inappropriate administration, and damage to the environment."

Hearing this, Tatiana said, "This is the first time I am hopeful about my country. Maybe the next step is to insist they make laws against stealing our money."

"And if they don't?"

She didn't provide an answer. One possible response would be, "We'll vote them out." This was suggested by a number of people, but Brazilian voters seem to have a lot of trouble getting rid of thieves. Then (4/29/09) the cover of *VEJA*, pictured a toilet with pull chain and read: "Pull to be free of them. The lack of honesty, shame, decorum, composure, and public spirit delegitimizes the Congress. Only the vote can banish the bad politicians without threatening democracy."

On the surface this makes sense. However, I once worked for an organization whose CEO was very popular with the staff and the board. Like Lula, he was "the man." But he was not, strictly speaking, truthful. At budget meetings, the accountant could be heard to mutter, "The fish rots from the head." Where is the head of the Brazilian government?

Brazil looks like a regular democracy. It has a president, a legislature, a judiciary, and people vote. However, Brazil's electoral system does not provide a straightforward way to vote Caligula out of office. Brazilians complain about the quality of the nominees for public office, as if only Caligulas entered the field. How does this happen?

A federal deputy told me that the parties hold internal elections to form the list of candidates. According to Samuels, "In seven of Brazil's eight largest parties, . . . the party statutes vaguely state something to the effect that 'state-level party conventions shall choose candidates for federal deputy . . . 'For legislative elections, all of Brazil's [27] parties' statutes provide for a decentralized system of nomination, . . . and state-level politics dominate the party conventions at which lists are generated. However, . . . party *leaders* [don't] control the nomination process. Instead, individual candidates have substantial leeway to decide whether to run or not . . . Parties rarely run the maximum number of candidates allowed, probably because of a shortage of female candidates. . . The quota [of female candidates] is *technically* 30% of the slots on a list, but parties are penalized for ignoring the gender quota *only when they nominate the maximum total number of candidates permitted.* "[60]

The deputy said that money plays a role in the formation of the list of nominees. A wealthy candidate has a better chance of getting nominated, perhaps because of the perception that he or she would have more success in the election. According to Samuels, "the more a candidate raises and spends, the more likely he or she is to win elections."

---

[59] Araujo, Alcione, "Ou restaure-se a moralidade ou locupletemo-nos todos," *Estado de Minas,* Oct. 5, 2009
[60] Samuels, *Op. Cit.,* P. 9

"In Brazil, party *organizations* are publicly-funded through a yearly appropriation, but political *campaigns* are not. Parties provide no funding to individual candidates for congressional campaigns. Instead, and in great contrast to most countries in the world and all others in Latin America, individual candidates are entirely responsible for raising and spending money for their campaigns. There are no effective limits on campaign contributions in Brazil, and campaigns are quite expensive . . . "

In an article about using public money for foreign vacations, we heard philosopher Roberto Romano say, "The Congress has succeeded in democratizing and making universal the theft of public money," and we learned that if the congressman were responsive to anyone, he would listen to the campaign contributor. This warrants a look at campaign finance.

This might sound like a dry subject, but it is actually very sexy. I know because many sexual terms are used to describe the relationship between the politician and the campaign donor. Bruno Wilhelm Speck calls the relationship *promiscuous.*[61]

Fabio Portela preferred *incestuous* to describe the relationship between politics and business.[62] In my involvement with the juvenile court system, I had the ill fortune to meet numerous practitioners of incest, and most had no idea what was wrong with the practice, other than it violated the law and other people got all upset about it. Campaign contributors probably feel the same.

Sexually speaking, the relationship between money and political power in Brazil may be getting a bad rap. After all, a wealthy oligarchy has ruled Brazil since the captaincies. One could say the relationship between money and politics has been more a marriage than either an incestuous relationship or an illicit affair.

Conventional wisdom maintains that unless the financing changes, Brazil will likely continue the old pattern of using public money to maintain an oligarchic and parasitical political structure. Among the various suggested reforms, Speck mentions the less severe attempts to limit conflicts of interest and the more sweeping, thorough measure of public financing of political campaigns.[63] Of course, to police such activities, one would need transparency with regard to political campaigns, a politically independent agency to investigate, and an ethical, efficient court system to process complaints.

According to Marinho, as deviant as the relationship between politicians and campaign contributors may be, in other countries neither public financing nor efforts to limit donations have brought down corruption. He observed, however, that "the degree of economic development, accompanied by urbanization, reduced social vulnerability, [increased] well-being, education, and access to information can provide the needed conditions to succeed against endemic corruption."[64]

Similarly, Abramo maintains that public financing would be futile, since the "objective conditions" that foster corruption remain firmly in place. What are these "objective conditions?"

Elections: The Open-, but secret-, list system

---

[61] Speck, *Op. Cit.,* P. 123-49

[62] Portela, P. 73, *VEJA,* edition 2113, ano 42, #29

[63] Speck, *Ibid.*

[64] Marinho, Andre, ËNxugando GElo," *Pensar Brasil*, Oct. 10, 2009, P. 15

The most direct way to get a crooked politician out is office is a recall election. However, since the 1988 Constitutional convention voted against the idea of recall elections, voters must wait until the next scheduled election to vote a rascal out.

Although it may change in the near future, the electoral system currently allows a vote for either a particular candidate or for a party. Candidates for the job of deputy appear on the ballot as though they were opponents. One would think that a vote for a new candidate who appears on the ballot opposing a crooked incumbent is equivalent to a vote against the crook. Lots of Brazilian voters think it works like that in their country, but it's not so simple.

To find out how it really works, I sought explanations from people who should know, and sometimes they contradicted each other. With regard to the election of federal deputies (not senators), most experts agree on the following points:

1) Parties nominate a list of candidates.
2) Candidates don't really run against each other. The contest is between parties.
3) Whether the voter casts a ballot for a candidate by name or not, both the party and the candidate get the vote.
4) Each party wins seats in the House according to the proportion of votes it garnered in the election nationwide. For example, if the combination of a party's votes and its candidates' votes amounts to a quarter of the votes cast, it has won a quarter of the seats. (Unlike the House, the Senate elects members by a majority of voters in each state.)
5) The party distributes seats to its candidates according to their place on the party's list of candidates. The place on the partyś list may or may not correspond to the number of votes he/she received.
6) One result is that Brazilian deputies don't exactly represent a district.

On voting day, 90% of Brazilian voters pick a candidate by name, not by party. According to the deputy with whom I spoke and most other experts, a candidate's place on the list is determined by number of votes he received in his own name, plus those received in the party's name. If candidates are chosen by name, I wondered, how do crooked politicians get re-elected? The answer is complicated but understandable.

For example, Deputy Sergio Moraes was recently serving as head of the Ethics Committee investigating the use of public funds by castle-building Deputy Edmar Moreira. Moraes said that he didn't care about public opinion on the matter. Actually, he said. "Public opinion is garbage." Since he had this attitude, I wondered how he could get re-elected. When I interviewed the federal deputy, I asked him to explain.

"Public opinion is generic," he said. "It is not the same as published opinion. The media condemns the deputy, but he only cares whether his district, his constituency, is satisfied. Local satisfaction among the voters in his region is important. If you serve your district, bring public works, and help your city, you'll get re-elected."

Secondly, under Brazil's open-list election method, a candidate like Moraes--or even Edmar Moreira, the castle-builder, himself--might win even if some appealing candidate runs against him and gets more votes. Yes, a corrupt politician can still get chosen for the House even if he gets fewer votes than another candidate from his district. He can win a seat if his *party* wins more seats and he makes the cut-off on his party's list. I needed an example to help me understand:

I'm told there are 513 deputies, and 2/3 (342) come up for re-election at any one time. Suppose that on election day honest candidate, A, got more votes than the thief, B, from his district. Suppose crook B's party won 33% of the vote and was therefore able to fill one-third of the seats (114) with the first 114 candidates on its list. Crook B could sneak in as the 114th top vote getter in his party. Whether or not honest A made the cut-off for his party's list, crook B goes back to Brasília to hire more relatives and build castles.

The deputy said that the scandalized candidate is a stain on his party and it may not want him on its list. But party membership is quite fluid in Brazil. If crook B's party doesn't put him on their list, he might secure the nomination of a different party. The voters might not even know he's running because they currently do not see the party's list of candidates when they enter the polling booth.

Describing this method of electing "representatives," Roberto de Toledo said the open list system currently is guaranteed to be a green light for the most dishonest and incompetent. When objections to this process mounted, Michel Temer reportedly suggested the party's list of candidates be written on the ballot. Plus, Temer preferred that the proposal not take effect until 2014.

Upon hearing about the delay, my usually polite girlfriend said, "XXXXXXXXXXXXX."

(She and I discussed whether I should leave in her comment or change the wording to soften it. She feared repercussions against me, a non-citizen, for criticizing the government, even though Brazilians, not I, were doing the criticizing. At first, I had no such concerns, as if my freedom of speech somehow crossed international borders. Then I remembered Rohter fleeing arrest for reporting the rumors that XXXX drank excessively. During the dictatorship, newspapers printed recipes instead of censored stories, but I can't cook.)[65]

New representatives are elected, but corruption thrives. Perhaps the problem is not the candidates or the elections. Perhaps there is something wrong with the legislative institution, itself. The legislature does not make laws or internal rules against many forms of corruption. Is election reform going to motivate the House and Senate to pass rules against their spending public money on vacation travel?

Hardly anyone thinks Brazil's system of government is healthy, even though House president, Michel Temer, said its institutions are healthier than ever. Perhaps the following joke, told to me by a Brazilian, sheds light on elections don't produce honest politicians:

A Brazilian politician died and found himself face to face with St. Peter. It is not necessary to say the politician was crooked.

"Where do you want to go, Heaven or Hell?" asked St. Peter.

"I don't know. What are they like?"

"Do you want to spend a day in each and see? Then you can choose."

"Sure."

The day in Hell was great: fine food, expensive clothes, good liquor, beautiful women. They had orgies, played golf, and best of all, his friends were all there. Satan was maitre d'. He went around asking, "Is everything okay?"

The next day the politician visited Heaven. It was nice, but boring. They wore simple robes, sat on the clouds, and played religious music on harps.

In the morning St. Peter asked which he preferred, Heaven or Hell.

---

[65] Rohter, *Op. Cit.*

"I'll go with Hell," said the politician.

"Okay," said Peter and he put the politician in the elevator and pressed "down."

When the elevator door opened, the politician was greeted by hellfire and the screams of the tortured. Satan was stoking the fires and cackling sadistically.

"Whassup?" asked the politician. "Everything was great yesterday."

Satan answered, "Yesterday was the campaign. Then you voted. This is the reality."

The politicians understand what the people want and they promise it. Once they get elected, everything has a way of staying the same. Sometimes the people want things to stay the same.

Institutional Vote-buying:

I asked businessman Ronaldo about correcting the problem of corruption, and he gave an answer which captured the Brazilian voter in a cynical net of self-interest at the nation's expense. He said, "Everyone is paying for the inefficiency and corruption of the federal government." However, he doubted that the voters, themselves, would vote for smaller government: "Lula has created fifteen new ministries (cabinet posts), including one for fishing. A cabinet post for fishing! With twenty million families on welfare and getting additional money for sending their children to school and one million federal employees, he has bought a lot of votes. These people aren't going to think about the future development of the country when their jobs and incomes are at stake. In this sense, his programs maintain poverty, not eliminate it. But it is difficult to correct because when Lula spends twenty million on welfare, forty million voters will vote for the continuation of benefits instead of the future of the country. Government workers will vote for the continuation of their jobs. This inefficiency is really another form of corruption. The political machine works to increase its power at the expense of the public good . . . It is hard to fix the machine."

"So it continues."

"The impunity of those in power is a leftover of colonial times as well as the dictatorship."

"Is the passivity of the people related to the Catholic religion?"

Tatiana looked up from her magazine and remarked, "The recent issue of *VEJA* says we should not blame the Catholic religion on the grounds that European Catholic countries are not underdeveloped."

I didn't buy that argument. "That just proves it is better to be a Catholic country than a Catholic colony. Spain, France, and Portugal were not stripped of resources and left undeveloped." I then cited an article which reported that countries with a Protestant tradition have less corruption than countries with a Catholic tradition because Catholics are more obedient.

Ronaldo stayed clear of this family argument.

Our casual digging among the weeds in the garden of corruption had reached the lower stem, if not the actual root. Some type of election reform (e.g., voting for individuals instead of parties, a closed-list system, public financing of campaigns, representation of districts, etc.) might help voters to flush crooked incumbents out of the system. However, these reforms might amount to nibbling at the nether regions of the rotting fish. The next chapter concerns the way the criminal justice systems encourages corruption.

The system (government) is bad?

No, the system is very good. It only needs money to take care of the problems that complicate the lives of judicial people . . .

What is the difference between the judicial people and the physical people?

You open up the physical people and they hurt like you. The judicial people are immortal.

Millor Fernandes

We are responsible for the changes and are its immediate beneficiaries. The omission is pure connivance and cowardice. Not to act is to lose.

Mario de Oliveira, Filho

Chapter 10: São Paulo—The problem of injustice

When I visited China, I never went to Shanghai. In 1970 I spent some time in Mexico City, but the metropolis had nowhere near 19 million people back then. I've never visited Tokyo, and I doubt I'll ever set foot in Mumbai. But I have been to São Paulo. In terms of size, with eleven million inhabitants and almost nine million more just beyond the city limits, São Paulo may have no other rivals.

The Federal University sent a driver to the airport to pick us up. He had the task of getting us to the hotel; but as anyone who's ever been there knows, in São Paulo a short trip can take a long time. As we sat in traffic, he explained that São Paulo is Brazil's heart. "Brazil's money is traveling these roads," he said. He was talking about finances, but Tatiana said it was true of the country's intellectual life too.

That night we attended a conference where a French writer talked about the psychology of war. Paraphrasing shamelessly, I learned that war requires the ability to divide the world into "us" and "them" and then feel justified in slaughtering "them." If a nation had a concept of humanity, it would treat a military attack as a crime; but it would not murder the criminal's relatives and neighbors. I believe she diagnosed my country to have a narcissistic personality disorder.

The professor who drove us to the lecture spoke to me in English, to Tatiana in Portuguese, and to the writer in French. With us traveled an army officer who said in French that no war is just, that all war is horrific and doomed to fail. A soldier said that. I was not in Kansas any more.

Both Brazil's money and ideas run through São Paulo. The judiciary serves the same purpose with respect to people's rights. One cannot understand violence and corruption without knowing how Brazil's system of justice fails its people.

When Rodrigo described the salve of cordiality, he downplayed the level of violence in Brazil. I told him that my first interviewee complained about violence before he mentioned corruption.

He argued, "The violence is low level. I take your radio. You give me your money so I don't damage your car. It is harmless."

I told him about the man who was shot during a carjacking.

He said, "Those things are rare."

I didn't cite the murder rates in Rio and Sao Paulo.

To the police falls the task of keeping people safe and arresting criminals. However, the people with whom I spoke didn't trust the police either. They considered them both ineffective and corrupt. In other words, the corruption of the very people responsible for cleaning up corruption represents a serious obstacle to reforming the way Brazilians conduct business.

Police Corruption:

The corruption of the police is indisputable, and one must ask why it persists. The question has to be narrowed. Brazil has a variety of police: Federal, State, Civil, and Military. The job of the military police is "to prevent crime, to secure the urban and highway traffic, the forests and rivers, and the activities related to the preservation and restoration of public order, civil defense, and the protection of flora and fauna." Sounds like they'd be spread thin, especially since the drug traffic in major cities is so heavy. The military police have big responsibilities and a bad reputation. Informants have told of their taking money to ignore a drug deal or forget a ticket.

Maybe the ticket was actually bogus to begin with. I've never witnessed this transaction personally, but Rohter told about his own wife's experience:

A policeman motioned her over as she drove and told her she could give him a tip and keep the points off her license.

She objected, "I didn't do anything wrong."

He answered, "I know, Madam, I know. But the minister has his whiskey, and I want my beer."[66]

A study of the military police showed that even the officers were not satisfied with the job they were doing. One as much as admitted to taking bribes and explained why he did and why he let criminals go:

"If we . . . arrest [the thief], . . . the [victim] remains at the robber's mercy . . . We cannot provide individual protection if we don't have an order from above . . . If there were only justice! There is corruption everywhere . . . Here, everything works on the basis of money. If you want to get something, you pay . . ."

As for the effect of this system, he said: "The military policeman is ridiculed . . . Going around in the uniform . . . is a source of shame . . . People don't like the police. People are even afraid of the police these days."

Most of the military policemen (21 of the 27 who had attempted suicide) complained of work conditions, such as the following:

1)   They complained of pressure from superiors: "I wasn't prepared to deal with the dictatorship, which is very castrating . . . The system discriminates against any form of weakness."

2)   Working long hours creates stress: "You know when you are going to work, but you don't know when you'll come home."

3)   Working nights and changing shifts created fatigue and endangered officers: "Working at night, I couldn't sleep. It changed my personality. I became irritable and aggressive."

4)   Unpredictable work schedules, complicated by poor communication with the superiors, brought this comment from an officer who attempted suicide:

---

[66] Rohter, *Op. Cit.*, P. 151

"What stresses me are the relationships in the station . . . To wait all month for a day off, and then it arrives, and the day has been changed--it throws a guy off."

5)	One suffered from the emotional fall-out from having killed a suspect: "The first crisis came shortly I killed a thief. After that my life was ruined."

6)	Defective or inadequate equipment created stress because the criminals were often better armed.

7)	Recognizing the danger of their job can come as a shock: "The two patrolmen began to shoot at the driver. One took at least ten bullets. I'd exchanged gunfire several times, but this was the first time I saw a policeman die."

8)	One officer was accused of a crime, which he denied committing. Stress was multiplied by the fact that the legal process lasted twenty years.

9)	With low pay and difficult work conditions, the selection standards drop, and recruits too often have pre-existing problems with depression, some other mental illness, or a history with drugs and alcohol. The brother of one said, "The problem was his drinking and the fear he'd lose his job at the military police."

10)	Some officers are troubled that the citizens are dissatisfied with their job performance: "At times someone is unhappy . . . We always want to give an immediate response to a call, but there are times we cannot."

11)	A number of problems result from the low pay of the military police, e.g., "I have a family but we have nothing. They cut my water and lights."

12)	When an officer tries to work a second job to supplement his income, fatigue results: "[I get] little sleep because I moonlight as security in a bar."

The policeman quoted by Rohter told us two interesting things about police corruption. He might as well have said, (1)"I make little compared to the government officials," and (2) " . . . if they are going to steal, so am I."

As I recall, for a period of time one particular U.S. police department (New Orleans) had the reputation of being both the most corrupt force in the country and the lowest paid police in any major U.S. city. So, what are Brazilian military police paid? In 2001 the monthly salaries for the military police in all but one of Brazil's major cities ranged from $150 to $401 dollars per month (at a 1:2 exchange rate). These salaries have probably less than half the buying power than those in the city which boasted the lowest-paid force in the U.S.

Being underpaid, the police have motive to steal. Being the arm of the law, they have opportunity. They also lack reasons not to. The supervisors could insist on their subordinates obeying and enforcing the law, but generally they don't.

External control serves as an adjunct to internal control within the police departments. The Public Ministry is responsible for investigating and trying cases of police misconduct, but it is not fulfilling this function. Even though people know that the Public Ministry of Brazil isn't doing its job, the situation hasn't changed.

Brazil has, however, produced thirteen police review boards to provide external control of police behavior. The police review boards came into being when allies in political and civilian life shared a goal. They took hold after calamitous events, like massacres of citizens by police. Civil society got behind the proposals and demanded a few, specific institutional changes. Police review boards "always lack the capacity or authority to do anything tangible to diminish death squads, despite being greatly concerned about them." They also can do no investigating or impose accountability on police officers. Perhaps that is why (1) they were allowed to come into being and (2) no Brazilians with whom I spoke knew the boards existed. However, the strongest and most independent of these thirteen have proved effective in increasing the transparency of the police, tracking trends of police violence, and involving civil society in police planning.

To be held accountable, an organization's behavior must be visible. Bruno Wilhelm Speck thinks, "The control of corruption ought to occur on two fronts. On the one hand, the individuals involved ought to be held responsible. This will reduce the expectation of impunity . . . On the other hand, it is necessary to develop systems of prevention, including transparency, auditing of accounts, and inspection of records, which diminish the opportunity for new corruption." Police review boards should help since they add transparency to police behavior. Nevertheless, Latin America's largest economy, Brazil, was in 2006 rated 62nd on the Transparency International Corruption Perception Index of 159 countries, placing it behind the likes of Cuba and Bulgaria.

In truth, without transparency, plots and schemes can blossom in the shadows, and corruption and brutality will flourish. Without transparency into government behavior, "neither the judicial system nor the internal disciplinary systems of the police effectively punish individual police officers, which creates the problem of impunity. The means by which governments control inevitable corruption—in addition to failures mentioned above—is through accountability mechanisms, which are lacking in Brazil."

Recently the House of Deputies passed rules requiring additional transparency. Rules are one thing. Compliance is another. An article in the paper said, "As of Saturday, in our first ten days of the new system of transparency in the House of Deputies, in which the securities and receipts to justify the spending of funds were supposed to be divulged, the accounts of [only] fourteen of fifty-three members of the bench had adhered to the process of giving detailed data."

Transparency may be an important tool, but maybe not a sufficient tool. For oversight to bring improvement in governance, the government must have the will to take action. Take that one picket on my fence, for example. A big chunk is missing from one side. The groundskeeper at my condo must have hit it with the lawnmower. The old picket must be removed and a new one nailed up and painted. I have the tools at home--a hammer, a couple of nails, and a paintbrush--but they are quite insufficient. I leave the toolbox open. I watch them. I can shine a bright light on all of the things that need fixing, but nothing gets done. That damn picket isn't fixed.

If some neighbor looks through her transparent window, sees my damaged fence, and tells me the picket needs fixing, I agree and agree, but the picket is still damaged. I wonder what is wrong. It is as though no one has bothered to actually pick up the hammer. Apparently these tools cannot power themselves. But I digress.

Brazilians can do transparency well when properly motivated. For example, Belo Horizonte has 320,000 pit bulls, or one for every seven people. In 2008, there were 1593 pit bull attacks. A frightened populace wanted the location and ownership of pit bulls to be more transparent. The city government looked for a way to motivate owners to be more responsible. They devised a system of which Speck would approve because it combined oversight with consequences. The law now requires that each pit bull have a chip installed some place in his body, and this chip allows the authorities to locate the dog. The fine for failure to do insert the chip is $553.50. The owner remains legally, financially, and eternally responsible for the actions of his dog.

If the same logic were applied to financial attacks by government officials, including policemen, who or what would motivate government officials to cooperate with their own supervision? Abramo gave the example to cameras recording traffic violations. (I once watched a U.S. trial in which the prosecution played a videotape of the accused man's arrest. It showed the officers following correct procedure and the defendant lying.)

As the military cop admitted, the people do not trust the police to protect them. Those who can afford it hire private security. Women who go out in traffic alone drive behind tinted windows and keep their doors locked. Men who wait for their wives in the car at the curb do so at their own risk. Young women who try to sell real estate in the evening hear rocks explode their windows and watch their valuable disappear into the night. Those who park their cars and pay no one to guard them lose their radio, whatever they have left in the car, and maybe the car too. Those who get on the bus with a necklace, debark without it. Those who are very unlucky lose their lives.

A license to steal:

After U.S. embezzler Madoff received a 150-year prison sentence for embezzling money from investors, the *Estado de Minas* ran his story on one half of the page; and on the other half, an article on the most recent scandal in the Brazilian Congress: "the million-dollar medical expenses aggravate the crisis in Congress. But no one has lost his congressional seat so far."

One way to steal tax money is to hire ones own relatives for unnecessary jobs. Will legislators voluntarily reduce the number of friends and relatives they can hire after the election? One need not speculate on this issue. My friendly, local, well-informed, outraged jurist confirmed that the legislature has as yet passed no law against practicing nepotism:

"With regard to nepotism, the Constitution (Art. 37) *implies* a prohibition against nepotism when it dictates that the entire system of government 'obey the principles of legality, impartiality, morality, openness, and efficiency.'"

The Supreme Court also weighed in against the nomination of a wife, companion, three degrees of relations, and so forth for government jobs. Thus, though neither the law nor the Constitution explicitly prohibits nepotism, the Courts have outlawed it. However, as the jurist said, "As Brazil actually functions, nepotism reigns supreme in the land," including within the Judiciary, itself, to a notorious extent.

Sometimes they don't even bother to hire relatives. For example, according to *VEJA*, First Secretary of the Senate, Efraim Morais, hired 52 ghosts to work in the Federal Senate. During the last four years of his tenure, millions of dollars disappeared in fraudulent contracts. In salaries, alone, the non-existent employees emptied the public coffers by $3.85 million ($3,850,000.00) over his tenure. In response he said, "I have done nothing wrong." Thus, there seems to little evidence that the thieves are rehabilitating themselves.

When I presided over a group home for teenaged criminals, I sat them down on their first night and asked what rules they thought the house should have. They drew up an impressive list. They disallowed any law violations, unauthorized absences from school or home, and also fighting and cursing in the house. None of us, them or me, expected they would follow those rules. Enforcement would be my job. On the other hand, when the post-dictatorship Constitution told the Congress to think up rules for themselves, they neglected to make any laws against pocketing tax money.

Nevertheless, the press and the public repeatedly express shock and outrage at the capacity of Congress to commit theft. The legislators diffuse the public's anger by castigating each other for their crimes. After weeks of behaving like the conscience of the nation, they vote to exonerate one another from having done anything wrong. The joke in Brazil is that the politicians put on a show of condemning one another and then go out for pizza together afterward.

The members of the Congress apparently don't want the public outrage to get out of control. As we've seen through their spokesman, Michel Temer, they warn that democracy hinges on their adherence to the Constitution (with its privileged immunity from prosecution). They argue that changes must be made gradually through political negotiation, and they reassure the voters that the violators are being severely punished despite their never going to jail and seldom losing their jobs.

The Weak Middle Class

In São Paulo a photographer told me that he had a great time visiting Buenos Aires. "At night, everyone is out walking on the streets. Music is playing. It is very safe." I asked why Argentina could be so much safer than Brazil, and he replied, "Because relatively speaking they have a larger middle class."

Apparently, he thought there was power in numbers; and when the numbers of poor overwhelmed the number of middle-class, streets became unsafe. An attorney and political scientist told me, "Machiavelli's discourses say a middle class is key to the survival of a State. Otherwise, it disintegrates into conflict between the self-interest of the powerless and the powerful."

Most of my informants represented Brazil's middle class. Though they were outspoken in their criticism of the government, most took no action to alter the situation. The clergyman explained, "Brazil never had a strong middle class, just a few rich and powerful families, a small, weak middle class, and lots of poor people. My parents' generation entered the middle class in 50's and 60's, but they lost a lot of money during the inflationary 80's. Inflation is not so hard on rich."

The middle class is often referred to as the womb of entrepreneurship. Small businesses employ most people in the U.S., and politicians of all stripes try to win the votes of that country's middle class. I wondered whether the Brazilian government was acting to strengthen the middle class. Then I read that Brazil recently announced an increase on the taxation of interest earned on savings. The threshold at which savings accounts would begin to be taxed was being lowered from $40,000 to $25,000.

On May 15, 2009, the headline in *Estado de Minas* read, "Savings: Mark of Inequality." The article said that a vast majority of Brazilians either (1) have no savings at all, but (2) among those who do, 99% don't have enough to be taxed: "More than 50.5 million Brazilians cannot save more than $50 . . . The accounts with more than $25,000 (those being taxed) belong to 1% of the total population."

It also said, "On the other hand, there is a small group of 3,822 people who have an extra $500,000 . . . Of the $7.45 billion belonging to this stratum of society, each person would, on average, have almost $2 million in his or her account." The article argued that these folks wouldn't be hurt by the tax increase on savings because this was just extra money to them.

The people who would be hurt are from that 1% (minus the 3,822 who have millions stashed away). By my calculations this group holds 35% of Brazil's savings. By lowering the taxable savings rate from $40,000 to $25,000, the internal revenue people are capturing the medium-sized savers with balances of $25,000-$39,999 and taxing them at the same flat rate at which millionaires are taxed. How does this promote the growth of an entrepreneurial middle class?

How about other taxes? Brazil taxes earned income progressively at rates ranging from 7.5% on $8,608-$12,900, 15% on $12,901-$17,200, 22.5% on $17,201-$21,492, to a maximum of 27.5% on more than $21,492. Considering that the highest rate of taxation kicks in at a very low income level, one could argue that proportional to disposable income, the middle class bears the brunt of the tax burden.

This means it bears the cost of fraud as well. When fraud siphons off at least 20%, the rich stay rich. The poor are cheated of hospitals, housing, and schools; but not actual money since they don't pay income tax. (They do, however, pay plenty in sales taxes, which is one reason some would like sales taxes to be made visible and why the press periodically reminds their readers what their total tax burden really is.) According to the clergyman I interviewed, "The poor don't have as much at stake because they don't pay taxes," but when services are stolen, so are their futures. I wondered why the government would target the middle class for increased tax revenue.

When I found myself sitting beside that Brazilian ex-pat on the plane, I asked, "If we assume that those who set government policy are not stupid, it would seem that they are behaving in a manner hostile to the financial, numerical, and political growth of the middle class."

He replied, "In the United States you can build wealth. You cannot do that in my country. First, I run my own business in the States. In Brazil I would not be paid as much, not nearly as much, and it would be very difficult to start up my own business in Brazil. Would the bank give me a loan? Would I be able to afford the cost of getting the government's permission?"

"Many international companies are located in Brazil."

"They figure the expense of bribes into the cost of doing business. It is hard to start up the business if you add in the cost of the bribes."

"Time is money," say the businessmen. Another cost to the Brazilian entrepreneur-to-be is start-up time for his business. An article titled, "Bureaucracy is still the major adversary," reported, " . . . at least 50% of new businesses die within two years after starting." They fall victim to a deadly combination of high taxes, excessive bureaucracy, interest rates that while on the decline are high by international measures . . . Brazil ranks 129th in the world in ease of starting a business."

Tax on the sale of property represents another piece of the wealth-growing puzzle. At a cocktail party I asked an unsuspecting victim, "Did you know that in the U.S. you can keep $250,000 profit on the sale of a home, $500,000 if you are married?"

"We don't have that in Brazil. You could really increase your wealth simply through home ownership."

"Exactly, and that's the point, to stimulate the economy by growing wealth. It gives the middle class money to invest. So, why don't they do that in Brazil?" This is the type of question that leads someone to find an excuse to refill his drink.

In Brazil the taxes on the profit from the sale of a home do not encourage home purchase in this way. An economist told me, "When a home is sold, the government taxes the difference between the amount you paid for it and what you sold it for up a certain amount." This would discourage buying and selling homes to build wealth.

The tax policies in the U.S. and Brazil with respect to home sales are opposite and create opposite incentives, whether for better or worse. Certainly the overzealous U.S. policy toward home ownership has had unfortunate consequences for the entire world. However, in the U.S. homeowners have been greatly rewarded for buying new homes, and it has created wealth for homeowners such as the ex-pat I met on the plane.

In Brazil, on the other hand, the taxpayer is punished for buying a more expensive home. He pays taxes at the time of purchase, and appreciation of the home is taxed at the time of sale. I wondered whether a change in policy might help the middle and lower classes to gain wealth and asked someone else at the party.

He said, "The Worker's Party wants to tax the middle class because they see them as the bourgeois."

"Okay, but in Brasília Lula's party has formed a coalition with other parties. Why would they want to deter the middle class from having enough money to grow businesses and wealth?"

When this partygoer couldn't answer my question, I asked it of the female journalist in the field of economics. She did replied, "We designate classes A, B, C, D, E, and F. Middle is C. The goal is to have D, E, and F become consumers, that is, to move them into C. Lula is the most popular president in history because he has been able to do this, with *Bolsa Família* (Family Purse) . . . "

Increased income for the poor helps them to buy things, but I heard no mention of helping the middle class to start businesses. As a matter of fact, Baer pointed out that the welfare payments going to the poor under Lula's Family Purse program are small compared to the amount paid to wealthy folks who loan the government money. He argued that welfare, while helpful to the recipient families, actually worsens the distribution of wealth. So, if welfare money is going to the poor, and interest payments are going to the wealthy, who is losing money?

Mario de Oliveira described the consequences of moving money away from the middle class and into the pockets of the wealthy: "the existence of privileges exists on a scale that consumes a substantial part of the resources which ought to be destined to investments . . . Here lies the reason for Brazil's lack of development. This 'burden of the privileged oligarchy' is the major impediment to the civic, economic, and moral development of Brazil."[67]

Would the oligarchy prefer that the middle class remain economically and politically weak? It seems like the bigger and stronger and richer the middle class becomes, the more it will demand the level playing field of a free-market economy. I wondered if this meant the oligarchy would really prefer a society comprised of many poor people to provide cheap labor and a politically and economically weak middle-class.

When I posed this possibility to a fellow partygoer, he asked, "So they are keeping me poor on purpose?"

"Well, I don't know what is in their minds, but if they wanted to reduce your taxes to grow the middle class, it would be pretty simple to do. They could reduce your taxes by 20% if they just quit stealing the tax money."

"That doesn't make it a conspiracy, though."

---

[67] Oliveira, Filho, Mario de, interview with *VEJA,* April, 18, 2007.

"I don't know if everyone in Brasília consciously thinks about keeping the middle class from growing in numbers and strength. Probably most are just greedy. But Renato told me to read Easterly about economic development, and I'll bet some of them have read it too."

I had borrowed Renato's copy and promptly spilled coffee on it. Between the stains I read how to prevent economic development (and keep wealth in the hands of the powerful): Award contracts regardless of merit and then don't honor them, ignore the law, inflate the bureaucracy, increase interest rates, raise taxes, in other words, employ 'policy tools that retard and inhibit people's ability to invest in markets.' Even if they only do it for greed, some of them have to understand the long-term impact of siphoning money from the middle class to the rich.[68]

Later, I asked an economist about the policy toward the middle class and got this reply:

"A definitive solution to poverty is economic development. Palliative measures can be taken in extreme cases, such as the Family Purse, but in the long run it is more important to create private-sector jobs with decent salaries." Is Brazil counting of the very wealthy to grow all the businesses and create all the jobs?

Economist Carlota Pérez told interviewer Diogo Schelp she thought, "The best is yet to come" for Brazil economically. In general, she said that recovery from the international financial crisis would require the creation of more and better jobs which produce and distribute the wealth according to entrepreneurial effort and production, rather than profit from speculation. She thought Brazil was in a good position because its specialization in life sciences and materials gave it an advantage during the coming technological revolution based in biotech, bioelectronics, and nanotechnology. She favored the size of its economy, the potential internal market, the diversification of industry, the technological capacity. She thought Brazil could excel in the sectors of petroleum, chemistry, metallurgy, livestock, and biotechnology.[69]

She also said that growth depended on entrepreneurship, not just the rich investing in established companies and products. Thus, I wondered whether the oligarchy was big and rich and savvy enough to start all of these new businesses. Could they carry the country's economy into the future?

Most economists and political scientists were saying, "No." One economist even pointed out that the opening of Brazil's economy to privatization and market forces has paradoxically resulted in increased concentration of ownership of its industries. Through their actions, the politicians were betting, "Yes," and the writers of *The Economist* agreed.[70]

Fisiologismo:

I hate it when writers in one language put words from other languages into the text, but only if I don't know the languages. Much to my chagrin, here I have written *fisiologismo,* a word invented in Brazil. *Desculpe,* as they say: "I'm sorry." I couldn't help it. There is no such word as *fisiologismo* in the Portuguese dictionary. *VEJA* had to resort to Wikipedia for a definition. It read, "*Fisiologismo* is a type of political relationship in which political actions and decisions are made in exchange for favors and benefits in the interests of the individuals."

In 2006 seven Nobel Prize-winning economists told *VEJA* that Brazil had one of the most closed economies in the world, due in large part to a "capitalism of godfathers" which favored certain sectors and economic groups, inhibited competition, ballooned the bureaucracy, and

---

[68] Easterly, *Op.Cit.* P. 324.

[69] Schelp, Diogo, *VEJA,* 27/5/9.

[70] *The Economist,* "Getting it together at last--special report on business and finance in Brazil," Nov. 14, 2009.

siphoned money away from development. For example, if a bureaucrat authorized a bank loan for a friend in order to build alliances, and that loan never had to be repaid, the money was not loaned for economic reasons and was likely not money well spent.

In theory, to stimulate growth a government should provide market-based incentives. I read that an economy which is free of political manipulation will cultivate cultural values like "hard work, savings and industriousness, honesty and trustworthiness, creativity, and responsibility. These are the bases of the wealth of nations."

Brazil's political leaders apparently prefer to stick to the well-traveled path of colonelism and oligarchy. Andrioli quotes Mario Amato as saying that the current concentration of wealth in the hands of a few is directly related to the political culture of the Brazilian elites found in the phenomena of colonelism and clientelism. According to Easterly, the sharp divisions in wealth and a weak middle class as seen in Brazil, raise the danger of social polarization, already well underway in the country.[71]

Fisiologismo is a tool of Brazil's oligarchy. The political party which dominates the legislature in Brazil, the PMDB, apparently has achieved this status with its absence of ideology, its complete pragmatism, its willingness to deal, and its single-minded focus on accruing and maintaining power. Having mastered the art of *fisiologismo* as no other linguistic group, the speakers of Brazilian Portuguese had to invent a word to describe their masterpiece. I had a number of questions about the practitioners of this 500 year-old art form.

An informant gave me this answer: "When you asked me why PMDB doesn't run a candidate for president, I thought it must be because they can have more power by bargaining with the President, and this article seems to support that. They can't win the general elections. Lula's Workers' Party got the most votes in the last two general elections; but in the Senate, the small, rural states in the Northeast gain disproportional representation; and therefore the PMDB gains a plurality. The president of the Senate, PMDB's Sarney, is a colonel."

Notice that this informant did not say Sarney was *like* a colonel. As we know, the concept dates back to the captaincies established by the Portuguese crown. After King Pedro II was deposed and banished, Brazil was declared a Republic, and elections were held, but these merely reinforced the power of an oligarchy because, as we know, these elections allowed merely 3% of the people to vote for the national congress.

Nowadays, as we've been told, "the influence of the colonels is based on two pillars: land and getting out the vote." Much of their power results from Brazil's high concentration of wealth in the hands of a few. In the past, wealth derived from land ownership; and arable land is still owned by a relative few. For example, in 2007 $15-20 billion was available for agricultural purposes. Eighty per cent went to the five hundred richest landowners, three times the total destined to Family Purse, the program to provide food for the poor, which received $5.5 billion.

Speck tells how colonelism spreads into urban Brazil. He argues that a major source of corruption is the amount of the federal budget which the executive branch has the discretion to spend. The executive branch uses this money "according to its interests at any moment . . . to corrupt [public policy]." As a result, wealth from industrial sources and urban life, as well as the wealth in rural areas, is among the most concentrated in the world.[72]

Thus, a confluence of factors makes the district of Brasília a veritable Fertile Crescent for cultivating power. When politicians have this much power, they can manipulate the economy,

---

[71] Easterly, *Op. Cit.*

[72] Speck, Bruno Wilhelm, "Corruption, prevencao e controle," TransparenciaBrasil.

and manipulation of an economy for political reasons " . . . inevitably creates an environment of corruption and privilege that wastes people's time, labor, income, and resources in just trying to bribe those with power. The political powers become wealthier and the society becomes that much poorer . . . "

Mario de Oliveira, Filho has also made the argument that the essence of Brazil's corruption is not new, but rather results from continued control of the country by an oligarchy. As a businessman, he points out that these oligarchies function as cartels which interfere with open markets and distort prices. He alleges that most of the three hundred biggest business groups are controlled by families which erect almost imperceptible barriers to prevent competition.[73]

An informant gave me a perfect example. The computer company for which he worked would have liked to bid against multinational companies on contracts, but they were not on the list of bidders. Why would a qualified company not be on the list of bidders? To get the lowest bid, one would want as many hungry, innovative companies as possible, right?

No, not if one were more interested in reducing competition and keeping one's friends in business. If the economy were really a private club, a new company would have to pay a hefty bribe to gain membership.

When I asked a businessman about the effect of this *fisiologismo* upon him, he said (Chapter 5) that the cost of bribes to enter a closed market discourages new businesses and interferes with rewarding the best products and services. In other words, the people who institute these corrupt practices impede economic development and prevent the less advantaged from prospering from the world's tenth largest economy. As we've been told, the money paid for bribes reduces productivity, causes the prices of everything to go up, reduces funds for government programs, increases insurance rates, threatens corporate reputation, and an increases the probability of employee sabotage. Overall, this results in a shift of wealth from the poor to the rich.

It also reduces the buying power of the lower middle class, which would be my description of someone who had no savings and worked three jobs just to pay living expenses and taxes. After a recent trip to the grocery store, my girlfriend, the self-proclaimed slave to taxes gave two examples which reflected lack of competition in the marketplace.

First, between trips the cost of *all brands* of paper towels had inflated from around $1.00 for two small rolls to more than $3.00. Secondly, pomegranates, which grow naturally in Brazil, had come into season. One of the fruits which had last cost $5.00 now cost $9.00. (Her actual words were, "$9? It's robbery!") There had been no loss of pomegranate trees to frost, no fires in the paper towel factories, just an opportunity to charge more. When I heard Walmart had signed agreements for a dozen or more stores, I wondered whether the chain's low prices would Walmartize Brazil or whether the cost of entering the market would have Brazilianized the world's largest retailer.

Some believe that as long as established businesses can limit competition, the cost of living will remain artificially high, the gap between rich and poor will remain wide, and other efforts to democratize the country will be ineffective. When the society lacks opportunity and economic justice, crime mounts. (Now, even dogs are stolen and held for ransom.) When the

---

[73] Oliveira, Mario, *Op. Cit.*, Three other examples offered by Oliveira included the wedded sale (to sell a product, a company has to buy something from its buyer), selective distribution (selling a product with restrictions on how it can be distributed, thereby reducing competition in its use), and predatory pricing (temporarily reducing the price below cost to drive out the competition).

lawmaker's, themselves, steal with impunity, no one respects the law. When there is no system in place to control crime, when the police can't be trusted and the courts are slow or corrupt, violence mounts.

Despite all of its difficulties, Brazil is considered one of the world's emerging economies, along with China and India. One informant expressed respect for the way her country has become independent of foreign imports. "Brazil now makes everything it buys. The cars are German, Japanese, Korean, or American, but the steel and the workers are Brazilian."

Playing the devil's advocate, one can assume Brazil will do nothing about corruption. Perhaps it will continue to develop anyway. I'd bet the oligarchy running Brazil thinks development can continue under its stewardship despite its cost-raising skimming. Perhaps they are right, and conventional economic analysis doesn't apply to Brazil where so much wealth is held by so few. Rather than comparing Brazil to a modern democracy or to free-market economies, perhaps Brazil should properly be compared to China where an oligarchy of party members controls the country. In China wages remain low by western standards, but China's economy is nevertheless expected to continue growing.

Perhaps if enough wealth is in the hands of the rich, investment capital isn't needed from the middle class. Maybe the very wealthy can continue to use high unemployment and dire poverty to keep the cost of labor down and thereby compete in worldwide markets. The business owners will grow their own wealth even though the situation for the millions of poor does not improve dramatically.

Wait! Are the people going to allow this? Didn't Tiradentes martyr himself for this in 1792?

Judiciary:

In examining the workings of the police, we learned that the Brazilian police cannot secure the safety of the citizen. The second part of the system is the courts: "In disbelief over politics and the politicians, the citizen puts all of his hopes in the Judiciary."[74] Indeed, in some countries the courts guard the rights of citizens and protect the populace from power grabs by the government, but not everywhere. My informants have told me that the Brazilian courts fail to protect their rights and deliver justice. The Constitution states a desire to promote the public good above all else; yet Brazil lacks a functional and fair law enforcement system. So, why would this be?

One reason is the failure of police to investigate crimes. "Consider the fact that the state of São Paulo maintains a civil police force of 36,000 members to investigate crimes, and there were 523,396 officially filed reports of crime in 1999, but only 84,519 police investigations were opened . . . the public ministry formally processed 25,300 cases, of which 12,102 began by capturing a suspect in the act, which does not require much investigative activity. In short, only 2.5% of all reported crimes reached a judge as the active result of police investigations . . . "

Then what happens? Lots of times nothing happens.

In the lower courts a manpower problem exists. Brazil has roughly one judge for every 23,000 inhabitants (while the U.S. has one for every 9,000). Informants complained because no one investigated the theft of their cars or because cases never reached a conclusion, which may at times be the result of a shortage of judges.[75] However, informants also complained about the lack

---

[74] Araujo, Alcione, *Op. Cit.*

[75] Gomes, Marcelo; Araujo, Ricardo de Melo, "Controle externo, "*Corrupcao--Ensaios e Criticas,* editoraufmg, 2008.

of punishment for white-collar crimes. A mother and her adult son had the following conversation:

Mother: "I've read about Madoff being sentenced to 150 years in jail in the U.S. Today the newspaper headline is something like, 'Out there criminals get 150 years in prison for their crimes, whereas here nothing happens with those who rip us off.' We have good laws, but they aren't respected. They aren't enforced. For example, a drunk driver killed a young physician and received a sentence of community service. The doctor's mother went to the prosecutor and told him she wanted to kill the man. He convinced her to trust him to pursue a second trial for a stiffer penalty."

I asked, "What happened?"

"I don't know."

"Was he the son of a rich man?"

"Certainly. This is how corruption works in this country."

I called their attention to headline which read, "Crime without punishment causes revolt in Ouro Preto."

"What is that all about?" I asked.

"Eight years ago [2001], a teenaged girl named Aline Silveira Soares was [allegedly] killed by four other kids in some kind of satanic ritual. The trial is still going on. I don't know what caused the latest delay. They are rich kids."

(Three of the defense attorneys failed to show up for the trial, and friends and relatives of the girl attacked the cars of the accused. The trial was postponed.)

The jurist with whom I spoke gave two other explanations for the failure to punish people who can afford attorneys. One was the Brazilian view of incarceration:

"Forget about white-collar crime. Those are never punished. Think about common crimes. We can't punish the common criminal. For example, there is the case of Pimenta Neves, a journalist who shot his girlfriend. He confessed, but he is free and will never be punished. He is not in jail awaiting trial with a high bond. In Brazil a person is considered guilty only after all the proceedings and appeals have been exhausted.

"We have two types of judges, the idiots of good faith and those who are dishonest and act in bad faith. The good faith idiots will say we should guarantee this person has his freedom even though he confessed. Freedom is the rule, and prison is the exception, even for the guilty. Even though there were witnesses and material evidence and he confessed, the killer is not considered guilty, and he has not spent a moment in jail.

"In North America when the police find ample evidence of guilt, a prosecutor will charge the suspect, and the judge will at the dispositional hearing decide whether to try, whether to hold the accused, and whether to set bail. Judge would take the socially responsible behavior of jailing a suspected killer. Even though we follow the first steps in Brazil, we then take a shift, and the killer goes free until the judicial process is completely done. The court procedures take ten to twenty years.

"Our rhetoric is based on the French Revolution's ideal of freedom. Judges consider it absolute. In my opinion, there is no constitutional principle which is absolute. For example because someone is assumed innocent until proven guilty doesn't mean men are essentially innocent by nature, nor does it mean punishment should be avoided if at all possible. The idiot judges take this 'innocent until proven guilty' literally, even if witnesses saw the murder and the killer has confessed."

Instead of pointing out the problem within the judiciary, the press often blames individuals for what they see as ethical lapses. In such an article, Escosteguy quoted Deputy José Genoíno when he complained, "Today, you are guilty until proven innocent."[76] According to the jurist I interviewed, the problem is just the opposite: No one is guilty until proved so over and over and over again. It is as though the judiciary is trying to protect guilty citizens from punishment.

The jurist is not the only one who has noticed this about the judiciary. *Estado de Minas* reported a perfect example on September 24, 2009. An ex-deputy (congressman), Hildebrando Pascoal, was convicted of the 1996 chainsaw mutilation and murder of a car mechanic and his 13 year-old son. He received a sentence of 15 years, plus three more years tacked on due to the accused man's previous record: In 2002 he was sentenced to 88 years for narco-trafficking, formation of a group which conspired to commit crimes, buying votes, and homicide. Wow, three extra years.

Despite the crime and the past record, the judge felt it necessary to justify the sentence. He found the circumstance of the victim's death to be "insensitive," and he probably got it right. Cutting off someone's arms, legs, and penis with a chainsaw seems insensitive. I wondered if he would be granted another trial and be back out on the streets until it was finished. It's worked for the past thirteen years. If another judge takes the retrial, will he have to explain that to anyone?

At this point, one might ask why "idiot" judges weren't removed from the bench. One answer would be, "The federal Constitution establishes the principle of oversight of public agencies (Article 34, VII, d)." In theory, it should be possible to evaluate the performance of the government, including the Judiciary. Despite the Constitution, no one measures the judiciary's performance or rates its efficiency. Data is not available. "The opacity simply feeds the suspicion that the ministers of the court system are compromised for political and economic interests . . . Justice is not the goal of the Brazilian Judiciary."

So, criminals go free. What is the effect?

One source answered, " . . . The slowness of the Judiciary feeds impunity and this fuels the greed of the holders of power in assaulting the public coffers. We don't put the white-collar criminal in jail to rot. We give him community service. With no real threat of imminent and effective punishment, corruption will never be effectively fought. Unfettered by the weak tools available to combat it, corruption becomes indestructible and impossible to purge."

One researcher argued that the judicial system was too predictably dysfunctional to be the result of individual cases of corrupt legal officials. Rather, the system purposefully facilitates fraud and impunity by creating complexity and irresolution. By failing to act against white-collar crimes, the courts allow the corrupt politicians, bureaucrats, and businessmen to establish a "cleptocracy," which tramples the Constitutional rights of the citizens.

Then the jurist divulged the second reason criminals with good attorneys go without punishment: "A soccer player killed two people driving drunk in Rio. It happened thirteen years ago and is still in the courts because the lawyers don't allow it to end. Three juries have found him guilty. Now they are on the fourth trial."

The case of the murdering soccer player has dragged on since 1996. What keeps it going?

"A judge's ruling can be questioned. He must justify his decisions."

According to the jurist, "If a judge does find someone guilty, his decision can be overturned endlessly. The soccer player was found guilty three times, but a fourth trial is underway. It is not like in the U.S. where only a higher court, an Appeals court, can review a case and order a retrial. In Brazil a case can be retried completely by a judge at the same level or a higher level, not just reviewed, but retried. In the Brazilian culture, the court does not have as much power as in the U.S., where a court is assumed to have performed correctly and a higher court will overrule only if a decision is absurd. Trials

---

[76] Escosteguy, Diego, "Ä etica dos incommuns," *VEJA,* Nov. 11, 2009.

can be infinite in number. Defense attorneys can endlessly petition for *habeas corpus*. In Brazil, half of the decisions are overturned."

"Why do the judges want to retry all of these cases?"

"There is no logic. The system considers punishment to be an evil and believes that you shouldn't fight one evil with another. Thus, if there is any chance someone is innocent, he should spend no time in jail. I don't agree. Letting a guilty person go free is also an evil. Sometimes punishment is constructive. Punishment exists to prevent future crimes by the guilty and to deter similar crimes by others. Those who commit crimes should be removed from society until rehabilitated.

"There is another mechanism by which the guilty go unpunished. We have 1900 trials awaiting conclusion. If someone is waiting in prison, he will have the right to trial before those who are free. This delays the trials of those who are not in jail. Since only poor go to jail, anyone who can afford a lawyer will be free. In addition, there is a time limit on waiting for trial. While a criminal waits for trial, the time limit may expire and cause the charges to be dropped.

"I know of such a case in a small town. The father of murder victim is waiting for the trial of his son's murderer, but it will never happen. He runs into his son's killer in restaurants and at the movies. He goes into the prosecutor's office every week to check on the progress of the case, but there is none. There are 8,000 cases waiting for trial. This trial will never start. I have been warned about giving out this information. People fear that if a journalist published it, people will start shooting each other in revenge."

This concern with "stability" reminded me of Temer's concern that civil war would break out if thieves were expelled from Congress. By withholding information from people, the people fail to act, and social ills are not corrected. This forces one to ask, "What good is stability if it serves injustice?"

Isn't it better to know the truth? In the words of Marcelo Cunha de Araújo, it is necessary that "the citizen have access to secret information about the practice of forensic law to someday become fully aware. The illusion of a neutral and egalitarian Penal Law ought to be refuted vehemently by key people who, by sharing a clear idea of the current state of things, can most effectively pursue a truly free, just, and harmonious society."[77]

Meanwhile, the local jurist was, himself, concerned about the judicial system's failure to address societal problems: "While the criminal justice systems concerns itself with minor issues, it is not taking responsibility for the lack of investment by society into areas that breed criminality. Until we do that, all of our efforts are merely as effective as drying an ice cube."

My girlfriend saw perversion again: "It is a perversion. Freedom is not the freedom to steal or commit crimes. People who break laws should lose freedoms."

After talking about criminal law, the mother and son shifted to civil law:

Son: "The problem is if someone does sue, it will take five years to go through the courts."

Mother: "Five? More like thirty! My friend's foot was crushed when she was signing something in a store and the table collapsed. The mall administrator made her sign a waiver before letting her call her husband or an ambulance. The bill was $25,000 even though her husband got professional courtesy from other doctors. The case has been going on for years. She will never get this money."

---

[77] Araujo, *Op. Cit.*, P. 219

(They weren't the only ones who talked like this. Earlier, the female journalist said Brazilian justice was slow and corrupt. "You must wait fifteen to twenty-five years to resolve a case." In Sao Paulo a Minister of Health was accused of stealing $322 million. It took ten years for a judgment to arrive.)

I asked, "The paper today (April 9, 2009) ran a headline which read, 'Citizens of Minas Gerais win millions in U.S. court rulings.' Why is this such a big deal?"

Mother: "Because in Brazil no one who wins a lawsuit will ever see the money. I know of a case in which a family sued over a death and won, but the bank had the power to withhold the money."

"Does a law give them this power, or is the Court's judgment being ignored?"

Mother: "I don't know. You need to interview a lawyer."

When I interviewed the jurist, he told me, "By itself, a bank can't overrule the order of a Judge. The bank cannot even appeal if the lawsuit does not target it. So, if a judge tells a bank to pay, the bank must pay."

In other words, if someone has won a case and no award has been paid, the case must still be under appeal, which appears to the observer as though "the lawyers are still negotiating."

On the same day *Estado de Minas* reported on the lack of justice in a murder of the young girl eight years before, it also told the story of one of Belo Horizonte's large housing developments. In 1988 Mayor Sergio Ferrara authorized the building of apartment houses on 519,000 square meters of wooded and protected land in front of a major shopping center.

"The mayor waived the protection without an environmental impact study. His successor tried in vain to reverse the decision, and in 1992 the Public Ministry filed suit to stop the construction." The court did not delay the construction until 17 years and 562 apartment houses later.

Finally, the court ruled, "Yes, there should be an environmental impact study," and *Estado de Minas* reported on May 22, 2009, "Belvedere III will have to present an environmental impact study."

I decided to do my civic duty and save them the trouble. I carefully examined the picture in the paper and found wall-to-wall high-rises, no plazas, and two lonely, scrawny trees. One tree grew from the ground. The other had become an apartment dweller, itself. Unless we count these two trees as a forest, I think we can assert that the apartment buildings have had a substantial environmental impact.

"I wonder if it cost money to get the mayor to waive the protection and delay the ruling?" asked my interviewee.

The jurist's discussion of white-collar crime soon morphed into another issue, the right to privacy: "The average Brazilian judge is stupid; and if he disagrees with a law, he will re-interpret it as he likes, rather than enforce it as it is written. The judge is more interested in his own concept of the law than in making it possible for things to happen as they should.

"For example, with the Supreme Court's current orientation, it is impossible to carry on an investigation of white-collar crime because the Supreme Court doesn't allow it. The Supreme Court prevents any investigation on grounds of violating privacy rights. Bank records are protected under a fundamental right for privacy. It is better to have one thousand guilty people found innocent than one innocent person's accounts inspected. It is a nice idea, but there is no other way to investigate, judge, and condemn white-collar criminals.

"There should be transparency in all this movement of money. If I am a public employee, why on earth should I have the right not to show my bank account? If I receive public money, I should be able to explain any deposit in my bank account. Politicians should be held accountable. They should show where their money comes from. The other day I was teaching graduate students; and when I said we needed financial transparency, the students, all professionals, didn't like it because it violated the right to privacy."

When I asked him whether his generation of lawyers would become judges and change the system, he said, "No, I gave a lecture to an organization of lawyers, and people booed me, as if I were in favor of torture or arresting people for no reason. I just want them to come to senses. It's common sense. Look at the obvious. There is a need for oversight."

In the university where he teaches, most of the professors are defense attorneys, and they have shaped the thinking of the students. They are very interested keeping things as they are because they make so much money. For example, his friend, a defense-attorney, makes $300,000 for one trial. "If I got that much I would not want it to change either." When he teaches these law students, they come to him believing that anyone who thinks differently is in favor of some kind of dictatorship against human rights. In his class, his students feel as surprised as if they had seen the other side of the moon, though some stick to their previous opinions.

Though he thinks the police should have access to the bank records of suspected criminals, this jurist is wary of too much police power. Recently delivered from a dictatorship, Brazil has mixed feelings about who is the enemy of the state. Policing agencies are feared as potential instruments of oppression. The jurist, himself, warns against this possibility. He says that in Brazil the police and Public Ministry could start oppressing the people. He does not believe the justice system is capable of keeping the police in check in any reasonable way, so they accomplish it by rendering the policing agencies impotent.

However, in the jurist's complex view of society, he sees the white-collar criminal as the enemy of the state as well. In his view, these criminals foster drug trafficking and homicide by misusing public money and exacerbating social injustice in Brazil.

"It is difficult to combat. The prosecutor never has the power to look at the bank records by himself. It always depends on a Judge's order to open the records. If a judge in one court gives prosecutor permission to check a bank account, the defense attorney will go to another court and get *habeas corpus* to set aside the order, and in the meantime his bank account won't be checked. An example is the case of Daniel Dantas (the billionaire banker who was accused of income tax evasion). If we look at his records, we will be sued by our professional organizations and called to explain our acts. The people being investigated will sue us for defamation. Commonly, when the judge and prosecutor have been sued, the sentence which has been given in the case is then nullified. Whenever a judge decides to check a bank account, he must be an idealistic guy. He is punished each time he does his job. He may do it once or twice, but after he gets burned a third time, the behavior will be extinguished. So, if the prosecutor doesn't do anything, he isn't doing his job; but he isn't punished. He goes on receiving his salary, and there is no more mess. Among professors of Criminal law, I am considered reactionary, like someone who doesn't fight for the basic rights, as if I were fighting for Big Brother.

"Another problem is that the prosecutors and the judges don't have the means and the staff to do a good job. In the case of Judge Nicolau, who stole many millions, if he took measures such as moving the money from account to account or passing some part of the money to relatives or other persons, it would become almost impossible to trace the money without law enforcement people experienced in those types of crimes. So, in theory the judges have the power over the banks, but in fact, if the criminals are well advised, they can keep the money even if they are convicted which, as I've explained, rarely occurs.

"Another example is Maluf, a politician renowned for dishonesty. He was convicted of embezzling millions, which he reportedly hid in accounts out of the country. He was sent to prison, but he got out in 30 days and got the right to run again. He won and got legislative immunity from prosecution again. Plus, he is seventy years old, so he has even more privileges due to his age. For example, he doesn't have to go no jail. At most he'd be put on house arrest. The money was never found.

A few days after this interview, the *Estado de Minas* (8/7/09), ran an editorial written by a State Deputy Alencar da Silveira Jr., titled, "Smoking is an Individual Freedom." After admitting that second-hand smoke is harmful to innocent bystanders, the article argued, "However, one cannot violate a Constitutional principle or the individual's rights while trying to protect another part of the population that doesn't smoke. Do those who smoke have fewer rights than those who don't?"

I asked a nearby Brazilian, "Isn't this like saying that jailing a thief takes away his right to freedom?"

"That's perfect!" she said. "This rhetoric reveals a defect in their thinking: They demonstrate an inability to weigh the damages of unlimited freedom. There is no concern for protecting the victim."

So be it.

Convinced that the court system was a mess, I asked the jurist, "Who has power to restructure the courts?"

"The legislature."

"Does it need to pass a law to do so??

"No."

"Being public employees, why would the legislature pass a law to open bank the accounts of public employees?"

"There will never be a law for a prosecutor to look in someone's bank account. You will keep on waiting. It will never happen."

This chapter began with a discussion of violence and police corruption and finished with white-collar crime. Is there a connection between the two? The military policeman told us, "If there were only justice! There is corruption everywhere . . . Here, everything works on the basis of money. If you want to get something, you pay . . . "

When police let criminals go free, they commit the same kind of white-collar crime as the government employee who takes a bribe to let a construction company get away with not finishing a bridge. If, as Araújo states, the government is a cleptocracy and the Courts are not up to the task of bringing it to a halt, one might ask whether the law of the land is actually the "law of Gérson." In the contest to gain advantage, the politicians and their partners in crime would appear to be winning the game.

Apathy, conformity, fatalism, and indignation in the face of politicians who only serve themselves to the country, but don't serve Brazil . . .

On April 21, Tiradentes was hung, then drawn and quartered, and his head was shipped to Ouro Preto, apparently to remind the discontented miners to behave themselves. One of them must have stolen Tiradentes' head because it disappeared and was never found.

JQ Jacobus

Chapter 11: Tiradentes—Where is the head?

The journey to the city of Tiradentes follows BR-040, the former Highway of Death, under construction and replaced in the headlines by a new Highway of Death, BR-381. The city bears Tiradentes' name even though he did not plot there (That was Ouro Preto), was not tried there (That was Rio de Janeiro on April 18, 1792), did not die there (He was publicly hung on April 21, 1792 on the Campo da Lampadosa), and his head wasn't sent there (It went back to Ouro Preto). But he *was* born nearby.

According to *Estado de Minas* on Tiradentes Day, 2009, artist Décio Villares gave the martyr idea a big boost in 1890 when he painted Tiradentes on the gallows as a Christ figure with long hair and a beard. Historians argue that a prisoner would not have been hung without a haircut and a shave. Hair apparently interferes with the rope's work. Then, to seal the deal Villares painted him as he lay in pieces. Our goal, on the other hand, is to inquire as to whether the political deal has ever been sealed.

The little city invites tourists and has much to attract them: nice hotels; uncountable shops with various handicrafts, including, I would find out, a sweater for a cold fall night; entertainment in the city plaza; horse-drawn carriages to take the curious around the city; well-fed, ownerless dogs; and furniture, locally-made from real wood. In a toy store while shopping for souvenirs for my grandchildren, I reached out to a blue-green dragonfly. He joined his six hands to mine in congratulations for something—I wasn't sure what—maybe a recent life decision, maybe surviving the trip on BR-040.

Tiradentes, the city, wants tourists; but at least one restaurateur of Italian culinary descent didn't think much of their intelligence. We hadn't ordered much from the menu, at least not much food, but we did sample enough to run the bill over $50. But over $100? It seemed a little high to me, but I didn't trust my calculation of the exchange rate and didn't want to look either stupid or cheap, so I plopped down my credit card.

"Would you mind if I took a look at the bill?" asked my very polite girlfriend.

Later, she stood nose-to-nose with the owner, a shameless blonde woman who argued that someone else's food must have found its way onto our check. We got the check corrected, and I left with the conviction that in Tiradentes, the namesake of Brazil's martyr for freedom to spend one's own money, the poor still hid money from the rich, only now any tourist was considered rich, and it was my money they were hiding from me.

Tiradentes, the man, became famous after the overthrow of Pedro II. Brazil's only hero inspires many questions, such as, "What has been gained from Brazilians eventual independence from Portugal?" Brazilians have a high tax rate together with extremely concentrated wealth and huge numbers of people living in poverty. Do Brazilians see themselves as free of rule by a privileged class, or do they think they work for peanuts and give their wealth to the rich? In other words, are Brazilians still underpaid labor for a new, homegrown ruling class?

In an early example of product branding, the military coup was equated with Tiradentes' pursuit of liberty. It looked like liberty; but as we have learned, the wealthy people of Brazil controlled the elections. It allowed the military and the landowners to rule without the interference of a slave-freeing monarch.

While not a fan of democracy, Plato didn't trust either soldiers or businessmen to have the people's interest at heart. About a state run by the wealthy, he said, " . . . such a State is not one, but two States, the one of poor, the other of rich men; and they are living on the same spot and always conspiring against one another."

The colonels and the military ruled over a century ago. Surely things are different now. We've learned how the government diverts money, but does it thwart the public will?

The headline read, "With the King in the Belly." The article said that in the middle of a supposed democracy, aristocracy lives sheltered by a Constitution written by the privileged and for the privileged. It concerned the likely outcome of the charges of corruption and nepotism against José Sarney, a man who was both former President of the country and reigning President of the Senate. Support for Sarney had come from none other than President Lula of the Worker's Party, a man elected to represent the working classes.

While away from Brazil, I received an email reporting that the recent issue of *VEJA* in which Lula said that Sarney's actions "must not be judged like those of a common citizen." According to the email, "The magazine criticized Lula's dividing Brazilian citizens into two categories: the 'common citizens' [that is, workers and tax payers] and, one would surmise, the 'uncommon citizens.'"

When I returned to Brazil to see for myself, I picked up the June 24, 2009 issue of *VEJA*. On the cover the headline quoted Article V of the Brazilian Constitution: "All are equal under the law without distinction of any nature." *VEJA* tested Lula's pronouncement of inequality by asking 100 people if they agreed that Sarney ought to be treated differently than ordinary citizens. None agreed. All of the answers were interesting. Some of the statements echoed explanations we've already examined.

The national character explanation by Aguinaldo Silva: "The Brazilian, generally speaking, has a flexible attitude in relationship to ethics." In the words of Paulo Eduardo Artaxo, "Brazilians tolerate corruption."

The political corruption explanation by Francisco de A. Barbosa: "If the president wants to avoid denunciations, it is because he fears one day he'll be the target."

The oligarchic explanation by John Emile: "In Brazil citizens don't have equal rights. Whoever has a better position . . . gets more privileges and benefits."

The attitude of hopelessness by Adriana Pereira: . . . [the denunciations] are always the same, but they remain free and being re-elected."

The movement to ban crooked politicians is represented by Maria Gonçalves: "The bad actors have to be banished from the political scene."

"We are nobody," paraphrased by Marcia Tiburi: "There is a tacit and pre-established agreement that Brazil is a no-man's land. Sarney counts on this. Lula counts on this. It's terrifying."

After Collor was impeached, most people blamed the politicians and thought that new leadership would eliminate corruption. Thus, when Lula's anti-corruption Workers Party (PT) was caught paying legislators to vote for their legislation, it was a big disappointment. Others shrugged and said, "Corruption in Brazil is an age-old practice that is fuelled today by the same sources as in the past." The institutional roots of corruption remain healthy in an unhealthy way, and nothing had been done to change them. Since there are no proposals for eliminating them, the problem should continue. Ribeiro suggested Brazil wasn't designed correctly to begin with when he said, "The Brazilian State is not built to function ethically." In what way was the Brazilian State built to function unethically?

It is true that Brazil's government fails to provide oversight. One expert argued that countries having a pattern of ethical behavior in their politicians have systems which provide close scrutiny. Brazil is not such a country. Brazilian public servants find themselves with access to billions of dollars and no one guarding the vault.

As if this were not bad enough, deeper in the Black Lagoon lurks something more sinister, a constitutional creature called *foro privilegiado*, or "privileged forum." Only the three attorneys in the survey identified this as the head of the fish. They asserted that, legally speaking, the rot begins in the Constitution of 1988. João Lopes Amaral, Jr., said, "It is absurd but the prerogative of parliamentary immunity gives benefits to the politicians." By this he meant that the privileged forum was an extension of parliamentary immunity originally designed to protect legislators from being punished for their votes or prevented from voting through incarceration. However, the creature has since mutated to protect not just legislators, but also more than 700 federal authorities. Naming the location of the problem, Fernanda Alves pronounced, "They should receive no *constitutional* protection because then impunity runs free."

At this point, one is reminded of the questions raised by Mr. Temer's interview with *VEJA* (see Chapter 8). Mr. Temer showed more concern for the job security of the deputies than did the citizens sampled for this article. More importantly, the portion of the Constitution which provides this immunity does not appear to reflect the wishes of the citizenry, which would make it undemocratic by the definition reported by Anastasia and Santana.

Inculpating the judiciary in the rotting Constitution, Gisele Schivo, said, "In Brazil there is a bureaucratization of the judiciary. The politicians in the legislature create laws to protect and benefit themselves. The distinction (between the ordinary and the extraordinary citizen] is unconstitutional," implying that the judiciary is not doing its job of correcting the problem.

I asked the jurist, "Do you think a legislator who commits a crime should be arrested and tried like any other criminal?"

"Yes."

"Why aren't they?"

"In our Constitution, only the Supreme Court can try Deputies and Senators . . . The Constitution protects the legislator from being prosecuted in any court but the Supreme Court . . . Under the 1988 Constitution, the Chamber and Senate can only render a political judgment by voting to expel members. Such a decision then allows the Federal General Prosecutor's Office (PGR) to bring criminal charges . . . before the Supreme Court (STF) based on evidence gathered with the assistance of the Federal Police (PF)." Furthermore, never in 180 years of its existence has the Supreme Court criminally condemned any authority covered by this immunity.

The jurist explained, "An end to legislative immunity will not solve all the problems in the government, but its mere existence is absurd, the ultimate distortion of a basic right. It is a cancer, a huge, metastasizing tumor. There are lots of things that must change--the right to condemn someone, sentence length, all that must change--but it must start with an end to immunity from prosecution. It is absurd!"

The process of trying a fellow legislator would have to start with a vote by senators and deputies to expel him or her. If every legislator were honest, maybe they'd vote out a crook; but if enough of them steal too, how likely is that to happen?

The congressmen could opt for a permanent solution and vote to amend the constitution to remove the immunity from prosecution. What are the chances the legislators will amend the Constitution to say that *they* can be tried in regular courts, can go to jail, and can be forbidden from running again?

Assuming they don't give up their license to steal, will a majority of deputies ever be able to resist the open treasury if they have no fear of prosecution? The final question was rhetorical.

Adverse suggests that corruption involves a lack of respect and disregard for the law. (He also warns that governments that disregard the law induce the same type of behavior in the people.) This definition doesn't fit Brazil. Though Brazilians like to say they "have good laws which simply aren't enforced," the truth is that much of the "corrupt" activities of the government are not illegal. No laws were violated when the legislators used public money for vacation flights to Miami.

However, surely laws are being broken when politicians participate in diverting at least 20% of Brazil's tax dollars from taxpayers' hands to unauthorized private pockets. These actions could be called corrupt, no?

By some definitions, but not by others. According to another definition, "Etymologically the word *corruption* comes from the Latin verb *corruptus* (to break); it literally means *broken object*." For Brazil's government to be called corrupt, something would have to have been good at one time and then broke.

The constitution allows government officials to commit crimes with impunity. When legislators like the castle-builder are suspected of fraud, they are not immediately indicted. The reason is simple and important: Immunity from prosecution. In other words, despite the democratic words in some parts of its Constitution, other key elements created a giant bureaucratic machine which is fueled by bribes and which can be unplugged by no one except the Supreme Court.

Suppose that a nation were never constructed to advance the common good, or at least not what the common man (like Mario) would identify as being in his interest. If this situation were created by the Constitution, itself, could the self-serving behavior by politicians be called "corrupt?"

"You can't define corruption without identifying values and norms," said a professor from Minas Gerais. An attorney and expert in legislative activities in the U.S. spoke to this point. When I told him about Brazil, he asked rhetorically, "If an entire society, like Detroit for example, does not value honesty in government, can you call its government corrupt, or is it just the way the system works?"

Architect Brandão argued that both the Brazilian society and government lacked a concept of the common interest. In his view, this meant the State had become corrupted. In a different chapter of the same volume, psychoanalyst Maria Rita Kehl added that corruption threatened to create a generalized absence of ethics at all levels of Brazilian society. The two articles taken together suggest that the Brazilian state has been perverted in the sense that it now violates its reason for existence.

Nevertheless, to cite Brandão's example, when a thief steals from the State, he does not corrupt it. Corruption occurs when the thief teaches the State to steal. To be called "corrupt" by Brandão's definition, Brazil would have to have at one time embraced the idea of common good, and then a corruptor must have brought a disease, an infection, into the State. However, in the view of many, the State of Brazil never embraced the idea of the common good. It always existed for an oligarchy.

Then, in 1988 a constitution established a government which in the words of one frustrated prosecutor amounts to a "cleptocracy." From the point of view of the military dictators who allowed the Constitutional convention to take place, as well as the men and women who voted in favor of the Constitution in its current form, how can their brainchild be called corrupt? Their cleptocracy functions as it was designed. They wouldn't say it's broken.

Over breakfast one morning I tried out my new view of Brazil on Tatiana. "Brazil is not corrupt," I said.

"What?"

"Remember the political scientist who asked, 'Can a state be called corrupt if dishonesty is the norm?' By establishing immunity from prosecution for government employees, the Constitution guarantees criminality. It creates a protected class, making it oligarchic to the core, so there is nothing honest and democratic to corrupt."

We had just watched the first *Men in Black* in which a giant alien cockroach with yellow eyes killed a farmer and hid in his skin. Since the bug was much bigger than the skin, the alien moved awkwardly, lurching along when he walked, and grimacing hysterically. It also appeared that the stolen skin was beginning to rot.

I reminded her of the cockroach and asked, "Can we say the bug corrupted the man when there is really no man inside? Brazil is like this alien. The government wears a skin of democracy like the bug wore a human skin. The Constitution protects and enshrines the oligarchy in the government. The only difference is that the oligarchy is not an alien like the bug. It is indigenous to Brazil, having come over on the original wooden ships."

Tatiana looked discouraged and said, "The politicians are elected, so it is harder to recognize that the actual system is undemocratic and is not affected by elections." Then she repeated her lament, "A dictatorship of thieves."

Speaking of fitting uncomfortably into a borrowed skin, my girlfriend and I began to notice that many of the most corrupt politicians were overfed white men who looked to us like pigs stuffed into suits. On May 20, 2009, the *Estado de Minas* ran a picture of six senators conferencing on the floor of the senate in the midst of a debate over whether there needed to be an investigation of the government-run oil company, Petrobras.

I turned to her quite innocently and asked, "I know a bunch of cows is a herd; geese make a gaggle; you can have a flock of birds and a school of fish; and someone I can't remember coined the term, a 'slouch of fashion models,' but what would you call a gathering of pigs?" Then I showed her the picture.

"I have to look this up," she said and finding a reference book, announced, "Ah, here. It's a congress, a congress of pigs."

I then asked, "Even if Brazil is not broken, can it be improved?"

"Of course," Tatiana answered. "Can't we all?"

Any illusions of my own perfection dashed, I replied, "I am not asking if improvement is conceivable. I am asking whether it is possible in Brazil."

She had learned to ignore such questions, so I asked the jurist, "If immunity from prosecution violates article V of Constitution, can the Supreme Court overturn it?"

"Yes."

The justification for the Supreme Court's striking down the immunity of the legislator runs like this:

1)   Public policy should flow from universal rules, not a social hierarchy or pre-existing policy.

2)   The Brazilian Constitution states some basic rules. For example, everyone is equal under the law.

3)   Therefore, "privileged trial" violates a basic premise of the Constitution.

"Why doesn't the Supreme Court strike this down?" I asked.

"The problem is interpretation. The Supreme Court has eleven ministers, chosen by the President to serve until 70 years of age or death, so forever. If one dies or turns 70, whoever is president chooses another one. Four retired for Lula and one died. Nelson Jobim, for example, is a politician. He was chosen because of political lobbying, by bargaining, while another judge, Carmen Lucia, was a professor at the Catholic University, an academic. There is no consistency in the choices, and decisions become political, not meaning conciliatory, but selfishly defending certain interests. They may trade a decision for something else."

There we have it from the mouth of a Brazilian expert. This is how the government thwarts the public will. The lawyers tell us that the license to steal is written into the Constitution in the clause granting the federal employee the privilege to be tried only by the Supreme Court. This creates an open door for the dishonest and an irresistible lure for the well intentioned. According to the lawyers sampled, the Supreme Court has not done its job by striking down this provision.

In other words, the lawyers are saying that Law of the land has infected the land. Rot has spread from the head to the body politic. Experts have pointed to many practices that spread the infection (political patronage, nepotism, failure of the judiciary to protect the populace from crime, lack of transparency, etc., etc.), but if the people don't recognize the basic structural cause, they will erroneously think that through the vote, they can elect people who will clean up the government.

Inevitably the Senate would drop the charges against Sarney. What had he done that other Senators had not done too? But the decision would not be finalized until some horse-trading could take place. Since Dilma Rousseff, the presidential candidate of Lula's Workers Party (PT), was also being investigated for other allegations, Sarney's party (PMDB) agreed to support Dilma in exchange for PT's supporting Sarney. Before the deal had even been struck, *Estado de Minas* published a cartoon showing some politicians feasting on pizza. Once the charges were formally dropped, some folks in São Paulo held a party and lunched on pizzas adorned with Sarney's likeness.

After Sarney was officially cleared by vote of the Senate Ethics Committee, a group with anti-Sarney signs protested some place in front of a camera. The crowd in the picture looked sparse and young. Over breakfast Tatiana staged her own small but loud protest against the vote:

"How can they do this?"

"What would you have them do?" I asked.

"He's guilty!"

"No, he isn't."

"Okay, not guilty of any crime, actually, since they never made a law for him to break, but what will stop this stealing?"

"Hey, I ask the questions. I have no answers."

"This is why I vote 'no.'"

(Voting is mandatory in Brazil. Everyone is supposed to go to the polls, but they have the option not to select a candidate. If someone makes no entry at all on the ballot, his vote goes to the leading vote-getter. But if a voter enters any number which is not taken by a candidate, no one gets his/her vote. If enough people did this, it would be clear how many people opposed all of the candidates, and it would not appear that a candidate had a majority when, in fact, he or she didn't.)

"There is no hope for this country," she said.

A few days later (August 22, 2009), the voice from behind the paper on the other side of the table complained, "What is this? That's it! I don't want you think I am any part of this!"

I busied myself arranging mangos over my granola. "Yes, dear?"

"Read this!" she said.

I did and found out that *Estado de Minas* reported on a "Movement against Ethics."

"What exactly does this mean, *cassar mandatos*?" I asked.

"The Senate wants to close down the Ethics Committee and leave everything to the Supreme Court, which will do nothing! They say it is undemocratic to nullify the choice of the voters by kicking out a corrupt senator."

"Sounds like it will save time and money since they never condemn anyone anyway," I said and began to eat.

"There is no place like Brazil," she mumbled into the paper.

To this point in history, Tiradentes' fight would appear to have been completely and profoundly lost. As I tried to understand whether the congress, itself, thwarted the will of the people, I read a quote from Senator Papaléo Paes *(Estado de Minas* March 24, 2009): "The wrongs ought to be punished and repaid, but we ought not throw out the whole institution [the Senate]." Like Temer, he argued that the institutions had to be preserved.

Preserved as they are? The Constitution's framers apparently found ways to protect the ruling oligarchy from both the voter and the Law. Okay, I understand the country is only twenty years from a dictatorship, and its people don't want to see cracks in the nation's foundation. Plus, the existence of corruption predates the current Constitution and Supreme Court. However, the lawyers interviewed by *VEJA* saw the legal system, starting with the Constitution, as the head of the fish. The Constitution, they said, provides the structure in which the corruption can exist.

None other than elder statesman, João Camilo Penna, concluded an interview with this: "The Constitution of 1988 . . . made Brazil noncompetitive by greatly increasing government expenses and creating unsustainable privileges. The situation requires a major Constitutional reform."

If Brazilians can't trust the Constitution, can they hope the Judiciary will fix the problem? In an article titled, "The Role of the Judiciary," Antonio Armando dos Anjos said, "The . . . [Judiciary] needs to act with all of its potential as an organ of the State to overcome the faults and limit the excesses . . . [with regard to] the dignity of the person (Article I, clause 3), [promoting] . . . a free, just, and supportive society and . . . the welfare of all (Article 3) . . . The law will not prevent the Judiciary from taking into consideration any . . . threat to the rights . . .

owed to the family, . . . with absolute priority to the child and adolescent . . . (Article 5, clause 35)."

If I understood him correctly, he said that the role of the court system was to protect the rights and welfare of the people against even the excess of the government, itself, or its laws. Then he quoted Celso de Mello as saying that as the Court tries to avoid judicial activism, it cannot become completely passive about correcting unconstitutional government behavior. The jurist told us that instead of grappling with the Constitution, the judiciary has focused on protecting the freedom on the convicted criminal and the privacy rights of the suspected embezzler.

Everyone from the man on the street to legal experts seemed to be giving the Judiciary the green light to hold the politicians to the same legal standards as everyone else. So what did the judiciary do in the Sarney case?

A court prohibited the newspaper, *Estado de São Paulo,* from publishing reports on a Federal Police investigation of Fernando Sarney, son of the Senator. One of the charges against Senator Sarney concerned nepotism. Apparently, conversations recorded with judicial permission revealed the senator and his son, Fernando, discussing the hiring of Fernando's daughter's boyfriend. However, if *Estado de São Paulo* were to publish the evidence against Senator Sarney, it would be in contempt of court. An opposition senator complained that this court order violated the constitutional protection of freedom of the press. It turned out that the judge was a close friend of the Sarney family.

Conveniently for my purposes, *VEJA* then published an article which discussed Antonio Toffoli, Lula's nominee for the newest Supreme Court opening. According to the article, the man recommended to "protect the spirit of the Republic's Constitution—the document that consecrates the principles and values of democracy and justice in Brazil," was not only young (41), in possession of a weak record of academic production, and had twice failed the test to be a state judge, but, but, but "he has twice been ordered by courts in the state of Amapá to return to the public treasury $350,000—money received 'undeservedly and immorally' through 'absolutely illegal' contracts." He did have one qualification: He was an attorney for Lula's party.

Three questions followed from this news:

(1) What kind of Constitution fails to require a clean criminal record from a Supreme Court Justice? According to João Camilo Penna, the Constitution is wanting, and lots of people know it.

(2) What kind of president nominates a convicted embezzler? This is similar to the question I asked the clergyman early in my investigations. He said Lula was the kind of president who supported a minimum wage and initiated a program of aid to the poor. As Guzzo told us, the kind of president who put these programs ahead of his anti-corruption rhetoric and formed a coalition with the PMDB to get his legislation passed is the kind who would then support his coalition partner, Sarney, when he was accused of nepotism and other things. In other words, President Lula would be a politician in Temer's sense: He would be someone who negotiated deals according to the guiding principal of expediency (Chapter 8).

Is such dealing necessary and therefore acceptable? Part of western civilization's rebirth involved new insights concerning politics. Even Machiavelli, the great teacher about the machinations of politics' princes, made the distinction between horse trading and horse stealing. According to Adverse, Machiavelli warned that political corruption eats away at the body politic and is fatal to the State.

Machiavelli suggested that a line exists between negotiation and corruption. But if corruption has infected the entire body of the State, how could a president get anything done without selling his soul to the devil? (That might be an overstatement. I will rephrase it: How could a president get his program through the legislature without agreeing to allow corruption?) If the President of the Senate were involved in nepotism, for example, accusations of nepotism might become a bargaining chip during negotiations with the President.

(3) How can a Supreme Court constituted as it is in Brazil help to clean up the government's corruption? In answer to the question, the jurist told us that a Supreme Court chosen for political reasons cannot and will not reform the system.

Wait! Do not despair. The problem has been solved. The judge who originally condemned Toffoli has changed his mind. He suspended his own verdict. Toffoli is not an embezzler, after all. Personally, I feel relief to know the treasury is safe once again.

Do such deals reflect the public will or thwart it? If the *VEJA* survey reflects public opinion, the people of Brazil want that their government workers to obey the law or suffer its consequences like the "common" citizen. The Constitution and the Judiciary think otherwise. If the Courts are not going to strike down the license to steal, will the Congress voluntarily give it up?

Concerning the airplane tickets for holiday travel, I asked the federal deputy, "Why would congress change the rules to give up impunity and make laws against itself?"

He answered, "Yes, why? The money exists to travel back and forth to Brasília. The rule does not say that only the deputy could use it. Now, since the scandal with girlfriends, etc., the House has changed the rules. There are two sides to the question of impunity. (1) Impunity exists to protect the deputy from political persecution. (During the dictatorship it was instituted to protect the legislator's freedom of expression and vote.) (2) The crook is stain on party."

The deputy didn't give unequivocal support for the repeal of the privileged forum, but our jurist took a clear stand. He said the immunity from prosecution was absurd and needed to be over-ruled. Would corruption disappear from Brazil if the immunity from prosecution were eliminated from the Constitution? The jurist might as well have said, "By itself, it won't solve anything." In truth, he said, "No, if the immunity from prosecution (*foro privilegiado*) were banished, it wouldn't fix everything. We must attack the legal issues," he said. To summarize his recommendations, the courts would have to change drastically their approach to white-collar crime by allowing search warrants for financial records, limit appeals so trials can end, incarcerate law-breakers after the first conviction, and sentence harshly enough to deter future abuses.

He expressed complete pessimism that the judiciary would make any of these changes. He expected the legislature and the judiciary to continue behaving just as they are. If the legislator won't take the first step and amend the Constitution, or the Supreme Court won't strike down clauses which contradict the spirit of the document, and if the three branches of government won't join together to make laws prohibiting the use of public money for private gain, won't reforming the judiciary, won't reduce the patronage system, won't institute transparency, etc., etc., what solutions are left?

After detailing examples of corruption, a politically conservative businessman said, "We need a revolution. But the military dictatorship here was horrible. Brazilians are much happier with corrupt democracy than with a dictatorship."

Despite Tiradentes' efforts, Brazil has continued to rely on oligarchs for over two hundred years since his death. Brazilians celebrate the day of his death as though he would approve of the country's current condition. One Brazilian publicly stated, "In this fraudulent country, what is most frightening is the ease with which the audience is fooled . . . "

How are they fooled? An informant complained, "Brazil is not a democracy." In her view, the vote does not a democracy make. In other words, can a government be called democratic if officials ignore the will of the voters?

Is the problem that Brazilians think their government exists to serve the public will? As we know, a very high proportion (82-92%) of Brazilians rank the end of corruption as their top priority for the government. A recent survey reported 73% of Brazilians thought corruption was very serious; and another 24%, serious. This would suggest they recognize the existence of corruption, but perhaps non-lawyers don't realize that corruption begins in the very foundation of the State, its constitution. Perhaps they don't believe that the government is constructed to serve the will of a few, not the will of the majority.

Mario de Oliveira, Filho, to name one Brazilian, does not believe the government functions in the public interest. He is therefore trying to spearhead a movement to democratize the country. His primary concern is the reduction of the power of a relatively small group of people who control the government and interfere with free market capitalism. If neither the Supreme Court nor the Congress will take the initiative to change the Constitution and then the government, can the people form a movement and demand action?

If someone from North America--home of a Revolutionary War, a Civil War, a violent labor movement, and a long and bloody struggle for civil rights--still expected that all of Brazil must be ready to rise up Iranlike against the constant siphoning of tax money by the government employees, themselves, a man named Rodrigo would set him straight. At a party for a visiting French academic, Rodrigo explained his view of the "national character:"

"I wish we could correct the injustces. I am working with lawyers to do this in a [particular] situation . . . but there will never be a revolution like in the United States. You have shown the world how to make things better, but in Brazil we never talk about the Constitution. If poverty gets worse, it only makes people more submissive. We admire the Civil Rights movement there, but the Brazilian people don't care about corruption . . . "

Wanting a second opinion, I later asked my lady friend, "Do you agree with Rodrigo about protests and marches?"

"Protests wouldn't work here. In 1982 we protested for the right to vote. Millions of us demonstrated for months, but nothing happened. The dictatorship picked the legislature, and the legislature picked the President, who was Sarney. We have been conditioned that it is hopeless to protest. We get nostalgic for someone to straighten things out, but we have to fight against a father figure who would be a despot like Chavez. If the Constitution is ethical, it should be followed; but if it leads to robbery, it should be changed. This is not a democracy. I don't want to live in a dictatorship of thieves! Maybe the younger generation will get upset enough to shut the country down with demonstrations, but it could never happen without someone organizing it, and who would do that?"

Indeed, her generation witnessed violent reactions by those in favor of the status quo. A recent survey of public opinion suggested a large gathering would be unlikely. On September 9, 2009, *Estado de Minas* reported on a *CNT/Sensus* survey in which 65.4% of the people gave the government a positive rating. The slight *decline* over the past month was attributed to the Sarney affair, the increase in swine flu, and the firing of Lina Vieira. If these statistics can be believed, Rodrigo is right: Brazilians don't really expect an honest government.

However, Oliveira did not specifically ask for marches and demonstrations. Other forms of "democratic insurgencies" exist. According to sociologist Leonardo Lamounier and Mozart Valadores, president of the Association of Magistrates of Brazil, the solution must come from civil society's organizing itself to pressure all levels of the government institutions to create a new order.

Back at the party Rodrigo was saying, "Soccer is more important than government. They can't tell you who their representatives are, but they know all the players on their favorite team."

"I hope so. Even I know the best players on Cruzeiro."

"Yeah? Good choice. We are content with our life. It isn't just the *jeitinho brasileiro*. We also survive by means of our cordiality. That is a willingness to help one another at a personal level without reforming anything, without changing the Constitution or protesting in the streets. I will help someone get a job. When the young guy asks if he can watch my car to protect it from thieves, I smile and say, 'Sure,' and I give him two or three bucks even though it is completely illegal. If someone steals the radio out of my car, I shrug and say I can get another one. Maybe I can buy mine back tomorrow at the market."

The architect talking at the family lunch would agree with Rodrigo that Brazilians are not going to coalesce into a popular movement, at least not the kind that produces marches. However, at the same gathering, a relative of the architect disagreed with him: "We have never actually waged a war for anything, but I don't think it is right to say we have no national identity or that we never fought for anything. Maybe we don't identify with the Constitution, but in the Northeast people fought off an attempt by the Portuguese to invade. During the dictatorship (1964-1985) there were many people, including students I knew, who fought against the dictatorship and were killed. Others simply disappeared. Anti-dictatorship guerrillas were massacred in Araguaia. Many of the opposition fled and just never returned to the country."

The architect then contradicted himself and came up with his own exception: When I asked him about the clause of the Constitution which protected the congress from criminal charges, he agreed with the need to eliminate this privilege but echoed what the computer guy has said about waving signs. He wasn't going out to protest against immunity from prosecution, but he did protest against the proposed visit by Iranian President Ahmadinejad.

The Iranian had just denied the existence of the holocaust while speaking to the U.N. President Lula, the man who is said to have his finger on the pulse of the Brazilian people, decided to invite Ahmadinejad on a State visit. Immediately, a congressman proposed a bill, making it a crime against humanity to deny the holocaust; and vociferous crowds gathered in São Paulo. Mr. Ahmadinejad thought again about taking time from his campaign for President and announced he would not be coming. (He was subsequently re-invited and did visit Lula in Brasília after Israeli Perez made an appearance. Protesters remained silent.)

However, I have witnessed many other demonstrations. Earlier we learned that deaths on BR-040 prompted demonstrations. A headline in the *Estado de Minas* said, "Residents of Caete close BR-381 for two hours in protest against a succession of tragedies. Enough!" The protest caused a ten-kilometer traffic jam . . . In the 108 kilometers between Belo Horizonte and João Monlevade, the stretch known as the highway of death, eighty-eight people died over the past year. In addition to an obsolete, sinuous design, deficient signals and signage, the erosion adds to the danger."

In other words, for people to put their lives on hold (and maybe on the line), the cause has to be right. Deaths in concentration camps merit a demonstration. In Rio the families of murder victims protested the levels of violence. In Belo Horizonte middle class people even wave signs about the poisoning of dogs. According to Pedrinho, "The people will take action if they (or their pets) feel threatened."

So far, I had heard no talk about protesting against crime organized by the government, itself. Then on April 26, 2009, the story read, "Military Police bar protest against violence on the corner of the street were the governor lived. 'We want to stop this corporation-like approach to government, this impunity, this trading of favors. We want them to be considered as [ordinary] citizens,'" said the protesters about their politicians.

Days later, I rode past a demonstration in front of Sindifisco, where people protested against auditing retired people. They were risking their employment in support of a woman named Lina Maria Vieira. Until recently, she had served as secretary of the Brazilian IRS. The President fired her. Lina says she was fired because she refused when Dilma Rousseff ordered her to bury an audit of Fernando Sarney, son of accused and recently exonerated Senator José Sarney. Dilma is Lula's chosen successor as president of Brazil. She, of course, denies the charge and gives some other explanation for the firing. No one with whom I spoke gave the slightest credence to Dilma's denials.

However, a poll revealed only 35.9% of the people thought Lina was telling the truth. Only upon reading this did I think, "It is possible that Brazilians might really be the most submissive people in the world, as reported by Malcolm Gladwell."

When I told this to Tatiana, she demonstrated less submissiveness than I and asked, "Do you really trust these statistics?"

"The government might be faking them?"

"Of course."

On August 25, 2009, a rebellion took place in Lina's agency: "Six superintendents--five coordinators in the area and one sub-secretary--offered their resignations in a letter to Lina's replacement. They apparently agreed with Lina's spoken preference for "finding the big tax cheats, rather than pursuing retirees and old people."

Another group expressed a similar concern for the poverty of retired people. Retired people have trouble living on their government pensions. On August 29, 2009, *Estado de Minas* ran an editorial cartoon saying, "Old people in Brazil should be congressmen, . . . bingo promoters, blood-suckers (a popular term for those who bleed public money from government projects), thieves, soccer coaches . . . " The punch line was that the cartoon was first run in 1996, and nothing had changed.

(As in all matters, retirement pay is subject to privilege. According to Mario, a retired farmer can earn less than minimum wage. On the other hand, other retires amass wealth at the taxpayer's expense. For example, some government workers can retire early and draw retirement while they continue to earn a living in private work. Examples include a former astronaut and one Supreme Court Judge who retired at fifty-three and returned to the practice of law.)

On the way home from the island city of Vitória, I had the good fortune to observe a protest close up. We arrived at the airport at 11:00 to discover our flight had been rained out. Then we obediently waited until 1:30 to return to the check-in desk for information about a 4:10 flight. When we stepped out of the restaurant at the far end of the terminal, we immediately found ourselves at the end of the stranded-passenger line. After four hours in the queue, we cancelled our ticket, got a refund from under-computerized but helpful GOL airlines, and caught a cab to the bus station where we bought tickets on São Geraldo bus lines' 9:55 p.m. semi-sleeper, overnight ride to Belo Horizonte. For five hours we passed the time happily, and at around 10 o'clock a bus pulled into the gate advertising Belo Horizonte as it destination.

Then the story became interesting and relevant. We could not board the bus. The rain had delayed the previous bus for over an hour, and it was just arriving to reload. Our bus had not arrived.

"Where is our bus?" Tatiana asked the driver.

"I don't know," he said.

"When will is it expected to arrive?"

"In a half an hour."

"If it is already an hour late and they don't know where it is, how do they know it will be here in a half hour?" she asked me.

I didn't know then, and I didn't know in two more hours when the bus still had not arrived. The twenty of us were the only passengers left in the bus station, and the employees of the bus lines were filing out of the building. All of the other passengers sat quietly, passively, just as their countrymen had said they would.

But the sheep arose. Tatiana found an employee of São Geraldo and complained our being told almost nothing, and nothing truthful. Minutes later, three angry men pounded on the door of the office until a young man came to the bulletproof glass and lied through the slot, "It will be here any minute . . . No, there is no way to reach the driver and find out where he is . . . I don't know if the bus had some mechanical difficulty," and then this: "The electrical problem has been fixed." Tatiana nailed him on that one: "What electrical problem? I thought you said you didn't know if there were mechanical difficulties."

On a nearby bench an attorney busied himself writing up an account of all this for an article in the paper and a lawsuit. Then he began to collect signatures on a petition.

Thus, six Brazilians were forming a plan: The press could be called, then the police, and finally the suit would be filed. Through some sort of mental telepathy, the young agent must have reached the unreachable brass because he came out of his fortress and reassured us the bus was on its way; and, sure enough, within ten minutes our bus appeared. Rather than gloat, the agent appeared sheepish. After we'd boarded, we found out why: The mysterious repairs remained incomplete, and we would "make a short stop at the garage."

That much was true. We spent a mere fourteen minutes at the garage and nine hours later arrived safely in Belo Horizonte. The moral of the story: Given enough shabby treatment, a minority of Brazilians will join together and challenge the way things are done.

If a common thread connected all of these brief demonstrations, could they unite to form a movement for an end to the rampant white-collar crime that drains funds from road repair, steals money from the taxpayer, and deprives the poor of services--practices that lead to life-threatening roads and by spreading corruption interfere with the protection of the citizenry from violent crime? Of course, I had no answer to this question.

Some interviewees had stated the view that corruption was just a middle-class worry, making a big national movement unlikely. When the objections to corruption focus on lost tax dollars, the concern may be shallower than when the problem is phrased in terms of absent sewers, deadly highways, unequal forms of criminal justice, long waits at the public clinic, and underpaid and corrupt police. When the spotlight is shined on the effects of oligarchic rule, who knows how large the opposition would be?

I certainly don't, but I could quote a bank manager who decried the frequency of theft in Belo Horizonte. He had just witnessed the theft of his neighbor's door. The thieves banged on the door in the middle of the night, and he awoke and looked out the window. By then, they were taking the door off its hinges. He called the police, and neighbors yelled at the burglars to try to scare them off. The men continued their work, freed the door from its moorings, and carried it off down the sidewalk. The police never appeared.

I don't know why they stole his door and nothing else. Maybe they planned to come back later. At any rate, the bank manager was both outraged and discouraged.

"Nothing will change," he said, "until the people watching from their windows take things into their own hands."

We know what we want: a Brazil where the institutions function and the governments are servants of the people, where the laws are respected, where the people prosper in safety, and public money is used to benefit the people.

Mario de Oliveira, Filho

People are always problematic. And the problems are always personal.

Millor Fernandes

Chapter 12: Brasília—Rules for the rulers?

Brazil's President Kubitschek conceived of a capital in the middle of the country where no large city previously existed; and he hired renowned architect Oscar Niemeyer to design its buildings. They envisioned a new start for the country, a pioneering national identity to replace the image of the pillaging Portuguese explorers. Joaquim Maria Moreira Cardozo, the engineer working with Niemeyer, saw the designs as true poetry.[78] The buildings may look like sculpture, but the city, itself, has been criticized.

"You've been to Brasília. What's it like?" I asked my interviewee.

"I've been there once in my life and thought it was horrible. I hated it. It's ugly. It has no green areas at all, just concrete, monotonous buildings, wide streets, empty public squares not for spontaneous meetings of citizens but for planned government gatherings. They built 'functional apartments' for government workers. Brasília was Niemeyer's socialistic vision: Everything should be equal by being the same, no individuality. But the leaders weren't going to live in a place like this, and they moved out. The rich--the elected officials, ministers, etc.--live in mansions on lakes outside the city. The workmen who came to build the city stayed and live in unplanned housing. So the city is divided into rich suburbs, the middle class in the socialistic hives, and the slums where the poor workers live.

"It completely violates the socialistic ideas of the architects who built it. Everyone was supposed to have equal rights. Inside each super square the citizen would have everything: apartment, store, playground, school. Everything was made to be the same so there would be no envy, no judging. They look like cages to me. I don't see any beauty in those buildings, just concrete.

"Brasília was built on flat, high land, so there is a lot of light; but in most of the buildings, the labs and offices are underground in basements, so scientists work with artificial light. I went to high school in a Niemeyer building, and it was suffocating, cramped, with no landscape visible from any window. What kind of design treats people like bees in a hive? He did two apartment buildings in Belo Horizonte. There are many one-bedroom apartments on each floor. The windows are small. The plan called for a laundry, a bank, and stores for each building. I don't know if it works like that . . . "

When interviewed, some current residents said they liked the building just fine; however, her opinion got some scholarly support from a social scientist who explained that the building of Brasília

---

[78] Altman, Fabio, Ä poesia concreta de Joaquim Cardoza," VEJA, Nov. 2009, P. 58

was driven by the philosophy of Le Corbusier. There are no neighborhoods in the planned part of the city, so its squares don't occur in neighborhoods. They are not places in which "thousands of unplanned, informal, improvised encounters can take place simultaneously." He argued that it "made no reference to the habits, traditions, and practices of Brazil's past or of its great cities" and represented a "disdain for what Brazil had been . . . In this sense, the whole point of the new capital was to be a manifest contrast to the corruption, backwardness, and ignorance of the old Brazil."[79]

Maybe so, but maybe it was very much the old Brazil with a new leader. According to the above author, the only people conceived as part of the plan were the government functionaries who were needed to support the government functions. There was no vision of industry, no life beyond the government. Interesting, he described as "a state-imposed city," as if Brasília, like the government which occupied it, was not designed of the people or for the people.

Thus, the plan of Brasília predicts an over-legislated society where "many aspects of life that might otherwise have been left to the private sphere were minutely organized, from domestic and residential matters to health services, education, child care, recreation, commercial outlets, and so forth . . .

"In the end, by 1980, 75% of the population of Brasília lived in settlements that had never been anticipated, while the planned city had reached less than half of its projected population of 557,000 . . . The irony is that President Kubitschek wanted to modernize Brazil . . . , the architecture, the design, a symbol of modernization . . . The real Brasília, as opposed to the hypothetical Brasília in the planning documents, was greatly marked by resistance, subversion, and political calculation . . . "[80]

How about corruption? I was told, "Now the term, *Brasília,* connotes corruption. For example, 'Those guys in Brasília' means, 'those guys who think only of their own profit,' and 'something typical of Brasilia' means, 'Everything will end up in pizza.' In other words, after a show of blaming and accusing each other, they will go out for pizza together afterward and no one will be punished." According to this view, Kubitschek wanted to leave the old, corrupt Brazil behind; instead he created an ugly new home for old, corrupt Brazil.

Lula arrived in Brasília after the 2002 presidential election. There are authors who would see the election of a president from the Worker's Party as a watershed and others who would consider Brazil to be imprisoned by its past.[81] Listening to Roberto Pompeu de Toledo, one might conclude that neither are true and instead might think Brazil is imprisoned by its Constitution, a document drawn up by the foxes to govern matters in the henhouse.[82]

One can find historical causes for the construction of Brazil's government as a money machine for the members of the well-connected oligarchy. There are also economic reasons (unequal concentration of wealth and high levels of poverty), cultural reasons (subservience to authority, *jeitinho brasileiro,* relative happiness), social reasons (poor public education), and institutional reasons (lack of Constitutional limits on power, privileged immunity from prosecution, and the opacity of government behavior). Some other realities have emerged: Congress won't fix itself, and the Courts have thus far been unwilling to redefine the nation.

We have heard that people in power cannot be expected to give up all of their privileges voluntarily. Furthermore, the people are not motivated to insist on a constitution that actually

---

[79] Scott, James C., *Seeing Like a State,* New Haven: Yale U. Press, 1988, P. 119.

[80] *Ibid.,* P. 129-130

[81] Robb, *Op. Cit.,* P. 291

[82] Pompeu de Toledo, *Op. Cit.,* P 134.

provides for a representative democracy. In the words of a businessman in Lavras Novas, "We have not achieved self-government." Not knowing how to solve the problem, people have become hopeless. They go to live in other countries if they can. They believe protests are for naught.

The media reports its depressing news day after day. "Nothing Changes with the Elite," announced the headline. "The Senate met to announce an administrative reform without displeasing the upper echelon of workers: the highest category of jobs will lose their titles but keep their salaries. It moves the hierarchy but not the purse." Gilnei Mourão commented, "They maintain their salaries but lose their status. The reduction in expenses is very little. It is not significant."[83]

Even criticism is criticized. On May 13, 2009, Marcos Coimbra opined, "Everyone knows that Brazil needs political reform . . . The problem, however, is exactly this, to use the idea of reform as a tool to distract the attention of society. Instead of moving forward, we move backwards."

Renato Janine Ribeiro mourned the failure of ethics and hoped education could improve the future: "The Brazilian State is not built to function ethically . . . " The awareness of this reality "is good, but I think very sad, because it means a renunciation of hope for ethics . . . Maybe a solution could happen in the long run, involving a strong educational process to spread ethical values to the new generation."[84]

What would the people need to learn through this education? Oliveira points to the need for education concerning civil rights and responsibilities. According to him, the power of the citizen originates from his constitutional and legal rights and from his contribution to the maintenance of the State, i.e., his payment of taxes. In Brazil such rights are almost unknown to the ordinary citizen and seldom divulged by the authorities. The citizen does not know how much he pays in taxes and therefore does not feel legitimate in demanding something back from the State. In this way, the rights and taxes paid become invisible to the eyes of the citizen and as a result he remains effectively powerless.

But what good is this information to a people without the will to change their government? Earlier a Brazilian reminded us that the German people elected their Nazi government. Recently, Stélio Lage compared modern-day Brazil to Nazi Germany. He described Brazil a country where impunity and nepotism rules and the institutions are lax, where thieves and scoundrels know they will escape punishment and laugh at the law. They use lawyers to exploit the infinite opportunities for acquittal in Brazil, generating 300,000 pages of trial records that no one will ever read. One scandal follows another. The risk is that everyone becomes hypnotized and the evil becomes banal, as in the holocaust.[85]

In despair, the son of one informant suggested dropping a bomb on Brasília. However, this approach would be messy and wouldn't correct the constitutional problems. Before Brazilians turn to the nuclear solution, two other measures have been suggested as possibilities.

Natural evolution of the marketplace:

Reduction in corruption could come from external pressure. An image of honesty is good for business, and Brazil under Lula is taking a prominent place on the world stage. Little affected by the world economic crisis, Brazil even loaned money to the international banking institutions.

---

[83] *Estado de Minas,* May 13, 2009

[84] Margalhaes Luiz Antonio, *Valor,* ano 9, #444, 19/4/09

[85] "Aberracoes Humanas, Entrevista com Stelio Lage,"Viver Brasil, ano II, #11, February 24, 2009, P. 112.

In addition, organizations like the World Bank favor transparency. As Brazil seeks a permanent place on the UN's Security Council, an open window into Brazil's corruption would not be good for the image it projects to the rest of the world. If they wished to refute de Gaulle's claim that "Brazil is not a serious country," the oligarchy would have to decide how much reform is needed in order to maintain the image of a democracy with a free-market economy.

Major events bring exposure. The World Cup of soccer will come in 2014, and Rio will host the Olympics in 2016. Ordinarily, as we have learned, road construction proceeds slowly, and money for such projects is diverted by fraudulent schemes. However, Brazil's government does not want the embarrassment of traffic jams during the Olympics and World Cup. Road construction has already picked up its pace, and crews work round the clock to prepare the access to venues.

The jurist suggested, "When corruption becomes imbecilic, Brazilian companies could lose foreign customers. International companies might retreat from the Brazilian market."

The jurist's professor asked, "If trading partners won't want to do business because of corruption, they might set limits on how we do business?"

"Exactly. Suppose a businessman from Finland is trying to do business in Brazil. If Nokia is doing business with colonel's family, it might not care that he is corrupt; but if someone from Samsung shows up and finds out Nokia is winning the competition because the colonel's relative has been paid to stand in the way of Samsung's entering the market, Samsung will not want to do business in that way. I think the financial interests will benefit from the current system for long time, but there will be a day when international business people begin to feel bothered. Then changes may happen." Maybe.

Grass-roots movement:

Must Brazil wait for pressure from the outside world? This story began with an attempt to understand Brazil's one national hero, a man who died for a principle and accomplished nothing. Does Brazil have no hero who met with success?

After breakfast I received an email, alerting me to a website which announced that a reform-minded independent candidate would be running for president. It turned out to be Mario de Oliveira, Filho. I told Tatiana, and she replied, "The thing that scares me about Brazil is that it isn't a particular government, this party or that party. It's any party. If a reformer gets elected, he will be corrupted too."

I acknowledged, "I don't know enough about Brasilia's inner workings to know how a reformer could achieve power and keep the country running while ridding it of corruption."

She shook her head grimly, but after she'd reflected for a moment, I heard optimism in her tone: "Things aren't going to stay the same. We are just beginning to understand the effects of corruption, all of the money that is being lost. It has all come out in the last eight years. No one talked about this before, maybe because it is so complicated."

In calling for a national movement outside of the current parties, Oliveira begins by agreeing with the jurist. He states, first, that the current system is so corrupt it cannot fix itself from within. The jurist agreed that people at the top of the power structure would not or could not bring reform to the government. To reach power in Brazil, he argued, one would have to compromise himself through bargaining and would then be hopelessly corrupted.

I asked him, "Will young lawyers eventually take power and change things?"

"No, because they won't arrive at top of system where change must come from without being compromised and corrupted in the process. When you have the power to make change, you don't want to make the changes."

Secondly, Oliveira's website contends that there are not enough principled, powerful people (what he calls the "elite") opposing the oligarchy: "It seems clear that we don't have a critical mass of this elite big enough to promote the development of Brazil . . . " The jurist concurred, "I am pessimistic. Nothing has happened over the past ten years because the pressure to prevent the Public Ministry from functioning is constant. Nothing stops people from creating mechanisms to disguise what they are doing and protect them from the Federal Police and the Public Ministry."

Here the optimistic Oliveira and the pessimistic jurist part company. Oliveira's website argues that it is up to the people. They must unite in a movement. Of course, my interviewees didn't believe Brazilians would form a movement, except in the direction of the kiosk to buy soccer tickets. The government apparently shares this view of its flock:

"Is the government concerned with cynicism of people?" I asked the jurist.

He answered simply, "No."

Wondering why people sometimes work for causes and sometime not, I remembered what one researcher told me: "Where do good ideas get the power to succeed? Is it politicians, masses, policy entrepreneurs, academics, what? I think my answer was this: networks of policy entrepreneurs who have a foothold that gives them resources to share ideas. Then, when a policymaker needs a solution to a problem, . . . he takes it off the shelf . . . He copies his contacts. That shelf of ideas was created by people who formed their mutual bonds, commitments, and such during Brazil's 70-80s democratization movement and they wended their way into NGOs, church groups, academia, local government, etc."

He also wrote the following:

" . . . Where civil society is weak, . . . [the] ability to get progressive reforms . . . will likewise be weak . . . [but] an active, networked civil society can actually accomplish a lot if they take advantage of . . . events that focus attention.

"What made these activists embrace the other? What activists became policy entrepreneurs and how and why? . . . [The] key techniques in their success were the development of better networks, the strategic use of leverage wherever they found it, the sharing of experiences, and the development of knowledge bases that turned the staff of these civil society organizations into true technical experts . . . "

"In Minas Gerais, the important political event that put police reform on the agenda was a 1997 legislative investigation . . . into human rights violations in the Minas Gerais prison system, which revealed horrors in police station jails (which are managed by the [civil police]) and in the [military police-staffed] prisons. Civil society came out in full force to endorse reforms, one of which was a . . . [police review board] copied directly from the São Paulo model."[86]

Brazil eventually produced thirteen police review boards. What other movements have produced results? Best known is the MST (Workers Without Land), the movement to put unused land in the hands of landless farm workers. More recently, the MT (Workers Without Roofs) has sought to use abandoned buildings as housing for the homeless.

---

[86] Reames, Benjamin, *Creating Accountability in Federal Democracies: The Diffusion of Police Oversight Policies in Brazil and the US.,* New York: Columbia University, 2006

The Workers Without Land movement arose in reaction to the concentration of Brazil's land in the hands of a relative few. According to the movement's literature, in Brazil 1.6% of the landowners control roughly half (46.8%) of the land on which crops could be grown; just 3% of the population owns two-thirds of all arable land. Another source said, "Half of Brazil's farmland belongs to just 4% of the population." Since this movement targeted the oligarchy's hold on Brazil's wealth, I wondered if it would have broad appeal.

I first heard about MST in a coffee shop in the U.S. where my tutor explained, "My uncle was a farmer in Rio Grande do Sul, and the MST came onto his property. He tried to make them leave, and they killed him and destroyed the equipment. The police did nothing."

The architect I interviewed at brunch wasn't about to sign up: "The MST, Workers Without Land, are criminals." (A few weeks later, *VEJA* would support his accusation in an article titled, "How the Movement of Rural Workers Without Land diverts public and foreign money to finance its crimes.") They come out of an outmoded, leftist idea of land management."[87]

Clearly, Brazil's attempt at land management has produced conflict, but could South America's largest social movement have degenerated into a bunch of criminals, an industry supported by organized crime? Dubious, I then heard the story of José Machado:

"He was a man with a small farm in Espirito Santo, a place where he lived, raised food for his family of five daughters. Not a rich man, he had a modest home and an old, beat-up pickup truck. He also had a small house on the beach which he loaned to people who visited; but he was so generous, he insisted on feeding us all three meals--breakfast, lunch, and dinner--every day.

"I remember when I was a little girl, José was visiting Belo, and in exchange for staying at our house and for eating lunch every day with the family, he would walk me and my younger sister to school. Every morning my mother would pull our hair into ponytails, and it hurt, and I hated it. Then José took us by the hand and we walked toward school, and as soon as we turned the corner, he would say, 'Okay, it's time,' and we would undo our ponytails. He would free our hair. Oh, it felt so good.

"I will tell you how José died. This was in the late eighties, right after the dictatorship, and MST invaded his land. This was not a big ranch. It was not unused land. He farmed it himself with one employee. He got up every morning and milked the cows. But what would MST do if they invaded unused land? They didn't actually farm, so they invaded nice land. This was twenty years ago, so José did not call his wife on the cell phone. He went into this little town to the police station, which housed its one policeman, and they returned to talk to the invaders. When José did not return at night, his wife became worried and went looking. She found the two bodies where they lay dead from bullet wounds in the head.

"José Rainha, the leader of MST, was arrested, was released, was arrested again, was released, until finally he went to trial. Evidence showed he had fired a gun. He was charged with the actual shooting, not just ordering it done. But back then MST was the Robin Hood, and its leader was acquitted."

I checked on Rainha's status. In 1997 a court in Espirito Santo sentenced him to 26 years and six months in prison. Apparently, he didn't serve out his sentence because in 2000 he was charged with burning down farm buildings, and in 2005 he was sentenced to ten years in prison.

---

[87] *VEJA,* Edicao 2128, ano 42, #25, "Como o Movimento dos Trabalhadores Rurais Sem Terra desvia dinheiro Publico e verbas estrangeiras para cometer seus crimes.

According to *VEJA*, other crimes eventually followed. A prosecutor who was fighting against criminal actions of the MST in Rio Grande de Sol abandoned the case after he received threats, character assassination, phone bugging, and even an attempt on his life.[88]

Where is Rainha now? Not in jail. He still helps lead the MST. In February 26, *FolhaOnline* reported that Rainha wished to speak with Supreme Court president Gilmar Mendes to explain that the movement is not a bunch of criminals but part of a democratic process.

Having learned all this, I better understood the feelings of the computer guy when he said, "The middle class does not trust the people behind these movements. The Workers Without Land started out as a way to get unused land into the hands of farmers. But they take land and don't farm it. They resell it for a profit. And their numbers aren't shrinking despite all of the land that has been confiscated. Why not? It has become an industry. The middle class doesn't want to stand in the streets and wave signs with the MST or the Workers Without Roofs (MT)."

Dateline 2016:

Seven years after the publication of this study, the Brazilian landscape has changed dramatically. Any talk of a middle class movement to change government is off the table. International Courts have punished Brazilian corporations for paying bribes to the operators of Petrobras, Brazils national oil company. Then-President Dilma Rousseff has been impeached for accounting irregularities which pale in comparison to the embezzlement of billions of dollars by national politicians. The former President of the Camara (House) has been removed from office and jailed. As of this writing, Former President Lula has himself been charged with five counts of embezzlement but has not been tried. The President of the Senate has been charged but remains in office.

I was summarizing for Tatiana: "For Brazil to dismantle its cleptocracy, the STF (Supreme Court)--politically appointed and well-paid (by the legislature)--would have to see its way clear to strike *privileged forum (foro privilegiado)* from the Constitution, perhaps on the premise that it violates of its violation of Brazils constitutional provisions for equal protection under the law. As now-president Temer pointed out, there is no protection of public money from private use by politicians because the legislature has never made rules against this practice. And they could demand that the legislators and cabinet members and administrators return all their bribe---"

"Stop!" she yells. They will never do that! Why would they?"

"Okay, they could declare all of those practices illegal from now on and let them keep all the money they've embezzled."

"You don't get it! They don't care what voters think. Voters have no control over nominations. They have to vote for somebody or pay a fine, and the party decides who gets in office. It would take enormous public pressure for them to give up this crime, but the truth is that the Brazilian doesn't expect his politicians to be honest. The Brazilian wishes he could have a job like that. Don't forget our national "hero,"Macunaima. He does not work and steals your money. My own uncle did that to my father! It is the foundation of Brazils culture."

"What is going to happen to the Lavo Jato investigation, then?"

"They have already accused Judge Moro of abuse of power. They will put him in jail, or he'll get away in time to join his wife abroad."

---

[88]"Abatido pelo radicalismo," *Viver Brasil,* ano 11, #11, Feb 24, 2009, P. 64.

Almost every Brazilian with whom I have talked is extremely pessimistic about the country replacing its cleptocracy for the rule of law." My glimmer of optimism remains for two reasons: First, though all Brazilians say their countrymen have the dishonest, lazy character of a Macunaima, none of the Brazilians I know are either dishonest or lazy. The people I know tend to be like Mario, the doorman. Eight years after we first talked about Brazil, I held out my recorder and asked an architect and a writer, "What would you change first about Brazil?" In unison they boomed, "Get rid of the Workers Party!" (That's the party which has held the presidency for the last four elections.) Both men thought that everything was poorly administered by this government and education, in particular, was being harmed by the Workers Party. Education is the key to progress," they said, and Brazil's motto is "Order and Progress," after all.

The next day, I read a report on strike being conducted by schoolchildren. Armed police had forced them from the school. "Why?" I wondered. It never occurred to me that government corruption had anything to do with rebellious middle schoolers. But the report maintained that a "Lunch Mafia" of politicians or bureaucrats or both had diverted money from school children's lunches to their own bank accounts. Brazil has Order and Progress, but apparently no money for school lunches.

The following morning, I took some coffee and a sandwich down to Mario, the doorman, pulled out my recorder, and told him, "It's been eight years since you told me your views of Brazil. What do you think now."

His words came fast: "We're in terrible shape. We have more poverty. We have no money. The health system doesn't work. I take my daughter there, and it's crowded with people, but there is only one doctor. It's filthy. We wait for hours and hours. It's infested with dengue-bearing mosquitos."

I reminded him that it wasn't perfect eight years ago, but it worked.

"Not any more. The country has no money. I work here; and on my days off, I wash cars. I like to work."

He'd told me that eight years before, and I'd observed him working every day, in the waiting room or on the street with a rag and a bucket, smiling, joking, getting a little greyer.

He went on, "My salary goes to taxes, and I have nothing left. The economy is stalled. No one wants to invest in this country. Dilma goes to Cuba and hangs out with Fidel (Brazil gave substantial sums for Cuba to improve Havana's harbor), and everything here gets worse."

Eight years ago he'd said, "We have problems, but all countries have problems. We need better leaders." Now he said, "All countries have problems, but here they are not being solved. My taxes go to police, but we aren't safe. Right here in this neighborhood (an upper middle-class, hillside neighborhood of high-rise apartment buildings), a guy on a motorcycle rides up to a bus stop, pulls a gun, robs everyone, and rides off. Later he robs Carrefour (the grocery store), the police catch him, but they let him go because "There's no proof." He comes out of the station smiling.

The night before interviewing Mario, the two university educated professionals had said that Brazil need to get rid of the Workers Party. Somehow, the doorman/car-washer with little formal education was perceiving things from a more systemic perspective: "None of the parties help. They are only after the money. The problem isn't political. The government is a mafia, like the School Lunch Mafia. We need a new constitution."

Eight years before, he'd said, "All countries have problems. We just need better leaders." Now he said, "Other countries have problems, but they solve them. After your crisis, Americans lifted your country out of the crisis. Other country's leaders take responsibility, but not here.

Who is returning the money for school lunches? A dam bursts, destroys a city, pollutes the countryside, kills a river, and sends pollution to Rio for the Olympics, and nothing happens. We are a big country, a rich country. We have money. We pay a lot of taxes, but where is the money? Why doesn't it solve problems? Our leaders don't take responsibility. Our constitution protects them.

"I work the entire day, everyday. I support my family. My children study. The oldest works too. We must work. Nothing will fall out of the sky to solve our problems. But we aren't building the country. The leaders aren't working to build the country."

"You were more optimistic in 2008."

"It's getting worse. China, France, Japan are growing and are ruled by law. They have politicians who steal, but they go to jail. Thieves and murderers go to jail. As a nation, we aren't working. We are trying to steal our way to prosperity. The Workers Party isn't going to solve this. No Party will solve it. Shut them all down! The country isn't functioning."

He says that the country isn't working, literally, not figuratively. Mario, the doorman who reads and compares countries, sees what smart, better-educated people don't see: This Brazil, this Brazil which is built to steal, is a failing state and will remain so without fundamental change. He thinks a working man should be paid a fair wage, receive efficient services for his taxes, with no skimming by politicians or bureaucrats, a country where thieves and murderers go to prison and cannot improve itself without a change in the constitution to stop the stealing. Instead of waiting for "better leaders," he says, "I just want an honest government."

When the first version of this book was begun in 2008, I took a humorous tone. Brazilian's complained but didn't express fear; and anger, only rarely. Mario's tone had changed. He lives in fear now, and he is angry. The doorman says what the Supreme Court has not yet realized, or admitted: "We need a new constitution."

Mario is one of just two Brazilians who told me this. The middle-class professionals I spoke to the night before just want more order and more progress. They feel like they are treading water, and that is apparently good enough. They do not want to go back to the days of military dictatorship.Mario, on the other hand, feels like he is drowning. He doesn't want it a little better, like getting rid of the PT but having master thieves like Cunha and Caldeiro running things, like stopping Petrobras-sized stealing but permitting bus stop-sized stealing. He wants law enforcement, a future in which poor children like his, not just wealthy children, can have a future.

When Lavo Jato began to pass out its indictments, patriarch of the colonels, Jose Sarney, complained that they were plagued by a "dictatorship of Justice." According to Tatiana, men like him, perhaps most Brazilians, don´t really want a rule of law, a society in which little "jeitinho brasileiro" is treated as a crime when it is. But most Brazilian I know do want an honest government.

Mario finally said, "It's getting worse. China, France, Japan are growing and are ruled by law. They have politicians who steal, but they go to jail. Thieves and murderers go to jail. As a nation, we aren't working. We are trying to steal our way to prosperity. The Workers Party isn't going to solve this. No Party will solve it. Shut them all down! The country isn't functioning."

He says that the country isn't working. Mario, the doorman who reads and compares countries, sees what smart and better-educated people don't see: This Brazil, this government built to steal, is a failing state and will remain so without fundamental change. Instead of waiting for "better leaders," he now says, "I just want an honest government." The man who never went to college gets the concept: "Brazil doesn't understand the concept of Law. "

While Brazilians, like Tatiana, feel pessimistic about achieving honest government, a glimmer of hope for Brazilś future can be seen in the presidential candidacy of oft-quoted Mario de Oliveira Filho, who ran for president in 2010. He was able to win the nomination from one of Brazilś minor, but established, parties. He received only a small percentage of votes, but at that time voters were focussed on politics. If people like Mario-the-doorman, and most other Brazilians I know, can focus on ending Brazilś cleptocracy, it is possible that they can someday elect honest candidates who do not fear the rule of law.

References
(In order of appearance)

Rohter, Larry, *Deu no New York Times,* Rio de Janeiro: Editora Objetiva Ltda, 2007, 416 pp.

Nunes, *Historia de Brasil,* Sao Paulo, Altana, 2000.

Robb, Peter, *A Death in Brazil,* New YOrk: Henry Holt & Co, 2004, P. 57-58

Hudson, Rex A., *Brazil: A Country Study*, ed., Washington: GPO for the LIbrary of Congress, 1997, http.//countrystudies.us/brazil.

Mann, Charles, *1491--New Revelations of the Americas before Columbus,* New York: Knopf, 2005.

Aquino, Rubim SAntos Leao de; Bello, Marco Antonio Bueno; Domingues, Gilson Magalhaes, *Um sonho de liberdade: a conjuracao de Minas, Sao Paulo*: Editora Moderna, 1998, 176 pp. Il. ISBN 8516021009.

Cheney, Glenn Alan, *Journey on the Estrada Real: Encounters in the Mountains of Brazil,* Chicago: Academy Chicago, 2004.

Holston, James, *Insurgent Citizenship: Disjunctions of Democracy and Modernity in Brazil*, Princeton: Princeton U. Press, 2007, P. 3-4, 33-34, 416 pp.

tupiwire.wordpress.com/2009/03/30/eliane-tranchesi-what-a-long-strange-trip-to-prison-its-been.

Kafka, Franz, *The Trial*, Sao Paulo: Abril S.A. Cultural e Industrial, 1979, 279 pp. P. 7.

Lima, Maria Elizabeth Antunes, Participacao do psicologo nos programas de qualidade total,¨ unpublished paper.

Oliveira, Fiilho, Mario de, *Brasil--o entulho oculto dos privilegios oligarquicos,* Sao Paulo: Editora Alfa-Omega Ltda, 2006, 384 pp.

Osava Mario, ¨chsallenges 2005-2006,: Corruption in Brazil--Old Tricks, New Dogs," transparency.org.

Reames, Benjamin, *Creating Accountability in Federal Democracies: The Diffusion of Police Oversight Policies in Brazil and the U.S.,* New York: Columbia University, 2006.

Araujo, Marcelo Cunha de, *So e preso quem quer!,* Rio de Janeiro: Brassport Livros e Multimidia Ltda., 2009.

Gladwell Malcolm, *Outliers--the story of success,* NY: Little, Brown, & Co., 2008, 309 pp.

Levi-Strauss, Claude, *Tristes Tropiques* (1955), trs. John and Doreen Weightman, New York: Antheneum, 1973.

Caldeira, Teresa, *City of Walls--crime, segregation, and citizenship in Sao Paulo,* Berkeley: University of California Press, 2000.

Sant´Anna, Afonso Romano de, Sarney e as capitanias hereditarias,"Estado de Minas, 2/8/09

Cabral, Otavio; Escosteguy, Diego, ¨A rendicao do ultimo coronel," *VEJA,* edicao 2124, ano 42, #31, 5/3/09, p. 64

Power, Timothy Joseph, *The political right in postauthoritarian Brazil: elites, stitutions, and democratization,* Penn State Press, 2000, 284 pp.

Baer, Werner, *A Economia Brasileira,* Sao Paulo: Nobel, 2009, 541 pp.

Rigueira, Jr., Itamar, ¨Inimiga da democracia,¨ *Livro da Editora UFMG analisa a corrupcao a partir da teoria politica, tratando-a em seus aspectos eticos e institucionais,¨* # 1633, Ano 35, 10/11/2008

Corrupcao--Ensaios e Criticas, editoraufmg, 2008

Scott, James C., *Seeing Like a State*, New Haven: Yale U. Press, 1988

Reames, Benhjamin, ¨Neofeudal Aspects of Brazilś Public Security," P. 61-96 in M.R. Haberfeld, ed., *Comparative Policing--The Struggle for Democratization.* L.A.: SAGE Publications, 2008

McCarthy, Cormack, *Blood Meridian.*

Benatte, Antonio Paulo, ¨E bicho na cabeca,¨ Historia Viva, #54, Editora Duetto, April, 2008, pp. 66-70.

¨Top criminals fixed Rio carnival result, say police," *The Guardian*, June 12, 2007.

Preto, Ribeirao, ¨A corrupcao no Brasil,"*JuNiN*, 27/11/2006, 23:39

Cabral, Otavio, ¨Chore, por nos, Senador," *VEJA,* ed. 2114, ano 42, #21, 27/5/9, P. 140-141

Preto, *Zonalatina.com,* ¨Political Corruption in Brazil.¨

Cicero, Paulino, *MercadoCommun,* ano XV, #192, 1/7/08.

Avritzer, ¨Corrupcao--Crime ou costume?¨ *Revista de Historia Biblioteca Nacional.*

Ribeiro, Renato, Janine, ¨As tres formas," *PensarBrasil, 10/10/2009.*

Plato, *The Republic.*

Speck, Bruno Wilhelm, ¨Corrupcao, prevencao e controle," *TransparenciaBrasil.*

Balch, Oliver, ¨How Corruption Inc does business in Brazil, *Guardian.co.uk,* 6/23/2006, 13.21 BST

Andrioli, Antonio Inacio, ¨Causas estruturais do corrupcao no Brasil,¨ *Revista Espaco Academico,* #64, 09/2009

Nunes, Sebastiao, ¨Introducao ao Direito Civil," *Historia do Brasil.*

Levi-Strauss, Claude, *Tristes Tropiques,* (1955), trs. John and Doreen Weightman, NY: Antheneum, 1973,

Raney, Adam; Heeter, Chad, ough Cut Brazil: Cutting the Wire, witnessing a land occupation, December 13, 2005, http://www.pbs.org/frontlineworld/rough/2005/12/brazil_cutting. html#.

www.ingramcontent.com/pod-product-compliance
Lightning Source LLC
Chambersburg PA
CBHW051944280526
45789CB00009B/3169